D0224035

Love in Modern Japan

This compelling and controversial book proposes to see the concept of love as a national state apparatus. By looking at key historical and social events in Japan, the book captures how men and women in Japan are made "loving" members of the nation, subjected to the state's intervention across the areas of life and death.

Ryang offers debate on ethnological case studies including ancient sexualized rituals and fertility festivals, the murder case of Abe Sada, the rape of Nanjing, the wartime institution of "comfort stations," postwar pure love and Miko and Mako's tragedy, the 1990s phenomenon of *enjokōsai* or aid-date, and the more recent wave of romancing a South Korean actor. By looking at love's transformation through the prewar and postwar period, with an additional eye on ancient times, Ryang touches upon the emergent process of the modern self and relates love to Foucault's concept of governmentality, biopower, and disciplinarity to give a wide-ranging historical and cultural analysis of love in Japan. Combining ethnographic, theoretical, and archival research, this seminal study will be of huge appeal to scholars of Japanese anthropology, feminist anthropology, and gender studies alike.

Sonia Ryang is an Associate Professor of Anthropology and the Stanley Family and Korea Foundation Scholar of Korean Studies at the University of Iowa. Her previous publications include *Koreans in Japan: Critical Voices from the Margin* (Routledge, 2000) and *Japan and National Anthropology: A Critique* (Routledge, 2004).

Anthropology of Asia Series
Series Editor: Shaun Malarney
International Christian University, Japan

Asia today is one of the most dynamic regions of the world. The previously predominant image of "timeless peasants" has given way to the image of fast-paced business people, mass consumerism, and high-rise urban conglomerations. Yet much discourse remains entrenched in the polarities of "East versus West," "Tradition versus Change." This series hopes to provide a forum for anthropological studies which break with such polarities. It will publish titles dealing with cosmopolitanism, cultural identity, representations, arts, and performance. The complexities of urban Asia, its elites, its political rituals, and its families will also be explored.

Hong Kong
The anthropology of a Chinese metropolis
Edited by Grant Evans and Maria Tam

Folk Art Potters of Japan
Brian Moeran

Anthropology and Colonialism in Asia and Oceania
Jan van Bremen and Akitoshi Shimizu

Japanese Bosses, Chinese Workers
Power and control in a Hong Kong megastore
Wong Heung Wah

The Legend of the Golden Boat
Regulation, trade and traders in the borderlands of Laos, Thailand, China and Burma
Andrew Walker

Cultural Crisis and Social Memory
Modernity and identity in Thailand and Laos
Edited by Shigeharu Tanabe and Charles F. Keyes

The Globalization of Chinese Food
Edited by David Y. H. Wu and Sidney C. H. Cheung

Culture, Ritual and Revolution in Vietnam
Shaun Kingsley Malarney

The Ethnography of Vietnam's Central Highlanders
A historical contextualization, 1850–1990
Oscar Salemink

Night-time and Sleep in Asia and the West
Exploring the dark side of life
Edited by Brigitte Steger and Lodewijk Brunt

Chinese Death Rituals in Singapore
Tong Chee Kiong

Calligraphy and Power in Contemporary Chinese Society
Yuehping Yen

Buddhism Observed
Travellers, exiles and Tibetan Dharma in Kathmandu
Peter Moran

The Tea Ceremony and Women's Empowerment in Modern Japan
Bodies re-presenting the past
Etsuko Kato

Asian Anthropology
Edited by Jan van Bremen, Eyal Ben-Ari, Syed Farid Alatas

Love in Modern Japan
Its estrangement from self, sex, and society
Sonia Ryang

Love in Modern Japan

Its estrangement from self, sex, and society

Sonia Ryang

Routledge
Taylor & Francis Group

LONDON AND NEW YORK

First published 2006
by Routledge
2 Park Square, Milton Park, Abingdon, Oxon, OX14 4RN

Simultaneously published in the USA and Canada
by Routledge
270 Madison Ave, New York NY 10016

Routledge is an imprint of the Taylor & Francis Group, an informa business

Transferred to Digital Printing 2008

© 2006 Sonia Ryang

Typeset in Times by
Florence Production Ltd, Stoodleigh, Devon

British Library Cataloguing in Publication Data
A catalogue record for this book is available from the British Library

Library of Congress Cataloging in Publication Data
Ryang, Sonia
    Love in modern Japan: its estrangement from self, sex, and
    society/Sonia Ryang.
        p. cm – (Anthropolgy of Asia series)
    Includes bibliographical references and index.
    1. Sex customs–Japan–History.   2. Rites and ceremonies–
    Japan–History.   3. Ethnopsychology–Japan.   4. Gender
    identity–Japan.   5. Japan–Social life and customs.   I. Title
    II. Series
    GN635.J2R93 2006
    306.7.0952 – dc22   2006011399

ISBN10: 0–415–77005–X (hbk)
ISBN10: 0–415–47926–6 (pbk)
ISBN10: 0–203–96703–4 (ebk)

ISBN13: 978–0–415–77005–7 (hbk)
ISBN13: 978–0–415–47926–4 (pbk)
ISBN13: 978–0–203–96703–4 (ebk)

For Samantha and Thomas

Contents

Preface and acknowledgments

This book follows my *Japan and National Anthropology: A Critique* (Routledge, 2004), its intellectual prequel. In that book, I asserted that anthropological studies of Japan in the West have been carried out in two completely opposite, yet intimately intertwined directions, both of which are epistemologically unsound: one is a tendency to generalize an observation of small corners and specific institutions that exist inside Japanese society into a general account of the Japanese and Japanese culture at large, with little painstaking theoretical exercise in between; the other is a trend to largely ignore the workings of the Japanese national state, when one talks about Japanese culture. I argued that such tendencies have created the situation where studies of Japan are seen as a specialty too special to make an impact on humanity at large.

In this book I look at one significant institution (or should I say concept), love, in close connection to Japan's modern nation-state—more precisely, its birth and maturity. By so doing, I intend to experiment on possibilities of ethnological inquiry into Japanese society and culture with the national state as an important—if not always visible—protagonist. I rely on concepts such as sovereign and biopower to explore such a possibility, hoping to make this study relevant to academic fields beyond the national confines of Japan.

Writing this book has highlighted one other reality that prevails our times—the realization that we live in dark times, in which one nation sends military force to another in the name of democracy and love for world peace, and in this very name other nations have joined in the act. Indeed, in the name of love for freedom, killing, torture, and suffering go on in the world. In the name of democracy, in government offices, incompetent individuals are given disproportionate authority through personal connections and rewards that they do not deserve. In the name of freedom, in ivory towers, decisions are made by a handful of individuals in power, whose interest focuses solely on benefiting their inner circles.

We do live in dark times and it is this realization that precipitated my pen to touch upon the subject of love, not because love is the solution or the opposite, but unfortunately, more often than not, because love comes in as a factor to push us farther into darkness—we have witnessed in the history of humanity that love has behaved in most unexpected and at times grotesque ways.

On a more mundane, yet no less important level, this book was born from within my profession as a teacher, which was embodied in one of the most successful courses that I have ever taught to date, "The Anthropology of Love." Every time my students expressed surprise, disgust, and compassion, I learned a great deal about love's plasticity, multidimensionality, and cultural relativity. As such, my students' contribution for this book is immeasurable.

Of the 500 or so students that were cumulatively enrolled in "The Anthropology of Love," if any were to read this book, he or she will soon realize that it has no resemblance to the course. Whereas the course encouraged students to read widely from sociobiology, psychology, and medicine to anthropology, sociology, history, and literature of diverse cultures and times, this book focuses solely on Japan, but my objective of trying to understand love among humanity remains the same.

The tale of the birth of this book, as with the nativity of any book, has been complex. Suffice it to say that Stephanie Rogers, senior editor at Taylor & Francis/Routledge, made it happen. This is the second time that I have worked with Stephanie and I wish to state that she is by far the best editor that I have ever known. Her style of letting the author blossom into her autonomy is simply remarkable and a true gift. Helen Baker, also at Taylor & Francis/Routledge, helped me keep up with the schedule with her excellent support.

Dr Don Cameron improved the manuscript tremendously through his remarkable copy-editing and critically informed reading with his trilingual ability in English, Korean, and Japanese. I thank Don for imparting me his talent and energy. I also thank Beverley Winkler and Sarah Fry of Florence Production for their editorial input.

Comments and suggestions by three anonymous academic reviewers as well as Dr Philip Taylor benefited the manuscript. Ongoing conversations with my colleagues and friends, including Linda Angst, Norma Field, John Lie, Gavan McCormack, Marlene Mayo, Karen Nakamura, Mark Selden, Miriam Silverberg, Janet Shibamoto Smith, and S. Hoon Song strengthened this manuscript. The special friendships I am privileged to have with Nancy Abelmann, Jan Bardsley, Haengja Chung, William Kelly, Crystal Kim, Julia Kim, Eleanor Kirkham, Matthew Kroot, Eunja Lee, Youngmi Lim, Charles Lindholm, Vera Mackie, Laura Miller, Jacqueline Mintz, Sidney Mintz, Tessa Morris-Suzuki, Jennifer Robertson, and Wendy Walker sustained and enhanced my work. Professor Alan Macfarlane's work was again a major inspiration for my ideas and interpretations.

The earlier version of parts of Chapter 2 was presented in a workshop held at the Center for the Study of Women, UCLA, and in seminars in the University of Pennsylvania, University of Pittsburgh, and Princeton University. I benefited immensely from feedback from Professors David Howell, Richard Okada, Amy Borovoy, and Sheldon Garon in Princeton. Part of Chapter 4 was presented in a panel organized by Christine Yano for the American Anthropological Association annual meetings in Washington, DC in 2005. I thank Chris for organizing it and Marilyn Ivy for her astute comment.

Inside "The Anthropology of Love," guest lecturers deserve special acknowledgment. Professors Charles Lindholm and Laura Ahearn visited my course and gave lucid, stimulating, and thought-provoking lectures. Their insight enriched the students' discussions as well as my research and was instrumental for inspiring many of my ideas.

The Gordon A. Prange Collection of the University of Maryland was an invaluable source of many of the key materials I use in this book. I thank the librarians there for their assistance.

I wish to acknowledge with gratitude Ms Yada Shōko, the executive editor-in-chief for Daiwashobō, who granted me permission to translate and use parts of the 1963 publication *Ai to shi o mitsumete* (Facing Love and Death) for Chapter 3. All translations in the book from this and other Japanese texts are mine, unless specified.

I omit the macrons for well-known Japanese place names such as Tokyo. Korean transliterations follow the McCune-Reischauer system, unless the author uses a different spelling for his or her name. When citing East Asian names, I follow the native convention of listing the last name first, unless the cited text bears the author's name otherwise, as in the case of the English text written by an East Asian author.

Finally, I wish to note how warmly my family supported me throughout the years of writing this book. My children, Samantha and Thomas, provide me with the meaning of my life and my partner, Bradley Kaldahl, continues to be the source of my strength.

While all those that are acknowledged helped me to make this book better, all shortcomings and faults of the book are mine.

Sonia Ryang, Baltimore
March 2006

Introduction

How should one write about love? Or can one ever write about love without writing also, if not more, about life—and death? What about power, gender, economy, beauty, language, body, and self, that is to say, about society? Some time ago, C.S. Lewis spoke of four loves: affection among familiar persons such as family members; friendship, or love between individuals as individuals, which was in his view the most noble and hence rare form of love; eros, or sexual love between lovers; and charity, love for one's neighbors. Strictly speaking, however, all four loves are about relationships and the self's engagement with them, rather than being an autochthonous ontology of the self as such. As Aristotle asked: "Do men love, then, *the* good, or what is good for *them?*" In other words, when we think about love, self's integrity is tested and self and society are faced with each other.[1]

The inquiry into mastery and care of self in Greek antiquity was closely related to the way in which men formed relationships with others, that is to say, others of certain socio-economic status and political membership. Men assumed appropriate self-care depending on the relationship in question, as different loves required different selves to be posited.[2] Love had to be thus situated in relation to the self and the care of the self. Love, therefore, despite all its seriousness and profundity, is not universal. No form of love—including agape, eros, philia, storge, *amour passion*, patriotism, filial piety, and paternalism—is supra-historical. But all love, even infatuation, comes in the guise of eternity, with a force that is beyond oneself, sometimes considered as madness and other times as sickness. Moreover, every love has its own story, structure and history, and its own social and cultural logic. This book is a study of love in one such context—Japan.

I must first clarify: this book is not intended to answer the question, "What is love?" Rather, it attempts to demonstrate, by looking at the way in which love is discussed, thought of, claimed and disputed, how the national state makes its population into "loving" national subjects. My task is a modest one: to suggest what an ethnological analysis of love as a modern state apparatus might entail. Although I shall be largely working around the concept of romantic love, I'd like to think about love here as a complex set of social functions. Rather than categorizing it as emotion or sentiment, which would inevitably create a separation from sex or lust, I shall maintain the broadest possible conceptualization of love and, as such, shall not divide it into categories such as romantic love, companionate love, passionate love, and so on. Instead, I shall attempt to reconfigure it in conceptually and historically specific ways in order to better describe love in the Japanese context. This means that I shall try my best to sustain the fusion of love and lust, or more precisely, ignore the distinction of love from lust.

In this book, I'd also like to approach love as political technology, maintaining my focus on the way in which love came to be installed and implemented as a state apparatus, shaping the population as self-policing, self-disciplining agencies of love. In this process, I use love to identify the efficacy of the modern Japanese state as a biopower, a form of power that aggressively concerns itself with the life and death of the population. I hold the view that the nation-state and its apparatuses are closely connected to the elements that are constitutive of modern self. Love is one such element, and a very powerful one at that. In moving from premodernity to modernity, Japan, like any other society, has gone through drastic changes in the formation and structure of self. This period has witnessed a metamorphosis of self from the passive, non-participating subject into the active, critically reflexive, decision-making, and self-determining agency. By looking at love's transformation, my exploration inevitably touches upon the emergent process of modern self.

As such, I relate love to Michel Foucault's concept of governmentality and systems of disciplinarity on one hand, and cultural specificities of life and death on the other. In the first connection, I take an approach attempting to locate the regulatory mechanism responsible for the creation of the "loving subject" in Japan. Such an inquiry necessarily requires an examination of how legal and cultural institutions and systems work on individual subjects. The historical shift of the topos of the sovereign from the restored ancient Emperor to postwar democracy is the key to this investigation. At the same time, it is also important to explore how individuals have responded to this process. In the second connection, and inspired by the works of Georgio Agamben, I consider the making of humans into a being with *bios* or a socially and politically meaningful life—and accordingly, death—through the institution of love and loving.

When using the term "love" in the work that follows, I shall be referring to both the narrow and broad senses of social relations, the state of mind and body, and the ideas and actions, which we associate with affection, beauty, tenderness, commitment, passion, and devotion. However, analytically speaking, as stated on p. 1, I am concerned with love as a social function and a political technology of the modern national state in parallel to what Foucault was concerned with in his examination of power.

Traditionally, scholars have treated love as pertaining mainly to the refined class or literate cultures and, as Bronislaw Malinowski implied, assumed that savages had only a sexual life. More recently, love has been studied in the context of discourses and poetics of emotion, as a global assertion of individuality, a material practice within the capitalist market, an expression of social relations, and the key to assessing historical change in a community.[3] In a subtle way, however, recent studies of love have implied a certain distinction between love and lust, romance and sex.

I should remind the reader of the point I made earlier: if my use of the term "love" appears to include or envelope what we might prefer to call "sex," that would be because in the case of Japan, the moment we introduce a divide between love and sex, romance and lust, and mind and body, the conceptual integrity of love appears to break down. From a different angle, Foucault, in writing *History of Sexuality*, turned the question of repression into that of the discourse of repression; hence, rather than asking why we are repressed, he asks: "Why do we say we are repressed?" The question remains: in a culture where sexual repression was not the issue, such as Japan, then, can we still talk about love? For, sexual repression or the discourse thereof became institutionalized on the basis of the love/lust distinction.[4]

I am not, however, asserting that in some transparent manner non-Western forms of love have no mind-body distinction, while Western loves are Cartesian. The distinction between love and lust exists in most societies, yet the rationale behind it differs dramatically. In the case of Japan, it is important to register that historically, love was an institution that included sexual consummation, and, as such, to consider them separately as we tend to do in Western (more precisely, Christianized) discourse is a misstep. It was Sigmund Freud who emphasized that all loving feelings are inevitably the reincarnation of sexual undercurrents of emotional tension.[5] This is not what I mean about Japan, either. Freudian theory is itself premised on the distinction between love and sex, and hence the denial of this distinction. When discussing ancient Japan, where this distinction was alien, it would therefore be a mistake to base an exploration of the concept of love on the presumption of such a denial.

For this reason, throughout this book I maintain certain skepticism or, shall I say, uncertainty about the possibility of defining love. When so-called Westernization, seen as modernization's conjoined twin, reaches and interacts with various traditions, inevitably, the alchemy leads to interesting and unpredictable results. The ingredients react to each other, not exactly as planned in the recipe—if there was one in the first place—and produce a concoction that is twisted, paradoxical, and unique. This might of course be seen as unvirtuous, decadent, or even perverted by some

observers, including those of differing cultures and of differing generations of the same cultural tradition. At times, judgments are reversed, with
younger members of a population either denouncing their antecedents as
defiled or conversely, celebrating the past as free and savagely noble. I
am trying to see Japan from this kind of angle—that of a synchronic
concoction, rather than a diachronic continuity. As such, the historical
framework which I adopt in this book can only be taken as a heuristic
device assisting the analysis.

However, there is no recipe or master chef. Rather, there are ideas and
institutions that react to each other in strange ways. The role of the modern
Japanese nation-state is decisive, but that, too, is not so obvious, since in
a mere 100-year period following the Meiji Restoration of 1868, Japan
underwent an intense process of change. Its political form, it is typically
argued, was changed from prewar emperor-worshipping militarist totalitarianism to postwar democracy. In the past seventy years alone, its
economy shifted from state-nurtured capitalism and colonial expansionism
to wartime mobilization, then to economic liberalism and later to affluent
late capitalism, currently facing recession after an extended boom period.
In the meantime, its population went through a generational shift combined
with various transformations in kinship structure and family composition.

Few better examples could be found in which to examine the state as
biopower as that of wartime Japan, where life as well as death was dedicated to the restored ancient sovereign, the Emperor. This period commenced not with the attacks on Pearl Harbor, but rather with Japan's
incursions into China at the very start of the 1930s, and constituted one
long state of emergency, one long state of siege, in which the power of
the sovereign became unlimited, ubiquitously perceivable and universally
visible. Wartime Japan's extremities, including the recruitment of "comfort
women" (i.e. sex slaves) for Japanese soldiers, the phenomenon of the
kamikaze bomber, the massacre and rape of Nanjing, and other unimagin-
able atrocities perpetrated by the Japanese military, need to be understood
in the context of this power. Meanwhile, at the everyday domestic level,
the National Eugenics Law of 1940 determined that individuals with "lesser
genes" (i.e. the disabled, the terminally ill, and the disfigured) should be
sterilized, and healthy women were encouraged to have an average of five
children, in order to achieve the national goal of populating Japan with 100
million "babies of the Emperor" or *tennō no sekishi*.

In wartime Japan, men and women loved each other via the Emperor's
love and reproduced children for Him. I call this love "sovereign love"
in Chapter 2. The notion of sovereign is particularly important to understanding love in the Japanese context. Unlike in France, for example,
where a rather clear replacement of the royal sovereign and the *ancien
régime* with national citizens' sovereignty had occurred in coordination

(in retrospect) with the intellectual trajectories of the Enlightenment, preparing the French population for modernity, Japan's modernity developed hand in hand with the reinstatement of the Emperor as the sovereign. Thus, Japan's first modern population assumed the form of the imperial subject. There were some exceptions; for example, many in the society's lowest strata failed to join the modern nationhood and participate in the national form of love, that is, sovereign love. To illustrate this point, I draw upon the 1936 incident of Abe Sada, a former prostitute who ended up murdering her lover and castrating him afterwards. I juxtapose this incident with what I see as the more orthodox aspect of sovereign love displayed by the Japanese military in the city of Nanjing one year later in 1937, and in the military "comfort stations," especially those operating during the height of the Pacific War.

Once we look at the love of the ancient Japanese, we know that the imperial gaze during the Heian period (late eighth to eleventh centuries) and that during the period from the Meiji Restoration until the end of World War II were two fundamentally different institutions. For Japanese ancients, as stated on p. 3, love meant holism: it included from the outset bodily fusion usually taking the form of sexual consummation. I try to show this in Chapter 1 by referring to the *Manyōshū* or the Book of Ten Thousand Songs, compiled in the late eighth century AD, by drawing upon the poetic and ethnological insights of Origuchi Shinobu, one of the most important twentieth-century Japanese thinkers, and by examining the historical and ethnological insights of Takamure Itsue, one of the most intriguingly original feminist scholars in modern Japan.[6]

I also address in Chapter 1 the ritual-like, sacred aspects of sexual play in festivals and in the marketplace, observed in diverse geographical locations and timeframes. Such practices included offering one's wife and/or daughter to a stranger that knocked on the door, seeking overnight shelter in a remote mountainous lodging, for example, or the custom of *yobai* (nightcrawling), which instituted a nightly rotation of males (married or unmarried) visiting females (married or unmarried) in the village—a custom that existed until postwar Japan in some areas. The notion of the sacred becomes the key to understanding these and other similar institutions. The polytheistic existence of the sacred, as illustrated in the existence of various little deities—gods of the street corner, gods of the intersection, gods of the village border, and so on—strictly speaking challenged the possibility of the monotheistic sacred, the best example being the restored imperial sovereign of Meiji Japan. Chapter 1 thus prepares the reader to see the anomalous, or should I say, following Hannah Arendt, perverted structure of sovereign love.[7]

War's end did not bring down the ethos and practice of the wartime state of siege overnight; rather, it reconfigured them—a fact which is often overlooked. The institution of *junketsukyōiku* (purity education) promoted by the Ministry of Education constituted one such reconfiguration. Purity education elevated female premarital virginity the utmost criterion of love, while the 1940 National Eugenics Law remained unrepealed until 1996. As such, the values and norms of eugenics lived on through the love and romance of postwar Japanese men and women. It is therefore no wonder that the national demographic goal continued to be upheld—though with the state now in the background as opposed to the incessant mention and reference to the Emperor in prewar times—and was finally achieved in 1967, reaching the 100 million population mark.

As opposed to sovereign love, postwar Japan's purity education came in the form of citizen's rights. Under the postwar US Occupation (1945–52), Japan's national education system was reformed, with hundreds of schools now becoming coeducational, while the burden of purity landing solely on the body of female students. The genealogy of the evolution of female students or *jogakusei* parallels that of Japanese modernity, and provides important clues to understanding love in the Japanese context. If, under the Meiji government, *jogakusei* symbolized civilization, modernization, and enlightenment, in postwar Japan, female students became a primary site to embody the nation's purity. With this in mind, in Chapter 3 I introduce what I call the national romance of Miko and Mako (nicknames), a model of pure love which ended tragically and prematurely with the death in 1963 of Miko, a beautiful college student whose face was destroyed by the surgery undertaken on the incurable cancer on her facial bones. This story, as will be shown, is exemplary in many ways of what the Ministry of Education's purity education demanded of Japan's young men and women.

The nation-state is not the only actor in determining the population's loving, living, and dying. Even in a so-called democracy, the population itself actively takes part in self-reform, self-policing and self-education in complicity, collaboration, and coordination with state apparatuses through their interaction with educational, cultural, and media institutions. Through such activities, individuals become law-abiding, rule-following, and producing-and-consuming members of the nation, and indeed, citizens. In fact, this process is more clearly visible in democracies as freedom of thought gives the population many different avenues through which to voice what it deems to be its own opinion and to assert its own lifestyle in terms of rights and entitlement. Furthermore, the state remains for the most part hidden in the background, appearing as an impartial and non-interventionistic entity, while in reality its role is precisely to condition individuals to think of the state as invisible. Love is one such context in which the apparatuses of the modern nation-state engage directly with the population, yet the population is made to (and is more than willing to, at the same time) believe that it is the person who is in love, and not that this very notion of love is one manufactured and promoted by state apparatuses such as the education system and the media.[8]

I use the concept of governmentality more explicitly in Japan's postwar context. Here, it is said, Japanese were granted democracy, and love became liberated from the imperialist state project and the Emperor's gaze and available, equally and freely, to citizens as their personal choice. However, while the end of the war brought an end to Japan's state of emergency, and a system in which the imperial sovereign possessed unlimited power, the national state came to replace this entity in its role of monitoring and policing the population in an omnipresent yet now largely invisible way. With the withdrawal of the state into the background, the sphere of the mundane came to be subjected more fully, to its last cell, to the operations of state apparatuses in such fields as education, culture, media, and public health. I shall further explore this logic in Chapter 3.

The continuation of elements of prewar demographic policy during the postwar period allowed Japan to avoid accepting immigrant workers in order to sustain the labor-intensive stage of postwar economic recovery. The exclusion of former colonial subjects who had remained in Japan after the war was rearranged, and this group, mostly Korean, was denied participation in the national sovereignty. They were abandoned to a precarious existence with no civil or political rights. More frighteningly, with no connection to the Japanese nation-state, they became "naked human beings" without human rights in a world where such rights were given only to citizens of a polity or sovereign nation—what Agamben called bare life.[9]

With this in mind, in Chapter 4 I present a study of a more recent time, in which the paradoxical long-term side effect of purity education makes itself known in ironic and twisted ways. I explore three contexts: the world of underage prostitution by female high school students or *joshikōsei,* conventionally called *enjokōsai,* which I translate as "aid-dating"; the novel *Shitsurakuen* (Paradise Lost), which details an adulterous affair and captured the imagination and desire of married men and women in Japan, selling three million copies in 1997 alone; and the phenomenon described by the media as "Yongfluenza" among middle-aged Japanese women in the early 2000s—a term derived from the name of the lead male actor, Bae Yong Joon, in the extremely popular South Korean *junai* (pure love) television drama *The Winter Sonata,* first aired by the publicly owned NHK network in 2003. I intend to explore these popular-cultural carriers of love in conjunction with the anxiety of the Japanese state in light of the crisis it is facing due to the continuing record low birthrate and the onset of the aging society. The manifestation of this anxiety comes in diverse forms, including the persecution of non-nationals such as Korean female students. Love, in this context, takes on yet another form—that of ambiguous denationalization. While the Japanese state is not abandoning the fundamental principle of its foundation—Japan being the nation only of the Japanese—ideas relating to how "Japanese love" should be and

how the Japanese should love and marry, for example, are being redefined around and beyond the national boundaries, albeit in an uncertain
way. An investigation of references to denationalized former colonial
subjects, Koreans in Japan, will help us see the process discussed in
Chapter 4. Let us see, then, how we can understand love and its transformation in modern Japan.

1 Sacred sex

Between the country of Tosa and Awa ... the mountain ridges meet
on a peak where a small shrine stands ... This was a meeting point
of two villages on each side of the mountain.

Every year, on a designated day, men and women from each village
spent a night here inside the shrine.

That night, those men and women, who had never met each other
before in their ordinary lives, slept together to make love. This reminds
us of *kagai* [the custom of entering into one-night sexual relationship
with a stranger]. Of course, this custom is widely known in other
provinces [of Japan]. But, this particular one deserves some attention
... since it followed the ancient formality of exchanging poems and
only those men and women whose poems tied even [i.e. formed a
unified poetic pair] went to bed together.[1]

In what reminds us of Herodotus's account of Babylonian custom inside
the Temple of Ishtar, ethnologist and poet Origuchi Shinobu reminisces on
the olden-day scene where Japanese villagers met as strangers at night in
the remote mountains. Whereas Babylonian men courted virgins "in the
name of Mylitta" and by throwing coins, Japanese villagers exchanged
poems as a precondition to sexual liaison.[2] Moreover, these poetic exchanges
had to follow specific rules as in any other games, in this case relating to
the number of syllables, rhymes, and semantic relevance. Unlike Babylon,
where all virgins prior to marriage were not permitted to leave the Temple
of Ishtar and get married until they had sex with a stranger, many Japanese
villages often involved men and women of all ages, both married and
unmarried, in sacred sex rituals during shrine festivals and religious fairs.

If love is a modern concept, and we are only accustomed to the distinction between what we now call lust and love, how can we understand the
fact that many ancient sacred rituals involved sex, notably, sexual intercourse with gods or goddesses, who, in all guises and variations, cannot
but be described as those of abundance, fertility, and above all, love?

Indeed, as in the cases of Babylon and ancient Japan, it was the custom that human bodies replaced godly figures, for the act of sex itself in the temple was the sacred offering and the sex between strangers celebrated gods and goddesses and embraced their fertility and prosperity. Thus, in Babylon, all unmarried women had to have sex with a man, any man, inside the Temple of Ishtar, "in the name of Mylitta," as a gift to the goddess. Without this ritual, marriage was to incur the wrath of the sacred and was therefore polluted. In order not to anger the goddess, a virgin had to give her virginity first to the deity that came in the form of a stranger inside the temple. This sacred act was at once ritual and cleansing, celebration and protection. In this picture, a virgin's sex did not primarily belong to her marriage with a human husband. It had to be first and foremost offered and sacrificed to the goddess, the sacred.

A set of questions immediately comes to mind. Why was sex sacred in the minds of the ancients? Why was it closely associated with deity? What was its position in the cosmological understanding of the ancients? Roger Caillois (along with many others) has remarked: "The sexual act already inherently possesses a fecundating power." Indeed, sexual sacrilege (along with dietary and material excess) is characteristic of numerous festivals and rituals throughout the world, where "the suspension of the ordinary rules of sexual behavior signifies nothing else than a temporary ascent to the beginning of the ancient time of creation." Referring to the creation myths of many cultures, in which the original birth and fertility were secured by brother-sister incest, Caillois reminds us that the breaking of the rules as witnessed in sexual orgies in festivals was a ritual or sacred act of return to the very beginning of the community.[3]

Seen from a socio-historical perspective, it is not too difficult to infer that the sacredness of sex was closely correlated with the weakness (or absence) of the notions of patriarchy and private property (including women and children). Broadly argued, ancient patriarchy, in this sense, was different from modern patriarchy, in that the patriarch's humanly claim stopped short in front of the temple. In a way, as Jungian analyst Nancy Qualls-Corbett suggests, the feminine element had as much validity and potency as the masculine.[4] Woman's sexuality was not placed directly under the control of the patriarch, but of gods, the divine, and the unknown. This could also be related to the polytheism of most ancient societies, as opposed to the monotheism of the world religions that later came to dominate human societies. It is interesting in this sense to remember that Japan is one society where even today polytheism and diverse religiosity are apparent.

In this chapter, I shall selectively discuss concepts and practices that historically have contributed to the emergence and transformation of the meaning of love in Japan. I must caution the reader that this chapter is not intended to offer a chronological and empirical study of history. Rather, it is an ethnological exposition of key concepts, figures, and practices pertaining to love. As such, I take a synchronic approach, tracing the sacred aspects of love and their later decline in Japan. Love, here, is meant to be a working definition, as discussed in the Introduction.

1

Kagai, the custom referred to by Origuchi Shinobu, is but one form of sexual encounter between men and women outside wedlock in ancient and medieval Japan that was institutionalized, ritualized, and consecrated. As recently as the late nineteenth and early twentieth centuries, there were many instances of practices that were akin to *kagai,* and other examples of offering "sacred sex." For example, in the Usukinu village of Ōita prefecture in southern Japan, every August during the festival of the guardian god, both married and unmarried women had to make love with three males. In the Hita district of the same prefecture, during the village fair in the Gomahime shrine, every night within the premise of the shrine, men and women were obliged to have sex, regardless of whether they knew each other or not. There were at least two or three other shrines in Ōita that practiced this institution. The famous pleasing-god dance festival (*kagura*) of the Sōraku district in the Aichi prefecture in central Japan lasted seven days and nights. On the third evening, after the dance of *tengu* (a figure with an elongated nose), men and women sought each other out and had sex. At the two-day October festival at Kumo shrine in the Sōma district of the Ibaraki prefecture in northeastern Japan, men and women had sex after the fair. According to local belief, this sexual encounter was seen as sacred magic to enhance women's fertility and men's virility, thereby inviting prosperity to the entire village. As late as the late 1920s in the Izu archipelago off the coast of Tokyo, on the day of *bon* (the festival of receiving dead souls), men and women sought sexual liaison in public, on the beach, on someone's front doorstep, on the street corner, in other words anywhere at all under all kinds of circumstances. Names for such customs included *kagai, okomori, zakone,* and so on.[5]

How are we to understand these instances of sexual excess? Is there anything sacred about these? The fact that these took place strictly within the premises of a shrine and exclusively during holy rituals and festivals is of significance—they took place only in front of, in the presence of, and with the blessing of the gods.

Some Japanese scholars deem it important that the ancients, referring to this kind of sexual practice, used the term *kamiasobi* or godly (sacred) play. With the presence of gods on these particular days in those particular places, no one was held responsible or morally reproached.[6] The play element here seems important. As Johannes Huizinga argues, play is serious, sacred, and rule-bound behind the façade that gives the impression of spontaneity. While being very primitive, play (for both children and adults) is a high intellectual and artistic activity for humans (and to some extent animals also). If any of the participants disregarded the rules or questioned the validity of fun, the game would fail or cease to exist. As such, play is highly ritualistic. Huizinga further emphasizes a parallel between play and seizure. Play makes one forget about oneself, buried in fascination and excitement, and as such, has similar attributes to the seizure in which one loses control of oneself or one becomes so self-absorbed that one loses touch with oneself. This rule-bound chaos, socially sanctioned de-sociality, and self-absorbed and self-oblivious passion generates the sacredness of ritual and play alike.[7]

At the same time, presuming too close or facile an association between play and the sacred would lead us to gloss over the delicate and complex relationship between sacred, fecundity-provoking sexual rituals and inherently unproductive activity such as play. As Caillois argues, in criticizing Huizinga, the overlap between play and the sacred is only partial, and it ends as soon as one begins to look beyond mere forms and formality. Caillois draws attention to the fact that whereas participation in ritual is mandatory, participation in play has to be based on free choice. Although both are rule-bound and exist outside the ordinary, many aspects of play are secular.[8] I would also add that despite their similarity on the level of morphology, they each have a different logic of economy. Nevertheless, as will be shown below, in the Japanese context, the concept of play or *asobi* becomes an important point in grasping the horizons of the sacred, or more precisely in elucidating *sacer,* the ambiguous double-facetedness of the sacred (see pp. 27–8). Similarly, in the Japanese context, sacred aspects of sex hold an important key for our understanding of love.

The ethnographic examples cited above direct us to register the "strangeness" of men and women that made sexual contact during the festival. In their ordinary lives, they were village neighbors and acquaintances. In many cases, sexual encounters were limited within the community during the days and nights of the festival. The only rule was that one had to have sex with *anybody*. A deliberate pretension or supposition of "stranger" existed here. Men and women pretended to be strangers, and had sex in the presence of the gods, reminding us of Herodotus's observation of the Babylonian practice as stated on p. 9. What does this say and what is the significance of "being strange"?

In order to respond to these questions, it is important firstly to know who was seen as "sacred." For this purpose, it will be necessary to take a slight detour, notably, through the world of *Manyōshū* or the Book of Ten Thousand Songs, since this will provide an angle to connect sex between strangers and love on the one hand, and love and sexual consummation on the other.

Compiled in AD 759, the poems in *Manyōshū* are grouped into different genres by later scholars. However, when discussing love, it is not at all clear where we can focus. For example, the genre of "mutually-longing songs" or *sōmonka* refers to the poems that were exchanged not only between individuals that were sexually involved, but also between individuals whose affections were not sexually oriented, including brother and sister or mother and son. Also, *banka* or the genre of "songs for the dead" is full of poems that express the feelings or sentiments that we would conventionally call love.

In today's Japanese language, there are three words that are commonly used to denote the English word love—*koi, ai,* and *renai,* the last being the amalgamation of the characters *koi* and *ai*. The term that *Manyō* poets used was *koi. Ai,* according to Itō Susumu, the author of *Nihonjin no ai* (Japanese Love), came to be applied to love only after the Meiji Restoration of 1868, primarily as a translation of "love," "*liebe*," or "*amour*" in order to accommodate encounters with Western literature. Itō notes that in *Manyō* songs, the character *ai* was used to denote beauty and qualifies it as not part of daily language, but belonging to the religious realm.[9] *Renai* is also a new word, created to match Western notions of romance and romantic love, although the meaning of this term is closer to that of *koi* rather than *ai. Renai* was much discussed by the first wave of Japanese feminists in the late nineteenth to early twentieth centuries, represented by Seitōsha or the Blue Stocking Society and its leader, Hiratsuka Raichō.[10] In today's Japanese usage, *ai* may be applied to a mother's love for her children, for example, but *koi* would not be used in this context, since it primarily has a connotation of sexual love, infatuation, or erotic passion. Depending on the context, however, *ai* could also be used with this meaning.

As stated above, the love that was expressed in *Manyōshū* is *koi*. But it would be an error to simply equate this term with the English "love." Just as the English term evolved over the centuries and just as it can refer to a wide spectrum of phenomena, emotions, and actions, including religious devotion, benevolence, liking, tenderness, affection, and material desire, in addition to sexual attraction, *koi* in *Manyō* poems has a breadth of semantic versatility and applicability.

Itō argues that the notion of love that *Manyō* poets expressed possessed two loci: self and other. The first locus is solitude. Love grows and resides in a lonely heart. The endurance of painful separation from the loved one (including the separation by death) or the deeply frustrating sense of longing for the inaccessible lover is the sentiment expressed here by the term *koi*. Often, a lone lover expressed his or her feelings in terms of *hitorine*: *hitori* is a lone person and *ne* comes from the verb "to sleep," *neru*. We can see that *koi* as expressed in *Manyōshū* contained in itself an indissoluble mixture of notions of bodily fusion and emotional union. By focusing on the term *kohi,* which is interchangeable with *koi* (given the tendency of *h* to become silent just like the French *h* muét), Itō suggests that *koi* for the eighth-century Japanese poets meant *ko* (alone) and *hi* (sad, sorrowful). In this interpretation, *koi* is the sadness of having to stay, live, or sleep alone.[11]

Where, then, does love begin? This is Itō's second locus. *Koi* in *Manyōshū* is not the result of one's own decision or choice, but of the captivating attraction of the other; it is the other's magical pull that causes *koi*. Itō shows how the term *koi* appears in relation to the concept of *ni oite* (in, within), denoting the locus, as in "... *ni kou*" (*kou* is a verbal form of *koi*). Here, *koi* is not something that one controls, but one is made captive to the other, or more precisely, one is (regardless of one's will) brought and bound to be in a *koi* situation.[12] Interestingly, it was male poets that often wrote about *koi* in this way, seeing the origin of *koi* residing in the attraction of the other, his beloved, and not in himself. In this perception, *koi* is not controlled by one's willpower—it is inevitable, a product of fate, a power that goes beyond human capacity.

It is possible that Itō's type of rationale unduly beautifies and distorts the picture of love of the ancients according to his own ideals of love. By contrast, when we read interpretations of *Manyō* poems from the Korean perspective, an entirely different vision, ethos, and concept of love emerges. Lee Young Hee, a renowned Korean literary scholar, author, and member of parliament, proposes to read *Manyō* poems combining old Japanese and old Korean. In her book *Mō hitotsu no Manyōshū* (The Other *Manyōshū*), which caused much controversy and animosity among Japanese scholars, Lee suggests a set of fascinating rereadings of key poems. Lee, inspired by the fact that *Manyō* poems as we know them today are the reinterpretation and transliteration of versions from eighth-century Japan, checked the original Chinese characters of poems against the old Korean usage at the times in which poems were composed.

Lee's endeavor seems to be historically substantiated. Chinese characters were used in both Japan and Korea (or, more precisely, in the kingdoms that existed in the territories now occupied by Japan and Korea) for dual purposes: for state-level documentation and in order to denote the sounds of native languages. Basically, no absolute rule was followed in the latter practice, and this almost semi-random use of Chinese characters, called *Manyō kana,* made it difficult for later translation/transliteration of *Manyō* poems into the post-Heian (eighth to eleventh centuries) Japanese language. This difficulty was compounded by the fact that the latter combined the newly invented vernacular writing system of *hiragana* (denoting sounds) with the existing use of Chinese characters.

The same method of using Chinese characters for the purpose of copying native sounds was also prevalent in Korea, where the invention of a vernacular writing system had to wait until the fifteenth century. (In both Korea and Japan, an all-Chinese writing system continued to be the norm for recording royal and imperial chronicles until the late nineteenth century in Japan and the early twentieth century in Korea.) During the fifth and sixth centuries, kingdoms in southern Korea used the writing system called *idu,* by which writers chose characters either to copy the sound of the indigenous word or to convey its meaning. In the first method, the meaning of a character was disregarded, while in the second method, the sound of a character was disregarded and although there was certain regularity, no rules bore absolute authority. It was therefore difficult for later interpreters to identify exactly what the writer intended to communicate.

During the same period, the two southern Korean kingdoms of Paekje and Silla fought fiercely over territorial hegemony, and eventually Silla won, forcing Paekje aristocrats to go into exile in the seventh century. The most obvious destination was Japan, and their arrival furthered the blending of cultures of the archipelago and the peninsula at that time. Indeed, there are poems of which location is not too easily determinable as to whether they are referring to Korea or Japan at the time. In this light, Lee's proposal to read *Manyō* poems by combining the knowledge of the *idu* system with the ancient Japanese usage of Chinese characters known as *Manyō kana* seems to be warranted.

In the context of our study, Lee's rereading enables us to see what we would call today the sexually explicit aspects of love during the *Manyō* era. Her work is particularly relevant to a key argument of this chapter, in that it helps us understand the "love" adored by *Manyō* poets not simply as emotion but as a complex fusion of mind and body, emotional longing and carnal unison, words and deeds, and as a set of social functions.

In one of the most loved and famed songs of the *Manyō* collection, we find the following:

*Akanesasu murasakino yuki shimeno yuki
nomoriwa mizuya kimiga sodefuru*

(Over the purple field, the marked field [of the Emperor], a guard is watching, is he not, you wave your sleeve [toward me].)[13]

The poem was composed by Nukatano ōkimi (Princess Nukata), who, by the time of reciting this poem, was one of the consorts of the Emperor Tenji (or Tenchi; reigned AD 661–72). This emperor used to be called Nakano ōeno ōji (Prince Nakano ōe), and defeated the powerful Soga clan in AD 645, heralding the era of literati-style reform under the imperial family, modeled after the Chinese system of law and order (*ritsuryō*). After the death of the Emperor Tenji, his younger brother suppressed opposition forces and became the Emperor Tenmu (reigned AD 672–86). Princess Nukata had been a lover of Tenmu, who used to be called Ōamano miko (Prince Ōama). When his older brother, the Emperor Tenji, demanded the princess, Prince Ōama had to give her up. As soon as he became the Emperor Tenmu after his brother's death, the princess returned to him, although the place of the empress was occupied by the deceased Tenji's eldest daughter, the Empress Jitō, who eventually succeeded her uncle/husband's reign (and reigned AD 686–97).

The above-quoted poem was composed when the Emperor Tenji went on an outing. Since it was customary for the imperial family and imperial consorts to accompany him on such occasions, Princess Nukata and Prince Ōama, as consort and younger brother of the Emperor, were both in the party and had glimpses of each other. Hence, her concern: is the guard watching you wave your sleeve toward me?

However, according to Lee, Princess Nukata and Prince Ōama did not simply exchange glances, but they made love. Lee rereads the poem with the *idu* system as follows:

> *Kokdoshong satch'i porasaekbŏl kane py'omalbŏl kane*
> *pŏlchik'isha anipojae kŭdae kasabŏlyŏ*

> (My fantasy lord's phallus cometh to my purple [female genital] in this forbidden field [marked by the Emperor]. I wonder if the guard watches your opening my scissors [thighs].)[14]

Lee's reinterpretation, not surprisingly, caused a hostile reaction among Japanese scholars of *Manyō* poems. (Did the fact that Lee was a Korean play a certain role in inflaming the hostility?) One linguist, Yasumoto Biten, called it a "sexual harassment" of *Manyō* poems.[15]

Upon further reading, however, Lee's reinterpretation does not depart radically from the Japanese interpretation. This relates to the prince's act of waving his sleeve toward the princess. And here is the key to our understanding of "love" in *Manyō* Japan. In order to lead to this, I'll have to make one more detour.

Ethnologist Origuchi Shinobu identifies the *Manyō* etymology of the term *koi* as deriving from magic. In ancient Japan, human life was perceived as incorporating *mi* (body) and *tama* (soul). Death was thought to be the departure of *tama* from *mi*. From this, if one could retain or bring back the soul that was about to leave or had just left the body, it was believed, one could revive the dead person. This magic was called *tamagoi,* a word consisting of *tama* and *koi.* Here, *koi* means "to beg" or "to plead," which is a homonym for *koi* (love). When put together with *tama,* it becomes *tamagoi,* rather than *tamakoi,* due to an elision-like effect. Origuchi places emphasis on this homonym, attributing to love a more active or action-oriented connotation, symbolizing the act of "taking" rather than passively "waiting to be given." According to Origuchi:

Kohi meant *shōkon* [inviting the soul back to the body] and this action is called *kofu*. Therefore, this is not only applied to the living humans. Death was understood to be the state in which the soul was evaporating, but as long as this soul was to return [to the body], the dead was to be revived. Since the ancients thought in this way, they often performed *shōkon* for the dead …

Later, scholars came to interpret *kohi* as love, as in inviting the soul of the person you love into yourself. After all, love was understood to be an exchange of the soul and this soul was believed to reside in clothing, or more precisely, the underwear and hence, the ancients exchanged their underwear. When the husband [who visited the woman during the night, according to the matrimonial system of the day—see the next section] left the woman in the morning, people called this parting *kinuginu no wakare* [parting of cloths]—this originated in the aforementioned belief [in the connection between the soul and underwear] … But [*shōkon*] was not merely a means of love—it was to invite the soul [back to this world].[16]

What does Origuchi mean when he emphasizes that *tamagoi* was not simply a means of love, but the act of inviting the soul, that is, magic? In the ritual of *tamagoi,* love is an action, rather than a feeling or sentiment: one goes out to fetch the soul of the loved one who had just died or had been lost. This is thought to be an extraordinary event. As such, this is a sacred act in the sense that it goes outside of the ordinary. Interestingly, in *Manyōshū*, it is female poets that wrote about *koi* in this way. Let us take a close look at the following poem by the Empress Iha (Iwa):

Kakubakari kohitsutsuarazuha
takayamano iwaneshimakite shinamashimonoo[17]

This song is usually understood as:

If I have to wait for you for this long, yet there is no hope for your return, I'd rather be dead and gone under the large rock on the high mountains.

Origuchi's interpretation is different:

My lover's dead and gone and my magic brings no effect. I'd rather be dead and lie down next to my lover between the rocks on the high mountains.[18]

He then hesitates whether to classify this poem as "love song" or "song for the dead." Eventually, he avoids the issue, and merely emphasizes the close relationship between magic and love, that is, the transfer or exchange of souls. In other words, Origuchi would seem to suggest, since both love and death involve the transfer of the soul outside the body (as in death) or to another body (as in love), the classification does not have to be so rigid. Instead, he further suggests, we should pay more attention to the way ancient Japanese poets saw the movement of the soul.[19] *Koi* in this light condenses diverse meanings such as "to long for," "to want," "to desire," "to possess," "to beg," "to transfer," "to go and fetch (the soul, dead or alive)," and "to absorb"—or "to love."

Furthermore, as Origuchi suggests, the exchange of souls was believed to be embodied in undergarments and this belief lay behind the practice of lovers actually exchanging underwear in the morning after their night of sexual liaison. This morning parting was called *kinuginu no wakare* or "the parting of cloth(s) or silk," as stated above. Importantly, Origuchi asserts that the act of waving sleeves or waving cloth also meant "lovemaking."[20] Although the poem actually cites *sode* (sleeve), this should be taken broadly (and euphemistically) to mean "clothing" or "cloth(s)," including undergarments. This act was a metonym for "love," which was not simply longing or sex, but a magical beckoning of the other's soul to oneself and equally magical sending-off of one's soul to the other. That is why the symbols of the previous night's consummation, the undergarments, were exchanged and then waved at one's lover.

From this, it should be clear that the field guard in Emperor Tenji's excursion party came to know of Princess Nukata and Prince Ōama's love-making: whether it was expressed through "opening [my] scissors" (*kŭdae kasabŏlyŏ*) or by "waving the sleeve" (*kimiga sodefuru*) is perhaps not so important. Lee is, interestingly, overly apologetic about having discovered the alternative, sexually explicit, Korean reading of what Japan's classical literary scholars treasure as the apex of national aesthetics.[21] Yasumoto, one of Lee's critics, was upset as he took her interpretation as sexual harassment in relation to the *Manyō* poems, as stated on p. 16. In my view, both are somewhat missing the point: love and sex were not separable and, as one, it was a serious cultural endeavor and wholesome passion of the *Manyō* era. Indeed, love and sex, inseparable and together, constituted an important component of life, addressing the question, "How should one live?" To get indignant about its sexual aspect as if it is unbecoming and to be apologetic about sexual discovery as if the act of physical union is degrading, are equally anachronistic, since these reactions reflect the prejudices and embarrassment of our own time, not the time of the *Manyō* poets.

2

As can be seen in the above discussion, ancient courtship involved an exchange of poems in set with sexual relations, just like the shrine sex on the mountain between Tosa and Awa. The subsequent sexual liaison, in its turn, was understood as marriage, albeit in a temporary and unstable form. Conversely, marriage meant primarily a sexual liaison. It is imperative here to understand kinship and marriage in traditional Japan. The matrimonial system prior to the Nara period (AD 710–94) was matrilocal (or uxorilocal) polygamy with the husband visiting plural wives and, to lesser extent, the wife receiving plural husbands, a practice called *tsumado(h)i* (visiting the wives). Children were raised matrilocally in the mother's family. By custom, women stayed in their (maternal) family home to receive the husband at dusk, sending him off at dawn.

However, referring to this system simply as "matrilocal," "uxorilocal," "polygamy," or "ploygyny," as if to assume that these well-worn (Western) anthropological terms can exhaust the nuances of ancient Japanese kinship and marriage, would be greatly misleading. For one thing, whether matri-locality was reflecting or closely connected with matrilineage or not cannot be easily determined, and if these were connected, how they manifested is far from clear. At the same time, after the introduction of the continental-style *ritsuryō* (law and order) system under Emperor Tenji in the seventh century, it became mandatory for children to be listed under the father's *uji* (clan name) on the household register, although the hitherto customary cognatic system of recording the mother's clan name first, accompanied with the father's clan name beside it, continued.[22]

The ethnologist and historian Takamure Itsue suggests that in Japan the shift from matrilineage to patrilineage took a long time. She cites various bases for this view. First was the existence of a strict taboo of mixing hearths between women of different matriclans. Second, the incest taboo was strictly observed among half-siblings who shared a mother but not a father. The practice of *tsumadoi* gradually shifted to that of *mukotori* (taking the son-in-law marriage), during the Kamakura period (1186–1333). *Mukotori* meant a reduction to only a few years in the period when the husband would stay at his wife's home before they moved permanently to his home. Nevertheless, the ancient taboo of not mixing the two matri-lineal hearths continued to be observed, thereby forcing the husband's parents to move out of the main building in the name of *inkyo* (literally, a hidden or withdrawn residence, denoting retirement). Further, until recently, there was no taboo regarding marriage between patrilineal cousins or that between patrilineal uncles and nieces, for example. Takamure attributes this, in a more historical perspective, to the lack of a strong, dominant presence of slavery in Japanese history.[23] In Rome, for example, slavery was structured in the idioms of patriarchy; in Japan, such an image of a patriarch claiming ownership of women, children, and slaves of the household appears only in the proto-modern period.

However, the issue of lineage, or more precisely speaking, the issue of determining lineage is, in my view, far more complicated and complex than Takamure appears to suggest. Takamure somehow connects matri-locality and matrilineage unproblematically. But, whether the matrilocality and incest taboo among children of the same mother meant matrilineage is not obvious. Furthermore, more fundamentally, what *is* matrilineage? In what today's Western anthropology sees as the typical matrilineal system, that is, the Trobriand kinship system as studied and depicted by Bronislaw Malinowski, lineage succession is materialized through special kin relations between the mother's brother (avunculate uncle) and son. In Japan's *tsumadoi* marriage, there is no male kin that plays any role. Of course, this is not to say that the Japanese *tsumadoi* is not matrilineal because it does not conform to the Trobriand type. The Trobriand type is only one among many possible matrilineal varieties.[24]

Under the *tsumadoi* arrangement, the husband and wife were not cohab-itants, that is, they did not share a living space, daytime activities, and child-rearing duties. While suspending the conclusion about matri-lineality, it is undoubtedly true that it was the husband that visited his wife, and not vice versa. Takamure (and many others, including Origuchi) notes that the husband was referred to as *maraudo* (read *marōdo*), *marebito*, or *kyakujin*, meaning respectively "guest" or "visitor," "rare or precious person" or "stranger," or "traveler." *Marebito* takes two characters of *kyaku* (guest, visitor) and *hito* (human). *Mare* in itself means rare, unusual, or precious.

According to Origuchi, the term *marebito* in the olden times also denoted gods that came to visit humans cyclically from *tokoyo* (see below) at the designated time. Ancient villagers supposed the sound of the door knocking from the outside (possibly by the wind) as *oto* (sound) and *suru* (to do), which had evolved into *otozure* (in today's Japanese, visiting or visit). Origuchi argues that this explains an old belief in Japan, regarding the sound of the door knocking with a sacred awe. In sum, someone who came visiting at night, knocking the door, was seen as a god from *tokoyo*.[25]

Origuchi gives us his interpretation of *tokoyo* as deriving from five different meanings. Although *tokoyo* in general meant *kaihigan* or "the (unknown) shore across the ocean," eventually it came to mean "the land of eternal darkness," "the sacred soil of eternal light," "the land of eternal youth and life," "the land of fertility and prosperity," and "the land of the sacred marriage." As such, one can see that while the term *marebito* mainly means "blessing" or "prosperous visits of the deity," equally it means negative, fear-provoking, and unknowable (and hence dreadful) contact with the deity or the supernatural in "the land of eternal darkness." It is important, I stress, to bear in mind that *marebito* came with dual, mutually contradictory meanings: sacred and prosperous on the one hand, and fearful, awe-inspiring, and calamity-inviting on the other.

In the logic of *tsumadoi,* time boundaries, it seems, were very important. Nighttime was thought of as the time zone in which gods were active, or more precisely, in which gods came to visit humans. From this perspective, the husband who visited the wife during the night was placed or treated as a god. As such, nocturnal sexual encounters between the commuting or visiting husband and the wife bore sacred meaning.

Feminist historian Kawazoe Fusae interprets this belief (which, for Kawazoe and others, is quintessentially a male-centered belief) as *shinkon-gensō* or "the sacred marriage fantasy." Referring to marriage in the period depicted in *The Tale of Genji* during the late Heian period (eleventh century), Kawazoe writes:

> Marriage in those days took the form of three consecutive nightly visits from a man to a woman. Since night was seen as the time for gods' activities and a man was supposed to visit a woman in the capacity of a god, he left before dawn, just like the gods would. From the woman's point of view, she would receive her man [a visitor-husband] as a deity.[26]

Along with time boundaries, spatial boundaries were also important. In *Manyōshū* we find:

> *Murasakiwa haisasumonozo tsubaichino*
> *yasono chimatani aherukoya tare*

> (Who is this person that I'm meeting [and having sex with] in this chaos of the fair?)[27]

Two characters are used to write the word *tsubaichi.* The first character, here pronounced *tsuba,* generally means "camellia," but can poetically mean "seasonal" or "of spring." More significant would be the second character, here pronounced *ichi,* which denotes "market" or "fair." Fairgrounds in ancient times functioned as ritual spaces, in which the ordinary order was suspended. Within these spaces, men and women often encountered each other sexually, and when they did so, they met as strangers meeting within the boundaries of sacred space, as we have seen earlier in this chapter.

Takamure infers, on the basis of her encyclopedic research, that throughout prehistory and up to ancient times, marriages took place in the presence of gods and often in extraordinary spaces such as at seasonal markets or deep in the mountains. These marriages, called *shinzenkon* or marriage in front of gods, were actually sexual unions presented to the gods—just like in Babylon. In Takamure's words:

> Marriages in front of gods must have taken place deep in sacred mountains which enshrined the mother-ancestor of the community ... gods of all sorts, including gods of *chimata,* important highway intersections, and gods of *sahe,* village borders, would have happily offered such a sacred location. These communal marriage sites were called *kunado,* I believe, consisting of *kuna,* an old Japanese word denoting intercourse, and *do,* meaning place. ... The god of *chimata* that stood on the road corners ... because [this god] offered the communal marriage site, was also the god of *kunado.* Eventually, *chimata* became the site for material exchange and thus, became the fair ground ... we know from old archives that both fair ground and deep mountains offered the site for *kagai,* a group marriage, so to say.
>
> [...]
>
> There is no doubt *kagai* is [a festival of] sacred marriage ... *Kagai* lingered on for centuries in our culture, but it is surely the legacy of group marriage in the presence of gods.[28]

As anthropologists are aware, kinship terminologies and systems of marriage in what Marxists would call primitive communes have been carefully studied and reconstructed by Lewis Henry Morgan and Frederick Engels, among others. For example, in the *punaluan* system, collateral female kin were seen as sisters and collateral male kin as brothers; excepting one's own brother(s) and sister(s), all these "sisters" and "brothers" were marriageable and did indeed marry.[29] In Japan as late as the Nara period (AD 710–94), kinship system strongly reflected the idea that men and women belonged to their natal clan for life, regardless of sexual liaisons, and therefore children belonged to the clan they were born into, that is, that of the mother. The *tsumadoi* marriage existed on the basis of this kind of idea about kin groups (or clans) and hence, the household registry often bore both names even after the imposition of the Sinized law and order system (*ritsuryō*), as stated on p. 19.[30] When we combine Takamure's insights on kinship ideology with her interpretation of sacredness, rituality, and deities—gods of intersections, gods of marriage sites, gods of village borders, and above all, gods of sex—we begin to see the logic behind *kagai.* In other words, festivals, rituals, and fairs revived and permitted a glimpse into group marriage or communal sex, which occurred only in the presence of deities, which in their turn celebrated and promised fertility and prosperity. At the same time, such practices effectively facilitated mating between men and women of different clans.

Unlike in the anonymous encounters of *kagai,* asking the other's name and telling the other one's own name in the ancient Japanese convention meant giving and receiving consent to enter into a (possibly long-lasting) sexual relationship. According to Origuchi, in the times of the *Manyōshū,* three terms existed denoting commuting sexual relations: *tsumamagi, tsumadoi,* and *tsumayobai.* The first, *tsumamagi,* meant the act of finding or locating a woman who would be appropriate as a spouse or long-term sexual partner. The second, *tsumadoi,* meant the act of commuting to that woman's place. The third, *tsumayobai,* was a means to move from the first stage, *tsumamagi,* to the second, *tsumadoi.* The term *yobau* means "to call or address by name." This can also mean to introduce one's own name or identify oneself. In other words, the act of *yobai* (the noun form of *yobau*) was part of courtship etiquette.[31]

In the *Manyōshū,* we find:

Tarachineno hahaga yobunao mōsamedo
michiyuku hitoo dareto shiriteka

(My name, the name only my mother knows, is never called, and who is this person that I see [meet sexually]?)[32]

Customarily, it was the man who would first tell the woman who he was, what his name was, which family and locality he belonged to, and so on. According to eighth-century norms, the name of a woman (meaning virgin) was a secret and only her parents (but more likely her mother alone, given the uxorilocal matrimony and matrilocal residence of children) knew it. Origuchi notes that: "If any man outside of the immediate family knew a girl's name, he would have the right to be her husband."[33] Thus, for a successful *tsumadoi* (wife-visiting), *tsumayobai* (wife-calling) was a prerequisite.

Interestingly, this term, *tsumayobai,* or more often simply *yobai,* was to be preserved for centuries, denoting the custom of "nightcrawling" that takes the homonym *yobai,* consisting of two ideographs, denoting *yo* (night) and *hau* (to crawl). This is a custom widely found in southwestern Japan even to the modern period, notably, a man's "crawling" during the night to the woman's house to have sex (see the next section).

The Japanese ideograph *kon* which now is used to denote marriage, *kekkon,* signified sexual intercourse in ancient Japan. The only taboos were that one could not have sex with matrilineal siblings and one could not have sex with a woman who was menstruating.[34] In the *tsumadoi* marriage system, the husband could acquire a second or third wife by commuting. The wife, on the other hand, could receive a visitor aside from her husband, when the latter was not around, which did not threaten the legitimacy of the marriage—since it was left to the will of the two people to decide whether or not to enter a sexual liaison. In other words, when they decided not to pursue the liaison any longer, the marriage was virtually over. *Tsumadoi* in this way denotes marriage between multiple husbands and multiple wives, and as a consequence, clear patrilineage was impossible to establish in this system.

Anthropologically speaking, and even up until surprisingly recent times, many provinces in Japan maintained the ritual of *shinkon* or marriage with gods, for females prior to their marriage to a human male, on the basis of similar logic to that found in Babylonian sacred marriage in the Temple of Ishtar. According to Origuchi, in many villages in Japan as late as the 1920s, when a girl reached puberty, her parents had to accept visits of young village men, initially very publicly and eventually, restricted only to the nighttime. If a visitor so wished, he would have sex with the girl. Origuchi infers that the origin of such an institution lay in the festivities that were ubiquitously found in Japan in various forms, in which men who pretended to be gods visited the homes of virgins in the village. This custom, according to Origuchi, was based on the logic that every virgin had to become a one-night-wife of the gods; unless and until this ritual was completed, no woman was able to become wife of a human male.[35]

In port towns and station towns (*shukuba*), when a traveler stayed at an inn, the custom dictated that this stranger be accompanied in bed by a daughter or wife of the inn-owner. In mountainous villages also, when a stranger-traveler happened to seek an overnight sojourn at a house, which was not necessarily an inn, a woman of the family (daughter or wife) slept with the stranger. These practices reflected the belief that strangers were sacred, that is, *marebito*.[36]

Another more recent scholar who emphasizes the sacredness of sexual liaison in ancient Japan is Saeki Junko. In her research, Saeki focuses on sexual liaisons outside wedlock, and locates the main protagonist in these endeavors to be the *yūjo*. Saeki pays particular attention to this term *yūjo*, which can be translated as "play women"; the first character that forms this word can be read as *yū* or *asobu* (to play), while the second as *jo* or *onna* (woman). The traditional reading of these characters would be *asobime*. It would be anachronistic, according to Saeki, to assume from this name that these women were simply prostitutes whose vocation was sexual play. In the ancient imperial system of Japan, *asobibe* or the Ministry of Play was the office in charge of rituals that concerned souls that had begun traveling from this world to the other and as such, *asobibe* officers were in charge of the time of death of the emperor. *Asobibe* offices were inherited matrilineally. Later, women in the *asobibe* diverged largely into two distinct vocations of *ukareme* (courtesans or prostitutes with artistic qualifications) and *arukimiko* (wandering shamans). Nevertheless, originally, *asobi* (play) denoted the phenomenon or event that exclusively dealt with communication with the other world, bridging life and death.[37]

According to Ōwa Kazuo, the *yūjo* are generally understood, under the sway of authoritative scholars such as Yanagita Kunio, to have their origins in the priestesses (*miko*) who originally served in the *asobibe* in ancient imperial Japan.[38] Fukutō Sanae counsels that, rather than simply identifying *yūjo* or *asobime* as shamans or priestesses, we see their emergence against the background of the rising patriarchal order from around the tenth century in Japan. In other words, according to her, *yūjo* as prostitutes are not related to the previously existing shamans (*miko*).[39] This view obviously severs *yūjo* from religious and sacred origins. In opposition to this, Saeki identifies *miko* (priestesses) and *yūjo* (prostitutes) as overlapping in their origins: rather than assuming that the *miko* eventually became *yūjo*, Saeki suggests the sex of the *yūjo* needs to be identified as the sacred sex of the *miko*. Saeki, in this way, proposes an ambiguous distinction between *miko* and *yūjo*, in the sense that they both belonged in the sacred realm and served as sacred prostitutes.[40]

I differ from Saeki, in that I regard that *asobi* or *asobime* were not simply women of sacred play; it is clear that they were also a cursed existence in ancient Japan. In Japanese terms, the notion of sacred or *hare* came together with the connotation of being cursed, and these women embodied both the sacred and the cursed. To see them simply as sacred would be to idealize ahistorically their marginalized, dangerous, precarious, and condemned existence, isolated and banished from ordinary society. They were seen with mystic awe and supernatural adoration precisely because they were unlocatable in terms of the ordinary social order and at the same time, precisely for the same reason, they were denigrated, excluded, and dehumanized in society.

According to Ōwa:

> The essence of *asobime* from the medieval *yūjo* down to the modern territory of red-light district stands in continuity. They are in a word *utsurofumono* [wandering ones]. As opposed to . . . *ke* or the ordinary, the extraordinary women of *hare* they were. In this regard, they were the existence closest to the deity. But, seen from the ordinary people, again, these women's cursed aspects came together with their sacred existence.[41]

Sacred and cursed. But these women of *hare* themselves were divided and continued to be internally stratified. Some lived closely with the emperor, loved by the emperor, enjoying privilege and stability; some were poor beggar-nuns who also engaged in prostitution, traveling from village to village. Some were entertainers who combined sexual services with their acts, and others were singers who practiced oracles and minor magic in exchange for meager payment. Under the rubric of *yūjo* or *asobime*, there were many different sub-vocations: *kugutsu*, women who specialized in singing performances; *asobi, asobime,* or *yūjo*, women who practiced artistic performances as well as sexual services; *bikuni*, nuns who traveled from province to province, prostituting; *arukimiko*, traveling shamanesses who also engaged in prostitution; and *shirabyōshi*, women who specialized in dance and also engaged in sexual liaisons, and so on.

The origins of *yūjo* aside, it seems problematic to compare the ancient priestesses who had official assignments and served the emperor in the capacity of female officials of *asobibe* in relation to death and mortuary rituals (most likely in order to protect the emperor from being polluted by the potency of death) to medieval *yūjo*, whose social, let alone official, status was far from stable. Furthermore, a handful of *yūjo* were loved and pampered by the emperor and enjoyed the patronage of aristocrats, while the remainder of the *yūjo* had to sell sex and perform in order to survive during medieval times after the tenth to eleventh centuries in Japan. By then, *tsumadoi* was no longer the dominant form of marriage, and the matrimonial system had shifted to what Takamure called *mukotori* (taking the son-in-law marriage), a precursor to the patrilocal and patrilineal *yometori* (taking the daughter-in-law marriage). Both of these stood on the premise that marriage was the concern of the family, differing from *tsumadoi,* which hardly concerned itself with the family or clan, reflecting chiefly the man's and woman's personal choice. With the decline of *tsumadoi,* when men wanted to have sex with a woman outside of wedlock, buying *yūjo* became increasingly the norm. No longer the magical power of love ritual of the *Manyō* era, the poetic exchange of love, and sacred group sex were the dominant love culture in medieval Japan.

If there was anyone or any man who still was seen as very close to the gods in medieval Japan, it was the emperor, whose foundation myth had it that he was the descendant of the Amaterasu or Sun Goddess, the founding mother of the Japanese nation. He or she—considering there were a number of empresses in ancient Japan—was the human male/female that most acutely embodied the deity.

In this light, the case of the Emperor Goshirakawa (1127–92) and his relationship to *asobime* is highly interesting. After his abdication in 1158, merely three years after commencing his reign, Goshirakawa became a monk in 1169, yet from inside the monastery he continued to exert full dominance over the sons and grandsons who succeeded the imperial throne until his death in 1192. Japan during Goshirakawa's lifetime was plagued by ongoing military strife between the Taira and Minamoto families, ending with Minamoto victory after a decisive battle in 1185 which closed the Heian period. As if offering a prophecy foretelling the future weakening of imperial power, toward the end of his life, the Shogun government was established in Kamakura, eastern Japan, and became an unprecedented source of challenge to the Kyoto-based authority of the imperial family.[42]

In the words of Ivan Morris: "[f]rom about the middle of the tenth century only two functions were left to the sovereign—the sacerdotal and the cultural."[43] If he was sacerdotal by birth, Goshirakawa chose his cultural terrain in an unexpected art. From his childhood, he became fascinated with *imayō,* a singing genre practiced by *yūjo* or *asobime.* One story has it that he was so much in love with this genre that he risked losing his voice by continuing to practice even with a bad throat infection. In his endeavors to improve his singing skill, it was *yūjo* that he admired and learned from as his teachers. He even had a prince by one *asobime* in 1169, and compiled what is now a valuable collection of *imayō* poems under the title *Ryōjinhishō.*

In the Japan of the Heian period (late eighth to eleventh centuries), the emperor and *asobime* existed above and below society—the emperor, above the ordinary social order, and *asobime,* below the ordinary social order. What was common between them was that they shared the status of not belonging to society. As such, the "sacred" emperor and the "cursed" *asobime* were placed in the same realm. The way the sacred and the cursed converge in this case becomes akin to the notion of *homo sacer* as portrayed by Georgio Agamben in his acclaimed yet controversial book, *Homo Sacer.* Agamben quotes from Alfred Ernout-Meillet's *Dictionnaire étymologique de la langue latine*: "*Sacer* designates the person or the thing that one cannot touch without dirtying oneself . . . hence the double meaning of 'sacred' or 'accursed.'"[44]

The notion *sacer* has distinct historical origins in Rome, according to Caillois:

> In Rome . . . [I]f someone becomes guilty of a crime against religion or the state, the assembled populace casts him out of its midst, in declaring him *sacer.* From this moment on, if there is any supernatural risk involved in putting him to death (*nefas est*), the murderer is at any rate regarded as innocent in terms of human law (*jus*) and is not condemned for homicide (*parricidii non damnantur*).[45]

This, needless to say, derives from the inherent ambivalence of "the sacred," which is seen with awe, veneration, and terror and therefore, becomes dangerous and prohibited; hence, taboo. According to Agamben, the double notion of sacred and cursed is closely connected to the position of exception of the sovereign, as the sovereign himself is at once law and non-law, inside and outside the law.[46]

The ambivalence of *marebito,* their topological exception from ordinary society,[47] overlaps strangely well with the existence of the emperor and the prostitute. In this sense, it is ironic to note that neither the emperors nor prostitutes possessed a history of monogamous marriage. When the encountering partners were both *marebito,* as in the case of Goshirakawa and his *asobime,* it confuses and compounds the sacred and the cursed to the extent that any inversion becomes possible. Their play, sex, love, and the art of *imayō* existed in the realm of exception. In this realm, the worldly order no longer exercises its effect—rather, it resembles a monastery itself where the temporal and spatial order assumes its own norms, independent of the rest of the world. In this sense, it is telling that Goshirakawa was a monk, and that *asobime* of the day often bore names such as *hotoke* or *bosatsu,* that is, respectively, Buddha or Bodhisattva.

3

Whereas the sovereign's sexuality remained an exception, the sacredness of this worldly sex, or rather, the ritual that made this worldly sex sacred within the spatial and temporal confines in the presence of gods during the festivals, was bound to change. It is well-documented that with the rise of the Tokugawa Shogunate (1603–1867), Japan adopted the Sinized Confucianist patriarchal values that came to dominate practices relating to marriage and love. However, historians' views are not unified with regard to the pace and mode of change. For example, Takamure Itsue locates the origin of patriarchal domination in Japan in the Muromachi period of fifteenth century. Amino Yoshihiko dates the emergence of patri- archal domination to around the time of the separation of the imperial court into northern and southern courts (during the reign of the Emperor Godaigo, 1319–31), and Fukutō traces the emergence of patriarchal rela- tions, at least among the aristocratic strata, to a much earlier period, namely the end of the ninth century.[48]

Important changes with regard to the meaning of fairs and markets are usually identified in the Muromachi period (fifteenth century). It is during this period that the sacredness of fairs in temples and shrine premises generally disappeared, to be replaced by a growth in the development of commercially oriented markets and stores. For example, according to the historian Wakita Haruko, the distribution of stores and the layout of market streets in modern-day Nara, an ancient capital city, largely over- laps with those which emerged in the fifteenth century.[49] The permanent and semi-permanent nature of the market rendered it ordinary, stripping it of its former extraordinary nature, accompanying sexual rituals such as *kagai.* Although the market remained and continued to be a site of ex- change, the material and monetary aspects of exchange came to overshadow what used to be an important role of the fairground—the exchange of souls.[50]

It is important not to be anachronistic at this point, however. Although it is true that the secularization of markets and fairs steadily progressed, in parallel with the rise of the capitalist economy, wedlock-ignoring festivals continued to exist, albeit in a semi-secretive manner, until a relatively recent period in Japan's history, long after the *Manyō* poems were written and exchanged. In this regard, the custom of *yobai* or nightcrawling and its persistence into the twentieth century cast an important light in our understanding of the changing relations between love and sex in Japan.

Nightcrawling means lovemaking by a man to a woman through visits to the woman's house at night, quietly knocking on the door, though with the full knowledge of the other members of the woman's household. Research by the ethnologist Akamatsu Keisuke is extremely helpful in understanding this practice. Born in 1909, after graduating from elementary school, Akamatsu became involved in communist-influenced anti-war, anti-government trade-union activities. Having lost his job with the postal service because of his arrest, and after completing his prison term, Akamatsu became a peddler in postwar Japan. While traveling, mostly throughout the southwestern area of Japan around Kobe, he collected oral data about sexual relations and practices and forms of social discrimination and stratification, among other topics, in agricultural communities undergoing modernization and witnessed that many communities still practiced *yobai*.

According to Akamatsu, there were some variations in the rules of *yobai* practices that he observed. He classified them into the open type, the semi-open type, and the closed type. In the open type, visitation rights to a woman's house were extended to any man, including men from other villages and travelers who passed through the village. Typically, this type of *yobai* involved all post-puberty males and females, both married and unmarried. The closed type strictly limited nocturnal visitation rights to village members. The semi-open type combined aspects of the above two in various ways. For example, in one such case, only widows and married women were visited, while unmarried girls were exempt from *yobai*.[51]

Those southwestern villages that practiced *yobai* typically had less hierarchical internal structures than those in northeastern Japan, which exhibited rigid social stratification within a powerful patrilineal group called *dōzoku*. Kinship systems were remarkably different in the northeast and southwest, with the former absolutizing patrilineage and the latter displaying a relatively egalitarian form of organization among lineages with regard to the internal government of the village. *Yobai* sex was more readily available in the southwestern villages with the weaker patrilineal emphasis, since such a practice as *yobai* would considerably obscure the patrilineal identity of children. Whereas the northeastern kinship type was characterized by a large stem-family or multiple-bilateral-family household, strongly oriented around the notion of blood relations, the southwestern type was characterized by a weaker emphasis on blood relations and strong neighborhood cooperation and association.[52] If a child was born outside wedlock to an unmarried daughter as a result of *yobai,* the child was normally absorbed into the mother's family matrilineally and matrilocally simply as another child of the senior couple, i.e. the parents of the mother/daughter. It is useful to remember that until the Meiji Restoration of 1868, Japanese commoners, the majority of whom were peasants, did not bear last names, making the identity of the father almost insignificant.

It might seem reasonable to note the genealogical similarity between *yobai* and *tsumadoi.* Inasmuch as it was only men who visited while women waited, it was accepted that men and women had plural sexual partners, and the formal notion of marriage carried very little weight. Both *yobai* and *tsumadoi* took place at nighttime by male "visitors" (read: strangers) who assumed the guise of *marebito* or stranger=deity. Let us remember that nighttime was sacred in terms of understanding the gods' activities. The way men knocked at women's doors, causing the sound, that is, *otozure,* was also part of such an understanding of the nocturnal visitor as stranger=deity. However, *yobai* in the twentieth century was fundamentally different from *tsumadoi* of the eighth century in the sense that it was now taking place in clandestine form, away or hidden from the interventions of the nation-state that now insisted on monogamous conjugal families. In other words, the tension between the practice of *yobai* and the modern nation-state's demand for a monogamous matrimonial institution needs to be born in mind: in the modern nation-state, there is only one order, that of the nation-state itself, and activities and customs such as *yobai,* which effectively create an alternative order during the night, are not acceptable (see p. 32).

Nevertheless, *yobai* and *yobai*-like activities persisted in Japan, especially southwestern Japan, for a long time after Japan's emergence as a modern power in the late nineteenth century. Akamatsu records *yobai* as occurring in some western Japanese villages until the 1950s. Indeed, he himself experienced it, arranged by a woman whose female friend—married with children—had to find a male mate to ritually cleanse her year of great bad luck, another instance of sexual intercourse carrying the sacred meaning. This encounter led him to a short-lived, yet romantic involvement with the woman.[53]

Furthermore, play-like elements persisted in sexually inspired customs. For example, Akamatsu records that on Awaji island off western Japan, the midsummer evening *bon* dance festival offered a venue for finding a one-night sexual partner after the dance was over. *Bon* is a festival to receive the spirits of the dead that would pay a seasonal return visit to the living family members. On Awaji, villagers participated in group dances on the night of *bon.* Only women danced, however, and usually, the dancing women wore a folded woven straw hat that covered the head all the way down to the cheeks. (This hat, called *kasa,* was widely found, with some variation, as part of the attire of *yūjo* and other *asobime* since the medieval period.) Men would identify under the hat a woman they desired and would approach her to make a proposition. Whatever happened that evening was never to be discussed later, even between husband and wife.

Mori Rintarō, a prominent army surgeon in Meiji Japan who contributed to modernizing public health inside the army and who was also known as Mori Ōgai, a great author of the day, wrote in one of his autobiographical novels, *Uita sekusuarisu* (Vita Sexualis), recollecting his childhood, which depicts the atmosphere of the *bon* dance very well:

> In my hometown, people loved the *bon* dance . . . Many people danced in a circle. Some stood aside, wearing masks, and when they had located a [female] dancer of their choice, they would enter the circle. I could overhear masked men say:
> "You went to the Atago mountain last night, didn't you?"
> "No, I didn't."
> "Oh, I know you did."
> . . . The third man jumped in:
> "If you go there in the morning, you'll find all sorts of things left on the ground."
> All the men burst into laughter. I felt as if I had touched something filthy and ran home as fast as I could.[54]

Akamatsu's data also tells us that in some villages, it was the custom that boys were initiated at a certain age into sexual knowledge by village female elders. Boys and women were paired by lottery and sent to a shrine for an overnight mating. Since the village population was not large, sometimes it happened that a boy was paired with his aunt or even his mother for this initiation rite.[55]

These customs were scarcely known to the West, despite the avid efforts of Japanologists from the late nineteenth century. This was mainly due to the Japanese state's effort to win the recognition of the West as a civilized nation, reflecting the need to rid itself of the unequal treaties that the Western powers had imposed on Japan in the nineteenth century. I am not suggesting that the government conspired to hide the inconvenient evidence; it was achieved in a structurally interactive and mutually informed manner through direct and targeted state intervention such as legislative reforms on one hand, and on the other, through conscious and unconscious weeding-out by participants in public discourse of information that would have culturally handicapped Japan in its competition with the West. It is interesting to note that while Western anthropological research relating to Japan started as wartime enemy studies during World War II (WWII), and was therefore often eager to characterize Japanese culture as different, strange, and barbaric, it nevertheless failed to record this kind of sex/love ritual in its documentation of Japanese cultural behavior.[56]

Of course, modernization was not aimed simply at pleasing the West. Since the nineteenth century, the Japanese state had systematically attempted to control (and profit from) sexual customs in various parts of Japan by the imposition of modern state controls such as taxation, medicalization, and other regulations onto traditional, locality specific sexual customs. The rise of the industrial economy and capitalism after the Meiji Restoration of 1868, combined with the new government's conscious effort to attain compatibility with the West, led to diverse sexual and initiation practices becoming subjected to the scrutiny of the legal and policing institutions of the modern(izing) nation-state.

However, it should be emphasized that Japan's modernization was founded upon the principle of the resurrection of the ancient sovereign. Following the Meiji Restoration, the population came to be registered in the household register or *koseki,* symbolizing the reorganization of Japanese people as the registered subjects of the restored Emperor of Meiji: most indicatively, the Emperor himself never had a *koseki,* because he was the law, yet at the same time, outside or above it, and therefore could not be his own subject. Since the implementation of *koseki* from early on in the Meiji period, the household came to bear ideological value and keeping one's *koseki* clean and untroubled vis-à-vis the Emperor's gaze became the duty of the household head, typically the male elder. Practices such as *yobai,* as witnessed by Akamatsu, persisted, it should be emphasized, under the combusting tension not only with the emperor-focused national-state but also within the household itself.

Regionally diverse matrimonial practices were reorganized under the Meiji state regulation, aspiring toward a standardized national system of monogamous patrilineage and patriarchy. The marriageable age without parental consent, for example, was set at twenty-five for women and at thirty for men. *Yobai* became unlawful, i.e. adulterous, and in its stead, state-licensed public prostitution designated in red-light districts became the lawful alternative for extra-marital sex.[57] Importantly, the hitherto localized and diversified deities were now unified under state Shinto or *kokkashintō,* part of the process of legitimating the emperor as the national deity. In this light, understandably, fecundity-related festivals within the shrine premises were suppressed and instead replaced with orderly and stately festivities.[58] Of course, it takes generations for categorical changes instituted by law to be absorbed into the realm of the mundane. In other words, from the late nineteenth century on, Japan became one large milieu where old sexual practices coexisted with the new legal regulations.

Moreover, it was not simply the legal system that tried to change Japan's sexual love practices. It would be interesting to see how the English-language concept "love" (*rabu*) came to be introduced into public discourse in modern Japan by literary scholars, Christian theologians, and popular magazines. Prior to Meiji, Edo literature during the Tokugawa Shogu-nate had focused heavily on liaisons between a man and a courtesan who lived and worked in a *yūkaku* (play quarter), the red-light district desig-nated and licensed by the Shogunate. In Edo literature, the famous head prostitute, *tayū*, in the red-light district, was typically every man's romantic ideal. The term that denoted sexual attractiveness was *iro* (color). *Iro* was lined up with *hana* (flowers), *cha* (tea), *kō* (incense), and *shoka* (callig-raphy and drawing). As such, as one branch of the aesthetic disciplines, the capacity to enjoy proper *iro* was a requisite element of an elegant and sophisticated life. It was, therefore, not simply about sex or carnality, pleasure, or debauchery. Rather, it was in set with the poetics and the beauty of life. If one needed to know about flowers and tea, fragrances and writing in order to appreciate good life, one also needed to know about *iro*—such was aesthetic of the Edo period preceding Meiji.

Whereas loving relationships in the world depicted by *Manyō*'s *koi* or Edo's *iro* took sexual union for granted or viewed sexual consummation as love's natural partner, post-Meiji literature came to posit *rabu* as a spir-itual relationship that excluded physical union between the individuals involved. Further, this *rabu* was translated neither as *koi* nor *iro,* but as *ai*. According to Saeki, *ai* in the Buddhist lexicon meant "obsession" or "greed," and as such, it had a negative connotation. Honda Masuko notes that in the early Meiji literature the character *ai* was accompanied by the *furigana* (vernacular writing) term *rabu* (or *raabu,* stressing the "o" of love) and the common usage of oddly mixed expressions such as *rabu shichoru* (to love or to be in love). Furthermore, the translation of the Bible opted for *ai* when referring to god's love, thus making *ai* "sacred."[59]

The above-stated changes, needless to say, did not happen overnight. Indeed, for a long time into the twentieth century, the term *iro* as in *iroonna* or *irootoko* (female lover or male lover) was used in popular discourse (see Chapter 2). However, steadily, *iro* became denigrated as a denominator of unspiritual, un-sacred, and base desire, as opposed to *ai* as sacred, spiritual, and noble love. As such, *iro* became inferior to *ai*, and was used to refer to the activities of so-called professional and profane sex workers, while *ai* became an emblem of the romantic sentiment resid-ing in the minds of refined and educated virgins. The courtesan was no longer the heroine of the aesthetics, the poetics, and the romantics; instead *jogakusei* or female students emerged as a new group offering the model of romantic leadership in the modernizing nation. As I hope to show in Chapters 3 and 4, a close examination of the historical positions that female students (and their various incarnations) have occupied in

Japanese society, together with an exploration of their role in changing the meaning of love and related practices, can provide clues to understanding how love was made into an effective apparatus of the modern Japanese state in controlling its population—a process that reflects Japan's emergence as biopower vis-à-vis its population.

In Japan's case, the axiomatic correlation between love and sex is closely related to Japan's shift from what Foucault called the sovereign state to the disciplinary state and helps to explain its relatively late occurrence. In other words, complex yet symbiotic relations between the sovereign power and disciplinary technology existed for a long time and well into the modern age. This phenomenon was closely related to the historical condition that Japan's emergence as a modern state was based on the restoration of the premodern, ancient imperial sovereign—rather than, therefore, being populated with modern citizens, *modern Japan emerged with imperial subjects as its population*. This had fundamental implications which affected every branch of life, including love: forms of love shifted only unstably and slowly within the framework of the sovereign-subject relationship.

In Chapter 2, I shall invite the reader to visit the years 1936–7 and then, wartime. This period witnessed the unthinkable juxtaposition of the two "loves." While occurring temporally adjacent to each other, in retrospect they could not have been more fundamentally opposed. This is the story of a prostitute and a "lust"-inspired murder which culminated in the posthumous castration of her lover; it is also the story of the rape, ravage, and massacre of the ancient Chinese city of Nanjing and the subsequent violation of women that were made sex slaves of the emperor's army. This discussion will allow me to explicate what I call sovereign love, or rather, the role that Japan's modern/ancient sovereign played in making love into a state apparatus and, in particular, how this love behaves in a state of exception such as during war.

2 Sovereign and love

That night . . . when Ishida told me that in order for us to start over together, we had to part with each other once, the desire to kill him came back, the desire which I first conceived when I had been away from Ishida from May 7 to 10. I thought if I were to leave him now, his wife would take care of his wounded neck just like I have done and I would not be able to see him for months, which I did not think I would bear, considering that a separation for only a couple of days nearly killed me. By whatever means I wanted to retain him away from his family . . . Since Ishida had just stabilized his business, I did not think that he would agree to elope with me or commit joint suicide. So, I decided: after all there was only one way to have him completely—I have to kill him.[1]

This was part of the confession of Abe Sada, a former prostitute, whose murder of her lover Ishida Kichizō became an unprecedented media sensation. It was 1936—four years after Japan took Manchuria by force, and one year before its soldiers raped and ravaged the entire city of Nanjing. Three months earlier, in February of that year, Tokyo had been gripped by tension as young military officers staged a coup, seizing the prime minister's residence. Indeed, Tokyo was still under martial law.[2] However, it was the Sada incident that captured the imagination of metropolitan residents, effectively diverting popular attention from the rapid militarization of society. This incident, and the detailed accounts of the particular aspects of the case, was to retain long-lasting interest and curiosity among the public as one of the most bizarre crime stories in modern Japanese history.

During the incident about which the above confession refers to, Sada put a length of string around Ishida's neck and tried to strangle him a couple of times. When Ishida finally told Sada not to let go of him halfway through, since it hurt more afterwards, she momentarily entertained the possibility that Ishida wanted her to kill him. After a couple of tries, Sada concentrated the strength in her hands and held tight her grip:

I cried, saying "forgive me," . . . Ishida uttered a moaning sound once, shook his hands wildly, and then became numb. I let the string go, but my body was shaking uncontrollably. So, I gulped down the bottle of sake on the table and made a knot in the string around the center of Ishida's throat, so he would not revive . . . I went downstairs to check the time: it was two o'clock in the morning.[3]

After she had killed her lover, Sada lay down alongside the body, which for her was no different from the person who had still been alive only a moment ago:

When I saw Ishida's lips were dry, I licked them so they'd be wet and I washed his face. It did not feel like I was next to a dead body. I even felt more affection toward him. I touched his penis and occasionally I placed it on my front [genital area] . . .

[. . .]

I knew I had to leave the inn. As I played with his penis, the idea occurred to me to cut it off and take it with me. I used my meat knife and started to cut it. It took a long time, since it was not easy . . . I also took out the testicles, which was not easy either . . . A considerable amount of blood kept gushing out . . . with that blood, I wrote on his left thigh 'Sada and Kichi, the two alone,' and I also wrote the same on the sheets.[4]

Sada was arrested two days later. According to the interrogation record, she wanted to kill herself, but was not successful. When she was arrested, she had with her Ishida's mutilated genitals.

Abe Sada was born in 1905 as the youngest of four children of a wealthy tatami mat maker in Kanda, in Tokyo's old town. By contemporary standards, Sada was a spoilt daughter. It does not, however, appear that she grew up with good role models: her older brother was delinquent and prodigal in nature, often stealing the family money to spend on women and alcohol, and her second oldest sister more or less competed with her brother in terms of waste and corruption. Since her childhood, Sada enjoyed being adored as a ringleader by her street peers.

After the Meiji Restoration of 1868, the Japanese state embarked on a deliberate and vigorous project aimed at Westernizing all parts of society, not least because it wanted to get rid of the unequal treaties that the Shogunate had entered into with the West. As was mentioned in Chapter 1, the most effective way to achieve this goal was considered to be to demonstrate Japan's level of civilization (that is, how close Japan was to the West). Japan was an anomaly among imperialist powers from the start—a bastard child of color. However, it was undoubtedly a furious fighter—first defeating China (1895), then Russia (1905), avidly participating in World War I

(WWI), and then joining the Western powers in the Siberian expedition against the Bolsheviks in the wake of the Russian Revolution. Japan emerged as the source of an unprecedented challenge to Western domination in East Asia, following its colonial occupation and annexation of Okinawa, Taiwan, and Korea (complete by 1910). By the early 1930s, Japan was showing its muscle—through the occupation of Manchuria, its withdrawal from the League of Nations, and its self-appointment as the liberator of Asia from the Western yoke. The Sada incident occurred ten years into the reign of the Showa Emperor (1925–88), at a time when Japan had begun to realize that the war of invasion in China could drag on for a long time, thereby extending the state of emergency. The young officers' frustration with the moderates within the military reflected such an ethos.

In this chapter, my focus is twofold: the notorious Sada sex-murder will be placed in close juxtaposition with the similarly shocking 1937 massacre and mass-rape of Nanjing by Japanese soldiers. A comparison of the Sada case and the rape of Nanjing will, I believe, provide us with a perspective, which allows us to see the connections—all too unexpected and not easily detectable—between the state, the sovereign, the self, and love. The key to understanding this lies in the state of exception or siege, which existed at the time, in which the law was suspended and unlimited power rested with the sovereign in the name of a national emergency.

1

First, let us trace the details of Sada's tumultuous life and of the murder itself, in order to understand the meaning of relying on her case as a reference point of our inquiry into love. At the age of fourteen, Sada was sexually assaulted by a college student. Subsequently, having suffered a long period of severe depression, she dropped out of school. In those days, a girl was viewed as fortunate if she was able to continue at school beyond the age ten or so; many would quit school after three or four years and learn practical skills such as sewing. After abandoning her formal education, Sada was sent to a wealthy family as a housemaid: her family's wealth had been depleted by then and Sada's parents did not want to have to support her. She found this situation intolerable, and eventually ran away from her employer, stealing the family's money, jewelry, and clothing, which resulted in her apprehension by the police.

When Sada was seventeen years old, her family moved to a town in the nearby Saitama prefecture. (Sada's older brother had taken a large amount of money from the family and this led to the end of the tatami business.) In this town, Sada was often seen in the company of men. As it was a rural environment, her dating escapades caused embarrassment to her parents. In the end, her father decided to send Sada away to an acquaintance of his in Yokohama, who would arrange that Sada be contracted (i.e. sold) as a *geisha*, i.e. an entertainer who would enter into sexual relations with clients. In her police interrogation record, we find: "I did not speak with my father in the train to Yokohama. I had made up my mind: 'my body is already filthy. I don't care any more. I'll never return to my parents.'"[5]

Sada was, perhaps, lucky considering that it was to Yokohama, and not Manchuria or Siberia, that she was sold as a prostitute. Many women like her in those days were sold to a red-light district abroad in exchange for a lump sum; in Sada's case the family needed it in order to pay their accumulated debts. In addition, many were sold, just like Sada, by their fathers, but also by their husbands, to the brokers who recruited prostitutes from Japan and dispatched them firstly to the north, to the Liaotung peninsula, Manchuria, the Russian border areas, and Siberia, and then to the south, to the Pacific islands, Indonesia, the Philippines, and New Guinea.[6]

While providing Sada with temporary accommodation before she was sold to a brothel, Inaba, her father's acquaintance and twenty-five years her senior, forced her to have sex with him. Later, Sada was sold with an advance of 300 yen to a *geisha* inn. Although Sada never received formal training as a *geisha*, she was better educated than the other girls who were available in the business and soon became popular, but she could never remain long at one inn.

According to Horinouchi Masakazu, her biographer, from the ages of seventeen to twenty-one, Sada was a *geisha*, from the ages of twenty-one to twenty-seven, a *shōgi,* and from twenty-seven to twenty-nine, a *shishō*. A *geisha* was not by definition a prostitute—she would sell her art (*gei),* such as singing and dancing, selling sex was not mandatory; a *shōgi* was a registered, tax-paying prostitute who was licensed to have sex in exchange for monetary payment; a *shishō* was an illegal, unlicensed prostitute who would typically work in a café as a *jokyū* or waitress, arranging meetings with customers at her discretion. For a fake *geisha* such as Sada, however, having sex with customers was an expected part of the service.[7]

Sada wandered from one place to another—to Tokyo, Toyama, and back to Tokyo, to Shinshu, Osaka, Nagoya, and back to Osaka again, then to Hyogo. By the time she reached Hyogo, her standard advance was over 2,000 yen, the bulk of which was taken by Inaba, who continued to act as a pimp. At one point, she was a concubine; at another, she was a freelance prostitute, yet, whenever she wanted to change inn proprietors and work as a *geisha,* she had to rely on Inaba, one way or another.

In 1935, Sada found herself in Nagoya again, as a maid in a traditional Japanese restaurant, where she became sexually involved with a high school principal. Nineteen years her senior, this man, Ōmiya, was also a member of the prefectural parliament. His refined manner, gentle speech and above all, financial generosity impressed Sada, but as her police confession would later reveal, she was not sexually satisfied. Nevertheless, Sada appreciated his patronage. Ōmiya suggested that Sada train herself as a restaurateur and eventually open her own restaurant with his support. This was an attractive offer: Sada was already thirty, which was middle age by Japanese standards of the time. Thus, Sada moved to Tokyo and became an apprentice maid at a restaurant where she met the lover she was later to murder.

Ishida, twelve years her senior, was the owner of the restaurant, a good-looking playboy, and married to a business-savvy wife who was older than he. From the moment Sada took room and board in his premises in February 1936, he paid considerable attention to her. By the end of April, they were lovers. According to Sada's interrogation record:

> I was told to serve a customer who occupied the detached room; there I saw Ishida seated as a customer. He told me that since he was abstaining from drinking outside his home, that day he decided to become a customer of his own restaurant . . .
>
> I sat by him and served him drinks; he would hold my hand, my body, and touched my front [genital area]. I was elated and let him do whatever he wanted to do to me. In a short while, a *geisha* called Yaeji came in, and I heard Ishida sing *seigen* [a traditional singing genre] for the first time. It was captivating and I completely fell in love with him [*mattaku horete shimaimashita*]. When the *geisha* disappeared for a short while, we had sex for the first time.[8]

Since their relationship soon came to the attention of Ishida's wife, who was in charge of the family accounting, their liaisons became increasingly difficult to arrange. Later in April, they eloped—if only temporarily: from April 23 to May 7, the two stayed in various *machiai* (the predecessors of today's Japanese "love hotels," the place where sex dates take place). According to Sada: "When we had to part once from the eighth to the tenth [of May], my feelings of jealousy and anxiety were so intense—I cannot think of any other time that caused me so much pain."[9]

Sada and Ishida's final liaison lasted from May 11 to 18, when they stayed at the Masaki Inn in northeastern Tokyo. For some unknown reason, Sada bought a meat knife, which she used to threaten, jokingly, to kill Ishida as a show of jealousy and love-madness. Ishida, according to Sada, enjoyed playfulness. On the twelfth or thirteenth, they experimented with strangulation while having sex, both having heard of the legend that the sensation would be intensified if one was strangled while having orgasm. At that time, Sada had a practice run with Ishida and nothing serious developed. On the fifteenth, she briefly left the inn to meet with Ōmiya, who gave her additional money, which Sada and Ishida badly needed. Ōmiya had no knowledge of Sada's elopement with Ishida, although he suggested to Sada that if she had someone in mind, he would finance her wedding.[10]

On the sixteenth, Sada "felt almost deranged" when she was embraced by Ishida: "I bit him while having sex and I just felt like strangling him . . ." and she put a string around Ishida's neck, occasionally tightening the grip while she made love to him on top. Sada told of this:

> When I tightened the string, his belly protruded and his penis moved convulsively, making me feel very good. I told him so, then he said, "if it is good for you, I'll put up with a bit of pain." Ishida looked very tired . . . but said, "no, I don't dislike it. Do whatever you like to do to my body."[11]

The following day, when they repeated it, Ishida almost passed out, telling Sada that his neck was getting very hot. Sada took him to the bathroom and washed his neck, which was showing a nasty mark around the area where the string had been placed. That night, Sada and Ishida had a little discussion: Ishida suggested that they go stay in a spa town away from Tokyo—this idea Sada did not like. Then Ishida started to review their relationship, telling her that she surely had known right from the start that he was a man with children. Sada recalled her feeling that:

> Ishida was trying to leave me, and I cried loudly. Ishida also cried and tried to say something kind to me . . . the kinder he was, the more annoyed I became and . . . just tried hard to figure out how I could possibly stay with him longer.[12]

Sada was despondent by midnight. What happened next we already know.

Describing Sada's arrest, Wakaume Shinji, writing for the journal *Bungeishunju,* wrote:

> Sada received cheers from the crowd, as if she was a triumphant general, when being transported from the Takanawa police station. The tram in front of the investigation headquarters, Ogu police station, was suspended and the place was jam-packed with people who wanted to have a glimpse of Sada . . . She was calm . . . her big eyes shined as if she knew no guilt and she smiled innocently. She looked intoxicated with supreme happiness . . .[13]

Would it be too outlandish to think of Sada's relationship with Ishida as incestuous and the murder she committed as patricide? Ishida was a patriarch in Sada's pseudo-household, in the sense that she lived in Ishida's household/business premises as an apprentice. It is often observed that, for example, in red-light districts, the madam of the house and her husband are referred to as *okāsan* (mother) and *otōsan* (father) by the women. Although Ishida did not play any fatherly role for Sada, she was at the mercy of his patronage and protection. Incidentally, it is interesting to note that Ōmiya, Sada's patron, also played the dual role of lover and father, offering, for example, to finance Sada's future and underwrite a proper wedding for her. These and other dimensions and events in the Sada case make one wonder about semantics of love, and I would like to take a detour in rereading the incident with reference to Freud, incest, and totemic taboo.

In thinking about neurosis, Freud was inspired by examples from classic ethnographies of "primitive" peoples. According to Paul Ricoeur, Freud's study stood on two postulates:

> On the one hand, primitive peoples give us a well-preserved picture of an early phase of our own development and so constitute an experimental illustration of our prehistory; on the other hand, because of their great emotional ambivalence, they are akin to neurotic patients.[14]

One has to be at once careful to bear in mind that Freud's use of the term neurosis does not denote a permanent pathological state, but is applied to a wider scope and in a way is neutral, thereby heavily overlapping with the so-called normal range of the psychic state. Nevertheless, it is interesting to see that Freud identified emotional ambivalence as love/hate feelings towards one's own—in this case, blood relatives.

Eating each other, or the anthropophagic devouring of each other's body, was an important part of Sada's relation to Ishida. Food and the use of the mouth, teeth, and tongue—such as biting, chewing, and licking—were common elements in their sexual play. Sada would dip a *shiitake* mushroom in her vagina and offer it to Ishida to swallow. Oral sex featured prominently in Sada's interrogation record; she recalled once checking on the degree of Ishida's love by making him give oral sex to her when she had a period. She would give oral sex to Ishida even when an inn maid was around.[15] Mutilating and possessing parts of Ishida's body—his penis and testicles in this case—could also be interpreted as metonymically digesting his body. In this sense, the penis was chosen, not only because it was a sexual organ, but also because it was something that Sada "ate" frequently during sexual intercourse with Ishida. Figuratively—and one might say subconsciously—eating Ishida's body was not only incestuous and hence, taboo, in social, historical, and cultural contexts, but also represented a totemic transgression of the prohibition of eating one's own.[16]

Freud appears to have used "primitive people" as an example of underdeveloped humanity in order to explain neurotic conditions rather than, as Lévi-Strauss does, the elementary structure of human societies in general. If ambivalent emotion produces neurosis, an excess of desire oblivious of prohibition is perversion, according to Freud: they stand in polar opposition, the neuroses being the negative of the perversions. Freud interestingly states that "in many families the men are healthy, but from the social point of view undesirably immoral [read perverted]: while the women are high-principled and over-refined, but highly neurotic."[17] On the other hand, it also needs to be acknowledged that the purpose of Freud's analogy between neurosis and the primitives is not so much to condemn the latter as neurotic, but to highlight modern pathogeny, since civilization's progress for him is a process of renunciation of primordial and archaic desire, such as in the Oedipal complex.[18]

The transgression of totemic taboo as displayed by Sada, then, becomes perversion, rather than neurosis—excess, rather than repression, of the sexual. Sada's transgression is, in other words, of a "festive" nature: Caillois presents totemic animal killing and incestuous sex as part of festivals that function to send the community back to its primordial, chaotic beginnings, renewing it and rejuvenating it through an excess of eating and sex.[19] But, of course, committed by an individual outside such communal-ritual time/spaces as festivals or carnivals, it constitutes a violation of taboos, and it is on this point that I shall focus when comparing Sada to Nanjing.

However, first we must attempt to grasp how Sada's discourse of love figured against the social conventions of her time. By the time she murdered and castrated her lover, at least in the realm of public discourse, virginity and sexual modesty were beginning to be regarded as the predominant female virtues. The terms denoting love, after the initial confusion with regard to translation during the early Meiji period, had more or less been set by then, at least in the manner reflecting class stratification inside society. The usage of *koi* as "falling in love" or "being in love" with sexual nuances, as opposed to *ai* as "to love, care for, and be affectionate," with the implication of sexual purity, was becoming the standard.[20]

In her interrogation, Sada was extremely economical in her use of the term *koi,* preferring to describe her love for Ishida using the term *horeteita,* the past consecutive tense of the verb *horeru.* Not easily translatable into English, this verb tends to denote the sentiment and status of "being stuck on someone" or "being head over heels for someone." While this term had formerly been widely and readily deployed, especially in verbal communication, if not in writing, it came to be seen as a rather vulgar and uneducated version of expressing love. Sada would call Ishida *irootoko,* the term consisting of *iro* (color) and *otoko* (man), which, as we have seen in Chapter 1, was an older, archaic version of the term denoting a male lover. Indeed, upon reading Sada's confession, it is obvious that she had never before had to discursivize her love. For her, there had been no exchange of love poems or love notes, no extensive discussion on what love was, and no in-depth verbal exchange with her lover, elaborating on their inner feelings and desires. All she had was to "have" men—sometimes with admiration, sometimes due to practical necessity, and only once as a result of a burning drive to love and possess a man completely, as in the case of Ishida. It would not be too wrong to deem that the process of interrogation and trial in a way forced her to characterize her affair deploying the discursive tools that were available for her—yet, let us note, she still did not use the term *ai,* which is an important marker, as we will see below.

At the time of Sada's arrest, Japanese society was being rapidly forced into the straitjacket of emperor worship. First thing in the morning, school children would line up and bow in front of the Emperor's portrait, pledging loyalty, reciting the Imperial Rescript for Students, and offering thanks for the Emperor's *jiai* or benevolent love. Women were organized under Aikoku fujinkai or the Patriotic Women's Association, received training in basic community defense skills, and were incorporated into home-front support systems. In a few years, men and women from the colonies began to be brought to Japan proper and beyond to work as miners, construction workers, and sexual slaves. Japan was bracing for the upcoming wars in the Pacific and southeast Asia. Except for a handful of committed anti-war radicals who dared to challenge the state, risking imprisonment and torture, everyone—men, women, old, and young—was made to participate in the imperialist war. Seen from such an angle, Sada appears to be remote from the social ethos then in force in Japan.

One would certainly wonder what had become of the feminists; for example, those feminists who had been so adamantly against the sexist treatment of women, resisting formulaic marriage and advocating freedom of love. At the time when details of Sada's affair were put on public display through her trials, Takamure Itsue, ethnologist, historian, and feminist, on whose important work on matrimonial systems in Japan I have relied in Chapter 1, was in asylum-like seclusion, focusing on scholarly research, withdrawn from public activities. This was in spite of the fervent public presentation of her views and her calls for "radical love" during the 1920s. By the 1940s, while Sada was in jail, Takamure re-emerged, writing to call for women's participation in Japan's sacred war against Western evil. Takamure called for women's participation in the military in support of national defense, strongly insisted on the necessity to defend Japan, the sacred land of the god, and advocated the sacredness of *renai*, love, in close connection to Shinto belief, regarding the latter as indicating the "right" way toward equality between genders.[21] In this sense, Takamure the feminist, along with many other scholars and thinkers, was well incorporated into the imperial sovereign order, while, ironically, Abe Sada, due to her extreme marginality, was outside this order. Sada's love, for one thing, had no reference to Japan's imperial focus.

Is it a strange feeling of *déjà vu* that we experience when we read Sada's story, when she tells the judge that she took Ishida's *fundoshi*, traditional underwear for men, since it smelt like Ishida, when escaping from the inn, putting it around her own waist?[22] Does it not remind us of "the parting of underwear," *kinuginu no wakare*, as captured by *Manyō* poets depicting the morning-after of the night of lovemaking (see p. 18)? Was not her act of laying beside the dead body, caressing and kissing it, part of this magic, wishing his soul to come back to his body just like in *tamagoi*? Is it too extreme to compare Sada with the ancients, for whom love and sex were inseparable?

This is not to say that Sada's love is identical to *Manyō* love or that it was somehow sacred. Nevertheless, imagining it in close juxtaposition with those concepts may not be so futile in order to remind us of the distance between Sada's love and the norms of her time. For, love in 1930s Japan, as approved by the state, was rapidly becoming "nationalized" through policies related to standardized compulsory education, population planning, eugenic marriage, and the supply and support of soldiers supposedly destined to lead Asia toward liberation from the West. One might, in a way, characterize the Sada affair as premodern or extramodern, in the sense that it was impregnated with the ethos of *tsumadoi*; love being purely a transaction between a man and a woman away from familial and societal constraints. She existed outside the order of the imperial sovereign.

For most Japanese people, the Emperor was indeed a man-god, *arahitogami*, who was believed to be permanently sacrosanct. That is to say, unlike the limited presence and occasional intervention of the ancient deities of *kagai*, shrine fairs, village borders, and highway intersections, this man-god was omnipresent, omnipotent, and ubiquitous. Worshiping the Emperor was done in (let us say) a secular manner, yet paradoxically, at the same time, his sacredness was the key to understanding this secular worship. It was practiced in schools, at village gatherings, in the workplace, and at home. The irony should be clear: the emergence of modern Japan presupposed that the premodern sacredness of the sovereign be democratically extended to all the population. The Emperor—the nation's men were to love him and die for him, while the nation's women were to love him and give birth to his children, *tennō no sekishi* or the Emperor's babies—thus, remained an exception, an exception from the existing this-worldly order, for He himself was the law.

Four years after the Sada incident, the Japanese government passed a law aimed at making Japan the leading nation of Asia through achieving a population of 100 million: according to the National Eugenics Law proclaimed in May 1940, it was ruled that individuals with so-called inferior genes (in this case, individuals with physical or mental disabilities, deformities, and incurable illnesses) would be sterilized in order to improve the composition of the national body, while healthy women should give birth to an average of five children.[23] The sacredness of the Showa Emperor thus spread without boundaries and limits, but where it proved to be most effective was among soldiers—it had to be, now that Japan faced the task of spreading the benevolent light of the Sun Goddess beyond the archipelago through sacred wars—and it is here that "sovereign love" came to play a decisive and perhaps most destructive role as political technology. If Sada's love was seen as perversion and transgression measured against the social standards of the day, the exception of the sovereign and the sovereign love prevailing in the military were the phenomena that defy the power of words.

2

Just as the state of exception allowing the sovereign to have unlimited power was nowhere more clearly manifested than in times of war, the subjection of the population to sovereign power was nowhere more methodical than in the army. It is here that physicality became a central concern for the state in terms of the political technology of power. Needless to say, the entire process of conscription (by the decree promulgated in November 1872), starting from the physical examination and extending to the discipline and training in the camps, brought the intense gaze of the state to bear on the body of the soldier, while life in the barracks constituted a total bodily subjection to the rules and ethics of the army. This totality, of course, also extended to the domain of sex. Sabine Frühstück, writing on the early formation of systemic sexual control of the population by the Japanese state, lists three subgroups as forming the forefront of this sexual subjection: soldiers, prostitutes, and children.[24] While not disagreeing with Frühstück, I would like to expand the horizons of our understanding beyond sexuality and suggest that soldiers were subjected to the technology of power *in toto*—including body, mind, sexuality, identity, namely life *and* death.

This spectrum reminds us of Foucault's notion of biopower. In one of the most readily available interpretations of this useful, yet elusive concept, we find:

> This form of power [biopower] is exercised on the body and it carries a specifically anatomical and biological aspect. It is exercised over members of a population so that their sexuality and individuality are constituted in certain ways that are connected with issues of national policy, including the machinery of production. In this way populations can be adjusted in accordance with economic processes.[25]

Again, though not disagreeing, I would like to shift the focus slightly in such a way as to envelope life and death as a totality, or a pair of extreme points of human existence, rather than highlighting sexuality and individuality, when setting the activating point of biopower. For this, I find Georgio Agamben's distinction between *bios* and *zoē* useful. Agamben states:

> The Greeks had no single term to express what we mean by the word "life." . . .: *zoē,* which expressed the simple fact of living common to all living beings . . . and *bios,* which indicated the form or way of living proper to an individual or a group.[26]

In this understanding, only those that have a political existence, or membership if you like, of a proper society, have life—*bios.* Thus, *bios* exists among citizens of *polis,* not among slaves. The same principle, it should be added emphatically, applies to death. For a life or a death to be socially meaningful, the human that bears (executes or fulfills) it needs to be a politico-civic being, whose membership of a society is both accountable and recognizable.

Some readers may think that what I am suggesting here deviates from Foucault's consistent attention to the body. However, my interpretation of the Foucauldian notion of body involves not seeing it as a simple material being, consisting of cells, blood, flesh, organs, and bones; the bodily being in Foucault's corpus is always understood to be a life-bearing being and, as such, it is not so much about the actual body in relative separation from, say, the mind, as an entity that contiguously contains life—and as a result, death. Unless we take this type of holistic approach, the very notion of technologies of the self, another important Foucauldian notion, cannot be properly understood. For, self is not a mere body or the smallest unit of the population. More concretely speaking, when Foucault talks about the shifting image of the soldier from the seventeenth to eighteenth centuries, from the stout, self-imposing figure to the docile body, he is not suggesting that the latter has lost its self or acquired a weaker self. On the contrary, the self of the docile body is a highly self-conscious, skilled, and sophisticated player in relation to state apparatuses and their workings, upholding public authority and therefore, ultimately sustaining governmentality.[27]

As stated earlier, Japan's modernity was founded on the premise of a restored ancient sovereign and the turning of the population from amorphous subjects of each localized lord into subjects of a centralized national power that now demanded devotion of a total kind, akin to the religious devotion to the sacred, as a condition of gaining *bios.* And it is in this sense that I shall maintain my focus on the concept of biopower, when approaching the notion of love in 1930s Japan.

In this connection, it is more than fascinating—and certainly no coincidence—that prewar militarist Japan actively organized its population around the concept of *kokutai* or the national body. This concept revolved around interlocking the unison and harmony of individuals with the nation, in such a way as to consume and subsume individuals into the national entity on one hand, while simultaneously turning individuals into loyal and willing guardians of the national sovereign on the other. Further, let us not forget, this otherwise egalitarian invitation to modern nationhood was closely connected with the way individuals were connected to the Emperor, the sacred heart of the nation. In other words, the modern Japanese nation stood on the foundation of the ancient hierarchy of sacred and religious kind. Let us not forget, either, that being a soldier meant functioning in organic connection to this sacred being as receiver of the Imperial Rescript for Soldiers, which taught that from primordial times, Japanese soldiers had been led by their supreme commander, the Emperor. Being a soldier, in other words, was to be a defender of the national body, which overlapped heavily with the Emperor's body. In a strange paradox, then, this is to say that in the case of Japan, the "social body" was not "social" as we might imagine, but first and foremost the body of the sovereign.[28]

By the late 1930s, the Japanese military was a formidable force, threatening to dominate the Asian continent. With key bases in northeastern China, Korea, Taiwan, Okinawa, Sakhalin, and the Pacific islands, Japan's army and navy were ready to expand northwards and southwards. On an international level, however, Japan's path to imperial military power was far from smooth—not least because of what we would call today racial prejudice and distrust of the Western powers. After the humiliating Three Powers' Intervention of 1895 (by Russia, France, and Germany) in the aftermath of the Sino-Japanese War, which stripped Japan of its war prize, forcing it to relinquish the Liaotung peninsula, Japan played savvy in diplomacy and entered an alliance with Britain in 1907. While Japan's participation in WWI earned it possession of some islands in the Pacific, which were formerly German territory, the rising dominance of US naval power in the Pacific led to increasingly unambiguous rivalry between the two nations. This state of affairs ultimately pushed Britain to abandon the Japanese alliance and side with the US. Japan's humiliation culminated in disadvantageous naval capacity quotas designated in the Washington Naval Treaty of 1922. In 1923, the Anglo-Japanese alliance was officially terminated.[29]

Japan's dissatisfaction with the West was manifested in its advancement to the Chinese mainland and, in 1931, its seizure of Manchuria. Its withdrawal from the League of Nations in the wake of the Shanghai incident of 1932 and Western criticism of its actions in 1933 were unmistakable portents of the looming ambition that was later to be crystallized in the form of the East Asian Co-Prosperity Sphere, aka the "yellow peril," to borrow the Western jargon.[30] Increasingly, domestic political power came to be held in parcels by military strongmen surrounding the Showa Emperor, although military leaders themselves were not in complete agreement either. As stated on p. 35, in February 1936, less than three months before the Sada incident, young officers who had been frustrated by the moderate faction, seized the prime minister's residence. Although the coup ended in failure and the officers responsible for it were executed, the so-called moderates were not disinterested in expanding Japan's territorial holdings by force.

Inside the military, soldiers were trained to live or die for the Emperor. But it is also true that brutality among soldiers within the hierarchy was widespread, and lynching and abuse of the lower ranks occurred routinely. The degree of discomfort, and the crudity of living conditions in the barracks, was intense. This was compensated by visits to comfort stations, that is, the brothels reserved for the army and navy. These visits were also seen as part of training soldiers into "manly" fighters. Unlike Western armies, Japanese military leaders were not familiar with the system of regularly replacing soldiers, sending them home temporarily after a certain duration of deployment and in turn replenishing the rank and file with the soldiers who had rested back home. In other words, for Japanese soldiers, unless they were injured or dead, it was a case of once in the frontline, always in the frontline.[31] Under such conditions, military comfort stations became the most obvious venue for soldiers to enjoy recreation.

In the 1930s, although brothels were widely available, and despite the fact that many Japanese women headed for northeastern China, either dreaming of making a quick fortune or being sold by their parents or husbands, the increasingly heavy Japanese military presence on the Asian continent meant that prostitutes were always in high demand. It is this line of argument that is often deployed when scholars try to answer the "why" generated by the horrendous mass rape of women (including children and elderlies) in Nanjing by the Japanese military in 1937—one year after the Sada incident. What I would like to do here is not establish the reason why the Japanese military did this—as if to suggest that there existed pre-imminent need (physical or otherwise) for soldiers, which was somehow not met sufficiently by using other means and therefore, consequentially caused the mass rape. Rather, I would like to explore the cultural logic behind this mass rape and ravaging. For, in my view, it was not a mad outburst of beastly desire—it was a methodical strategy, the conception and execution of which were necessary outcomes of the Japanese state's emergence as a modern biopower with the Emperor at its apex. To do this, I find the concept of love one of the most important determinants, and it is on this point that I shall closely juxtapose the rape of Nanjing and Abe Sada's sex murder.

But first, let us recount the scenes from Nanjing in 1937. It is yet to be determined precisely how many were killed, raped, and brutalized in Nanjing following the entry of Japanese soldiers to this ancient city on December 13 and during the subsequent six weeks of occupation. Calculations vary between 38,000 and 430,000, although researchers most frequently agree on a figure of 250,000 to 300,000.[32] Upon entering the city, Japanese soldiers competed to rape as many women as possible and after raping, many killed the women. At least one photo shows a very young female body with legs wide open, showing naked genitals and belly cut open with intestines pushing out. Some took a picture with the woman they had just raped, who was ordered to show her naked lower body by holding up her blouse. Children and babies were shot in scores, pierced by swords, thrown down against the pavement, beaten to death, kicked to death, burned to death, drowned, strangled, squashed, bludgeoned, and sliced. Before reaching the city, the massacre had already started: two Japanese soldiers, Mukai and Noda, started a competition—the one who had had slain 100 Chinese with a sword first would win. As of November 30, 1937, Mukai had scored 106 and Noda, 105.[33]

Iris Chang draws our attention to the "impalement" of vaginas in Nanjing. Vaginas indeed became a focus of brutality and violation, not only by Japanese penises but also by bamboo spears, sword blades, guns, glass pieces, bottles, and other elongated objects; all kinds of phallic substitutes were used to ensure that vaginas in Nanjing were injured and violated—alive or dead, that is. Chang calls it "sexual perversion."[34] But was it? Was it a perversion, or was it a systematic, methodical, and measured act of making known the power of the Japanese sovereign? Was it not the case that every soldier's penis was in fact not out of control, but acting exactly as its mission called upon? In other words, did not every soldier's penis embody that of the Emperor, making the latter enter (by force) the bodies of Chinese women? Was this excess not supposed to be the exact way to disseminate the Emperor's benevolence? Perhaps it would not be too much to infer that Japanese soldiers acted as sovereign, embodying the sovereign power whose "love" the Asian neighbors were to appreciate. And it would not be coincidental that the restoration of the ancient sovereign as the head of the modern Japanese state carried a distinctly familial (incestuous) tone: the Emperor was the direct descendant of the Sun Goddess, while all the rest of the Japanese were ultimately to trace their ancestry to the same goddess, rendering the Emperor into the head of one large household. Seen in this way, sexual violence committed by the Japanese soldiers in Nanjing (and elsewhere) was not a perversion, as perversion implies a deviation from the normal. On the contrary, seen from the perspective of the imperial sovereign of Japan, it was normal, expected, and scheduled.

But, of course, seen from one step outside the imperial sovereign order of Japan, it was profoundly perverted. We may infer, according to the imperial sovereign order of Japan, that the logic behind the Nanjing massacre was that because Chinese (younger) brothers were not behaving by not welcoming the Japanese leadership in Asia, it was necessary to punish China, since such resistance would go against the ideal of the Japanese imperial order in accordance with the family-state model with the Emperor as the household head. If the Chinese were the younger brothers, raping Chinese women would be nothing but brother-sister incest. Here again, rather than the "emotional ambivalence" of incest prohibition, as proposed by Freud, what we see is a logic of excess—the perversion as the neurosis's positive—in parallel to Abe Sada's totemic incest.

On an empirical level, it is important to register that the China War that Japan undeclaredly entered into in the early 1930s was the beginning of a long period of devastation that led to Japan's ultimate defeat in 1945. The duration of war and misery under the increasingly militarized domestic order, I should add, had a great impact on the lives not only of the colonized, but also of the majority of the ruling nation, the Japanese themselves. It is important to note, as stated by Agamben, that it is during times of war that the sovereign most effectively possesses unlimited executive power. In the name of war, his decision-making power bypasses existing legal scrutiny and, in the name of the law, the law itself is often suspended.

What does it mean to have unlimited executive power from the point of view of a head of the state? It means that he has the authority to investigate individuals as the law sees fit, incarcerate and torture if necessary, and above all, terminate their lives, if that is deemed appropriate. And who decides?—he does, since he is above the law and at the same time, he *is* the law. In this schema, he is absolutely protected; the only way to stop him is to kill him, and such an act would not, incidentally, constitute homicide in the regular sense, since such a killing would also operate outside ordinary law and be treated in a different framework, such as treason. In the context of wartime Japan, the Emperor was not the sole agent making decisions; the cabinet, strategic headquarters, and other offices were also involved. But what the Emperor himself actually did or what kind of person the Emperor was is irrelevant, since it was his *topos* being the law and above the law at the same time that bestowed on him such power. Hence, war (and all the atrocities and violence committed) was carried out in the name of the Emperor. In other words, the war, the ultimate state of emergency, was authorized in his name. It was this point of authorization that ultimately made him powerful. In the words of Carl Schmitt, "Sovereign is he who decides on exception."[35]

What is notable in the context of this study is that the relationship between men and women came to be shaped in the mold of military operations and the national state of emergency, being channeled through the notion of masculine conquest and feminine support, all in the name of the Emperor. In sum, men and women entered a relationship under His gaze. In this realm, all men were soldiers, past soldiers, and future soldiers. The slogan of *kokuminkaihei* or the militarization of the entire national population was to reach its peak as the war went on. In this sense, it should be relevant for us to examine, in conjunction to the Nanjing massacre, the notorious institution of the army comfort station, since I believe this institution is revelatory in terms of understanding the love of the sovereign.

Senda Kakō, a former Japanese soldier who published in the 1970s the first postwar recollection of the deployment of sexual slavery inside the Japanese military, emphasizes that there was a fundamental difference between the Meiji military establishment and that of Showa. Whereas close to 80 percent of the officers were familiar with international laws pertaining to war during the Meiji period, in the Showa period only one among twenty officers knew that international laws existed regulating the treatment of prisoners of war (POWs).[36] Senda also testifies that it was around the Taisho period (1912–26) that the philosophy of "securing supplies in enemy territory" became dominant in the army. By the time of Showa, the army was ruled by the ethos of "winner takes it all"—all here including human lives, their sexualities, fertility, and dignity. It was in this spirit that the Japanese army entered the city of Nanjing. Indeed, the winner took it all, not only lives, but proper burial rites, sanity, humanity, and future. Soldiers were instructed by superior officers to resolve their sexual desires "locally" and, after the rape, destroy the evidence—by killing the victim.[37] One former soldier testified that in a small, incredibly poor village which Japanese soldiers passed through after the Nanjing massacre, they found a girl of about fourteen with her mother and grandmother in the family's cave-like dwelling. Despite the desperate pleas of her mother and grandmother, soldiers gang-raped the girl in front of them until she lost consciousness. In another recollection, a soldier testifies that on the way to Nanjing, he saw dozens of Chinese women lying on the roadside, raped, violated, and left half naked by the Japanese soldiers who had entered the village before his unit reached it.[38]

It used to be a commonplace assumption that the emergence of army comfort stations originated in the aftermath of the ravaging of Nanjing.[39] However, recently, the genealogy of this institution has come to be considered in tandem with the conditions under which the modern Japanese military was organized as well as by the way in which the modern Japanese state controlled and regulated prostitution since the restoration of the Emperor of Meiji. Whereas the Tokugawa Shogunate's policy toward red-light districts allowed brothels relative autonomy and self-government with the connivance of the Shogunate, which enormously benefited from the tax revenue, post-Meiji prostitution became regulated directly by the state, through supervision by prefectural governments and the police authorities. The most efficient way of subjecting prostitutes' bodies to state regulation was the implementation of routine and compulsory checks for venereal disease (VD). This measure itself was, according to feminist historian Fujime Yuki, directly modeled on the contemporaneous Western practice, and was consciously adopted in order to appease Western eyes that often regarded Japan as otherwise barbaric and uncivilized. Following the 1853 opening of certain Japanese ports to the Western powers, Western enclaves were established and intercourse with Japanese prostitutes became part of daily life for Western males staying in Japan. The concern over VD, therefore, was real—the only difference being that Western men in Japan were not subjected to compulsory, regular check-ups, while Japanese prostitutes were required to undergo such examinations in exchange for government-issued licenses.[40]

Once military action in China started in the early 1930s, the establishment of army comfort stations became an open necessity due to the uncontrollable spread of VD in the army, especially the one witnessed during the Siberian intervention. This may have been the original logic behind the setting-up of comfort stations with facilities for the regular medical examination of both women and soldiers on the basis of the preceding experience of check-ups of prostitutes. The organization of comfort stations became larger in scale and more systematic after the Nanjing massacre. Now having women transported with the army, following the latter's transfer, became the norm, although rape of the most hideous sort was perpetrated repeatedly by Japanese soldiers, regardless of the existence of comfort stations. When transported, women were classified along with horses and ammunition, that is to say, as "goods." As stated, in the prolonged warfare on the vast territory of China, the Japanese military had no routine of replacing soldiers periodically, by returning them home for recreation and rest and "rest and recreation" were to be gained solely by means of the comfort stations. This practice inevitably intensified the burden on each woman, while necessitating more efficient recruitment—often by force. Senda testifies that, in theory, the army estimated that women were recruited at the ratio of one woman for thirty-five to forty soldiers. This statistic conforms to official records.[41] Thus, by the time the Pacific War worsened, young Korean girls (who had the reputation of being virgins due to Korea's strict Confucian morality) were lured, coerced, or simply kidnapped in their tens and scores, and sent to comfort stations in Manchuria, the Pacific, and Southeast Asia as military "comfort women."[42] The IMTFE (International Military Tribunal in the Far East) ignored this crime against women of multiple nations. As a result, silence was firmly imposed on the former "comfort women" and the abuse they had been subjected to for decades after the war.[43]

But if, as I suggested in Chapter 1, sacred sex between strangers celebrated the deity and invited good luck and a good harvest, cannot the logic behind establishing comfort stations and implementing regular sex as part of military discipline be understood, at least analogously, to be related to the beckoning of sacred power to Japanese soldiers? Can this not be understood also as a celebration of the Emperor's awe and sacrament? Perceptive readers will understand that I'm not saying this in order to mystify (let alone justify) the sexual violation of women by the Japanese military. It is about the love *of* the sovereign needing to be reciprocated by the love *for* the sovereign. Soldiers' duties—from the rape of Nanjing to frequenting comfort stations—were to return the benevolence of the Emperor with total faith and the embracing of imperial authority, which they celebrated by making love to (namely violating the bodies and the persons of) women, before, during, and after they fought against the enemy. In so saying, I am by no means suggesting that therefore, individual soldiers were exempt from war crimes and moral responsibility and all faults fell on the Emperor—the question of moral-historical responsibility is an important task, but it is beyond the scope of this study, although it is truly wondrous how the Emperor of Japan was exempt after the war from all blame for the miseries that Japan brought to the lives of millions of human beings.[44] Here, I am asserting a structural logic behind this heinous situation.

Sex at the comfort stations was part of actions taken in the state of exception where, in the name of war, women at the comfort stations were enslaved directly under the Emperor's gaze. Oddly, hand in hand with the state's institutionalization of the monogamous conjugal system as the norm, the same state instituted the military prostitution system as an important component of disciplinary life of the imperial army. It should be clear that far from being seen as adulterous or immoral, the comfort stations were established by the Emperor's army as part of a strategic operation that was deemed necessary and legitimate in the state of siege. As with all other honors and duties soldiers received from the Emperor, "comfort women," too, were the gift of the Emperor. To deem the comfort station operation as uniquely Japanese, as if to suggest it was part of the national culture or that excessive sexual mores were inherent to Japanese men, therefore, is not correct: it is a product of a historically formed and conditioned state of exception under the resurrection of the ancient sovereign.

"Comfort women" were indentured servants/slaves of the Emperor and, therefore, not the private property of soldiers: in the comfort stations, violent behavior, alcohol consumption, and other forms of abuse were not allowed in theory, since the women's bodies were the gift of the Emperor to all soldiers. On the other hand, the women in Nanjing were the war booty won by individual soldiers. Thousands of them were brutally raped

and killed, their bodies considered disposable as they had not been consecrated by the Emperor. Killing of "comfort women," however, was to
constitute a crime against the Empire (if not against the women themselves). It is, therefore, only logical that "comfort women" had to die
along with the soldiers, in the manner of *gyokusai,* literally meaning
"crushing a jewel," which indicated honorable death for the Emperor in
the face of imminent defeat at the hands of the enemy. Of course, this is
only a logic. In reality, many "comfort women" were abused, brutalized,
and even murdered.[45]

The use—or abuse—of "comfort women" constituted part of military
discipline. It is no coincidence that soldiers routinely were given one
condom each with the brand name *totsugekiichiban* or "attack and blast"
(condom use having been made mandatory) after which they would, with
hardly any foreplay, swiftly insert their penis into the woman's vagina,
rubbing fiercely, and ejaculating at lightening speed. According to the
recollection of one Korean "comfort woman": she lay on the floor for
seventeen hours without a bathroom break and received three hundred
men.[46] Men waited in line right outside the entrance to her room, and
left as soon as the act was over. To carry out this kind of assembly-line
sex act, soldiers must have had to first have an erection, then put on a
condom, and ejaculate on time. Doubtless, it required considerable discipline to do this. One can recognize to what degree soldiers' bodies had
been made docile and productive. Indeed, indoctrination works precisely
in this way: it makes bodies docile, devoid of original thinking, making
them into a mere bundle of reactions and responses. It is this docility that
is exploited to the maximum under a state of exception.

On another level, as long as the logic of violation of the female body
was concerned, both "comfort women" and the rape of Nanjing served
soldiers who defended the sovereign. Soldiers' lives and deaths depended
on the sovereign, and the sovereign's power was exercised by them—their
fighting, their raping, their killing, their violence, and their sacrifices
embodied and carried the crest of the Emperor. The more they violated,
the more they injured, and the more they killed, the more sacred did the
Emperor become. Soldiers were, in other words, not modern citizens, but
the Emperor's subjects. Their *zoē* became *bios* only through their subjection to the sovereign. In the name of the Emperor, every soldier acquired
a political or proper form of life, that is, *bios.* This form of life in its turn
equipped soldiers with the technology to cultivate and discipline the
"proper" self, the self that knows how to return the sovereign's love to
the sovereign, by killing, raping, torturing, and above all, dying.

Abe Sada's act of murder was purely self-oriented, while the Nanjing
rampage was focused on the imperial sovereign. Both involved the
rhetoric of love and passion and violence of a distinctly sexual kind.
Both were oriented around death or murder, though on different scales.

Both were accentuated with mutilations and genital references. Sada's affair represented the last remaining threshold of self-absorbed, private love, while Nanjing heralded a new era of love and passion, oriented around the relationship with and loyalty to the sovereign; as such, this latter form of love was quintessentially public and political, yet at the same time, internalized by the individual self. By sexually violating Chinese, Korean, and other women, including Japanese, Japanese soldiers proved their prowess and loyalty to the sovereign. The Emperor's army's virtue was to be strong, manly, invincible, and able to do anything extreme and unthinkable (such as suicide bombing) in the name of that sacred being.

The rape and massacre of Nanjing was the beginning of what turned out to be a long, painful loyalty contest among soldiers, which continued until Japan's defeat in 1945. Sex here was no longer a pleasure—it was well and truly part of one's duties, tasks, obligations, and sacrosanct assignments. In this perversion, *bios* was turned into a grotesque abnormal life in which the right and wrong of life and death were deeply twisted and so inverted that human self-destruction was mistaken as dignity, hatred with love, and *zoē* or the simple life of all beings with *bios* or a socially meaningful life. Such an extreme distortion was possible because of the deep love, utmost loyalty, and unconditional self-sacrifice for the sovereign Emperor, which, in turn, was secured by the promise of immortality, sustained by the belief that individual death was to be compensated by the eternal life and immortal body of the nation. Such a logic of sacrifice also belonged to the state of exception, the national state of emergency.

An important difference between Sada and Nanjing is that Sada did not succumb under the Emperor's reach. Indeed Sada, by committing herself to the personal cause of love, resisted the increasingly all-encompassing military ethos of the time. Sada's actions constituted infidelity to the sovereign love of prewar Japan, where everyone was related to each other via the Emperor.

When the war ended, Japanese soldiers returned from battlefronts via various detention camps to Japan. These marriageable or married men brought home not only bloody war experiences vis-à-vis the enemies but also the experience of sex with "comfort women." Their understanding of their relations with "comfort women" was multiply determined. Upon recollection after many decades of silence, many soldiers called comfort stations *kyōdōbenjo* or (and allow me to be literal) communal shit house. Some recalled their relations with women as the only human element in the duration of the terrible war, while others were indignant of the fact that foot soldiers were given foreign women (such as Koreans who were deemed as subhumans), as opposed to the officers, who always got Japanese women.[47]

The experience of mass sexual enslavement at the comfort stations in that desperate, insane, life-threatening battlefield environment became the foundation on which man-woman relations in postwar Japan was to be formed. More precisely, a conspicuous lack of critical reflection for many decades in postwar Japan on "comfort women" and many other issues including wartime atrocities, colonial responsibility, and other crimes against humanity, came to condition many things including the nation's romantic relations (see Chapter 3).

Suffice here to say that it is interesting to note that the systemic and practical procedures involved in setting up the comfort stations was swiftly inherited by the defeated government with no moral introspection. One of the first things the Japanese government did in order to receive US Occupation forces was to create the RAA or Recreation and Amusement Association. Founded on August 26, 1945, eleven days after Japan's surrender, the RAA was responsible for establishing and managing comfort stations for the US forces and providing prostitutes, in order to protect other Japanese women, without whose reproductive capacity the nation could not have been rebuilt.[48] This organizational routine, that is, the offering of women (or more precisely, certain women) in receiving the powerful or the dominant, had been thoroughly internalized by Japanese of various ranks and positions under the imperial order by the end of the war. For example, when Soviet soldiers advanced to Manchuria, the Japanese Manchuria expedition unit or Manshū kaitakudan chiefs selected young, unmarried women from the community between the ages of thirteen and twenty and assigned them to provide sexual services to the Soviet soldiers, in order to appease the latter so as to protect the rest of the Japanese remaining in the unit; ironically, these women were also referred to as Joshi teishintai, translated as the unit of women who devoted their bodies (for the Emperor), the name that was also used for the army "comfort women."[49]

The women that were offered, i.e. devoted their bodies, formed one of two streams; the other was constituted by the women who bore children. During wartime, while certain women were headed toward military comfort stations, inside Japan proper, other women were assigned to bear the average of five children, as noted earlier, in order to meet the ever-increasing demand for staffing the Emperor's army. The National Eugenics Law of May 1940 set the goal of bringing the total Japanese population up to 100 million by the year 1960. This population policy was formulated in line with a set of proposals made by the Japan Racial Hygiene Association or Minzoku eisei gakkai, a grouping dominated by physicians, in 1936; ironically, the year of the Sada murder incident.[50] It is interesting to note that, in a way, this 1940 law was structurally upheld by the Japanese through to the 1960s, a decade marked by high population growth. Indeed,

despite such drastic historical events as the war, Japan's defeat, the crum-
bling of the divine authority of the Emperor, and the foreign occupation,
the population maintained consistent growth in accordance with the 1940
goal. Of course, any good historian knows that the mere implementation
of a new law does not automatically and immediately bring about social
change. The law has to be internalized by subjects as a dominant norm
of life, and this process is a time-consuming one, while once internalized,
even the most drastic revolution cannot completely and swiftly undo the
norm and assumptions that have come to be built inside subjects, as this
also takes time. In this sense, it is hardly surprising that the 1940 law
finally delivered its aimed outcome in the 1960s.

Hannah Arendt states: "Because of [love's] inherent worldlessness, love
can only become false and perverted when it is used for political purposes
such as the change or salvation of the world."[51] The rhetoric of unifying
Asia with the benevolent love of the Japanese Emperor as represented in
such mythico-religious slogans as *hakkōichiu* (meaning one cosmos under
the Emperor's sagacity) precisely fell in this category of perversion.[52] Let
us recall that the sacrifice of totemic animals is a practice accessible for
the entire clan on ritual occasions, but committed by individuals, it would
be an irreparable crime. Sada's transgression was a crime—although
deemed a crime of passion and resulting in a relatively light punishment,
that is, a six-year prison sentence—while the rape, massacre, and destruction of the entire city of Nanjing was seen as a glorious national victory,
a sacrifice for the sacred order of the imperial benevolence, a carnival for
the sovereign, and a festival for the subjects. One cannot resist asking:
which is more perverted, a woman who commits a crime because of over-
passioned love or a nation that commits itself to bloody rape of its neighbor,
also in the name of love? Perhaps it was fortuitous that Sada's love was
shielded from the national state of emergency, precisely because of the
criminality that was ascribed to it by the state, since killing one man
outside the sovereign order was a crime, while killing, mutilating, and
violating hundreds and thousands in the name of the Emperor was a glory.

The target of Arendt's remark was totalitarianism, which normally (and
perhaps necessarily or inevitably) comes with the language of love.
Winston Smith had to obliviously and selflessly adore Big Brother climbing
up the ladder of the execution scaffold.[53] Amidst starvation, North Koreans
today still call their leader "Dear Leader" and tearfully sing songs praising
his love and care.[54] Just as totalitarian regimes are often supposed to be
contemporaneous to us, in that they are often "modern," however anomalous they can at the same time be, Japan's prewar sovereign state was
also intended to be modern, albeit with the restored power of the ancient
sovereign. It is here that sovereign love becomes relevant to us and to
postwar Japan. For, love in such a society is reciprocated only between
the sovereign and the subject, and not between subjects.[55] Postwar Japan

therefore, faced the need of having to build love among citizens, a fundamentally different kind of love from the one that the sovereign and his
subject used to share exclusively.

3

Abe Sada was released from jail in 1941, having served four years and
four months. The reason for the reduction in her jail term from the original
six years was due to her good behavior and the amnesty granted in connection with the commemoration of 2,600 years of the imperial reign.[56]
Upon her release, the prison offered her automobile transportation with a
driver, due to the sensational coverage she had received from the media
at the time of her arrest as well as during the trial. While in jail, Sada
had received approximately 10,000 fan letters, in addition to numerous
marriage proposals and motion picture production offers. After her release,
Sada used a pseudonym and tried to live a quiet life. She entered a (brief)
marriage and, with her husband, sought refuge in the countryside during
the Allied bombing of Tokyo. After the war, Sada came back to Tokyo
alone and, just like everybody else in Japan, tried to reinvent herself in
a society that was in the process of renewing itself. This attempt, however,
was not easily achieved.

As Japanese society reconstituted itself under the US Occupation
(1945–52), one of the important changes was related to freedom of speech,
which the Japanese did not have before. This notion encompassed a
wide spectrum of ideas and forms of expression, including Communism,
ultra-nationalism, the labor movement and trade unionism, sexual explicit-
ness, and bizarre and grotesque crime stories, typically under the headlines
of *ero* (erotic) and *guro* (grotesque). In this "free" atmosphere, ironically,
Sada's 1936 crime of passion became the subject of renewed attention,
with exaggerated pornographic emphasis, culminating in the violation of
Sada's privacy by writers and publishers of pulp fiction. In the remainder
of this chapter, I shall briefly recapture how Sada's feminine agency was
transformed in accordance with postwar Japan's love culture, since this
will provide us a bridge to the study of love in 1960s Japan, to be discussed
in Chapter 3.

In 1947 alone, at least five books were published depicting Sada's affair
with Ishida and the subsequent murder, with disproportionate attention
given to sex scenes. At least one of them blatantly fabricated the line
that Sada had told the author the story herself. Sada was offended, having
noticed that her case was reported in a newspaper, radio shows, and
journals that specialized in pornography and sex crime stories, in addition to the aforementioned books. She filed a lawsuit against some
publishers and published a memoir herself in 1948.[57] In her memoir, Sada
writes: "My relationship with [Ishida] was such a beautiful love (*utsukushii*

renai) that no sex book can possibly deal with it."[58] Note here: she uses the term *renai* that she never had used during her trial when referring to her relationship with Ishida.

By retrospectively recounting her act during the interrogation after her 1936 arrest, certainly Sada had a chance to render her affair with Ishida more meaningful. But at the same time, the need to have to render, discursively, her affair within the scope of comprehension then available meant that she had to rework and reframe her deed. The most obvious genre she could utilize was a crime of passion. But as we noted earlier, she demonstrated a crude use of terms relating to love, and not that of an educated person. In the meantime, the media in 1936 conferred upon her the image of a terrifying, yet irresistible femme fatale (see Wakaume's comment on p. 40). This image became exaggerated in the postwar revival due to the atmosphere of free love and free sex, as I have just mentioned. And as if it were some kind of vicious circle, the publication of her memoir, along with the lawsuit and related media coverage, gave Sada yet another chance to publicly make a statement regarding her past affair. But, now Sada was no longer a perverted criminal, as she had been in 1936; her story was, instead, molded into the acceptable repertoire of postwar Japan's love story. So what *was* this repertoire that Sada's 1936 affair now had to be reinvented in?

A *taidan* (conversation) between Abe Sada and Sakaguchi Ango, carried in a 1947 issue of the journal *Zadan,* would be an appropriate context in which to contemplate this question. Sakaguchi was an avant-garde novelist who had openly opposed the war, disregarding his conscription notice.[59] Let us first examine the conversation:

Ango: Have you, by the way, ever regretted that incident? I personally do not think it was a bad incident.

Sada: No, well, not really. I don't think I regret it. Sometimes, yes, I wonder if I should not have done such a thing, but well, still, okay, I don't regret it at all. I am sorry for the dead [Ishida], I am . . . I don't know why I feel this way.
     [. . .]

Ango: I believe that [what you did] was something that every individual thinks about doing. You just *did* it. That is why everyone was terribly sympathetic to you. You must not try to make up some excuse for it.

Sada: No, I don't try to come up with an excuse. I don't try to explain why I did such a thing to him. It was it and I am satisfied about that. I don't even think I should not have done it. But, I am not happy about the public who thinks that I did that purely because of desire of flesh.
     [. . .]

Ango: I think you are the purest person of all. You just have to say it
           [to the public] without any falsity. That will never become porn.
           The total purity would never make pornography.
Sada: But, you would wonder how strange it might sound when I say
           that I don't regret that incident.
Ango: Absolutely not.
           [. . .]
Ango: Have you ever fallen in love, when you were young, with a man
           of your dreams?
Sada: I was . . . raped . . . It [the affair with Ishida] was my first love.
           I was thirty-two. It was the first time that I really fell in love with
           someone [*koi*].[60]

Sakaguchi added to the article a monologue reminiscing about his
meeting with Sada:

> Sada-san's prison term was . . . too long. I thought it should be three
> months or half a year. Although she took a life and disfigured the
> body, there was no criminal element [in her behavior]. Only pure love
> [*junai*]. I feel pity. She was a victim of the age. Her behavior was
> scandalized in the age of militarism and that is why she had to suffer
> from the additional imprisonment on the basis that her act went against
> the morality [of the time] . . . The case of Sada is a sad love, consist-
> ently pure [*junjō*], deeply sad, but warm. Her love will eventually
> become an eternal savior for everybody.[61]

In Sakaguchi's perception, Sada, now a middle-aged woman, was almost
disappointingly plain and ordinary—far from the image of a notorious
femme fatale. Sakaguchi, however, does not patronize Sada in the conventional way; he does so with subtlety, empathy, and respect. He privileges
Sada's experience of love as honest, courageous, and non-hypocritical. In
Sakaguchi's mind, Sada is pure, innocent, and immersed in love, a love
that was to serve only her lover and herself—a role model for lovers in
the new, postwar Japan, in contradistinction from the subjects whose love
was only devoted to, and to be reciprocated by, the sovereign Emperor.

Whereas in the past, Sada's act was understood to be an excess—an
excess of emotion, an excess of physical engagement, an excess of play,
an excess of passion—in Sakaguchi's depiction, Sada's act becomes an
exact act, an act which he viewed as just about right for modern, free,
liberated lovers, motivated by adoration of the partner of one's own choice;
in his word, "pure love." What we have here is a new woman created as
a pioneer of this new form of love—love that is free from the sovereign's
gaze, love that exists completely for two people only, that is to say, love
that is born between equal and free-thinking citizens, and this love now

has to be "pure." Although Sakaguchi does not appear to imply "pure" as relating to sexual purity, the introduction of this term in contrast to pornographic implications (as stated in the conversation) brings it into opposition with carnality. This is how Sada's love was recreated: in 1936, she was unable to separate love from sex—her term "*horeru*" meant to love, to do love, to make love, not to talk about love—now in 1947, she was talking, talking about love, separating it from sexual passion. Is it the case that within little over a decade, Sada the prostitute/murderess was reborn as Sada the citizen?

The post-Meiji feminine subject in Japan emerged in the figure of *ryōsaikenbo,* the good wife and wise mother, in the wives who would support their husband's devotion for the Emperor and the mothers who would willingly send their children off to the battlefield. This femininity was normatized and was highly productive in terms of female participation in the imperialist cause as the subjects of the Emperor.[62] In 1940, as I have already mentioned, the government proclaimed the National Eugenics Law and divided the population into the healthy and invalid, now assigning the healthy men and women to ideally reproduce an average of five children in order to meet the ever-increasing demand for demographic growth in light of the war.

Sada's anomaly was precisely that she stood as an antinomy to these idealized character-types. She was no wife. She stole someone else's husband (not just once) and often, someone else's father. She was no mother. Her sexual endeavors were indifferent to the motives of procreation or the preservation of the Japanese as a species let alone its physical improvement—her sex was dangerous, wasteful, and destructive, particularly when viewed in the context of patrilineal and patriarchal principles; after all, she was a castrator. She was no national (at least consciously) or imperial subject; in her all-absorbing love, she was quite oblivious to the sovereign order and the national and international crises Japan faced. Sada's sexual identity was at the margins of the marginal, excluded from the national-normative loving feminine practice of *ryōsaikenbo.* The very perception of Sada as perverted may have had less to do with castration or sexual violence than with the fact that she embodied an existence that stood outside the sovereign order of the Emperor. Love that was not dedicated to the sovereign was not accepted in Japan under the state of exception. In this order, love between two individuals for each other was not love.

From a feminist point of view, we can strive for the following interpretation. What we have here is a woman whose sexuality and gendered identity were placed, perhaps temporarily, outside the patriarchal order of the sovereign's divine rule. Considering that the sovereign assigned both men and women the equal duty of dedicating themselves to him, while the content of their duties was gender-specific in such a way to empower men in the public realm as opposed to women's exclusion from it, Sada's kind of sexuality could not have been accounted for even as "the oppressed" or "discriminated against" in the heterosexist feminine scheme, where men are the dominators, normatizers, and canonizers, and women, the dominated, the regulated, and the encoded, within the rubric of patriarchal gender relations. What comes to my mind is Monique Wittig's view—that only women bear sex, not by being born but by becoming women, while men are general, in the way that only people of color bear race, while white people do not have it—but it is also important to remember that hardly any Japanese feminists contemporary to Sada showed interest in her act of subversion.[63] One can say that Sada's prewar sexuality was excluded from the existing heterosexist order: the masculinist order which would exclude her, thereby rendering her sexuality meaningless and undefinable, could not find a place for it—just a threat of castration was enough to refuse it. At the same time, her sexuality did not belong to the existing feminine genre, *ryōsaikenbo*, as a derivative of the male original, that is, the authentic national subject of imperial Japan. From this point of view, Sada's femininity, at least at the time of her killing Ishida, did not have gender, as it did not constitute the notion of the feminine that was available at the time.[64]

But then, why was it that when Sada's 1936 affair was located in the repertoire of non-sovereign love by commentators in postwar Japan, it became different from what it actually was in 1936? In the postwar context, Sada rendered her 1936 act comprehensible by actively seeking participation in public discourse (though also finding herself its unwilling object at times). Sada's postwar manifesto provided the language to describe her act and transformed its locale from the margin (or outside) of the patriarchal sovereign order under the Emperor to the inside of the contemporary sociality, turning her gendered identity and her sexual position into something that the public could comprehend, categorize, and deal with by using the existing vocabulary, in tandem with the voluptuous and liberated romantic desire of the postwar Japanese public. Her love, in other words, was revamped as a love that was exciting, fascinating, but ultimately safe, unlike her love in 1936, which was dangerous, poisonous, murderous, and above all, undefinable. As Arendt aptly states: "Each time we talk about things that can be experienced only in privacy or intimacy, we bring them out into a sphere where they will assume a kind of reality which, their intensity notwithstanding, they never could have had before."[65] By being placed in the realm of public discourse and popular language, Sada's 1936 affair, as it were, assumed many realities, every one of which was different from her original act.

The role played by Sakaguchi Ango, seen in the conversation above, is instrumental in the transformation of Sada's 1936 affair. Indeed, in Sakaguchi's rendition, nothing about Sada's act was inexplicable: her gendered identity, sexual behavior, and love were all domesticated in the postwar public discourse of new love—pure and innocent, separate from sex. The appropriation of Sada's image by an avant-garde novelist and other "free-spirited" pornographic writers, the arrival of "freedom of the press," and above all, the reconfiguration of the defeated national identity, were phenomena not coincidental or mutually isolated in their contemporaneous occurrence. Especially in the postwar context, where the Emperor all of a sudden declared that he was no longer a god, but a mere mortal, and where sex and love were no longer Emperor-bound or sovereign-focused, Sada was restored as a "woman" again, the woman that fitted the existing genre of femininity. Furthermore, her form of love was enthusiastically promoted as "new love," love between citizens, not between sovereign and subjects, in Sakaguchi's lucid wording.[66]

If we go back to the dialogue between Sada and Sakaguchi, it is evident that it is Sakaguchi who defines Sada's act, describes her emotions and, indeed, her love, elaborating on her muddled and somehow hesitating fragments of words. Her wording is obscure and at times confusing and contradictory, while Sakaguchi corrects her, coaches her, in the process reshaping her account. Sakaguchi authorizes Sada's experience as pure love at such speed and with such lucidity that Sada herself cannot even object. What we have here is, in a way, a conversion, or more precisely, modernization of Sada's love: Sada's kind of love, the love that consummates in a pre- or extra-linguistic way, destructive not only for the other but also for the self, is not compatible with a modernity that presupposes a rational, critical, and reflexive self and, above all, productivity, yields, and return. The basis of this modern love was the separation between "love" and "sex," as in sex being the reward of love. Let us see this more in Chapter 3.

3 Pure love

I think our love can simply stay within just the two of us . . . But, I also wonder if [our love] can give strength to those people who were disappointed in love because of their illnesses and disabilities. But above all, I'd love to let the whole world know that there exists a man like Mako who possesses such wonderful love.[1]

A few months after writing these words, Miko died of cancer in her facial bones. She was twenty-one. All of Japan was drowned in tears as it followed the tragic story of Miko (Ōshima Michiko) and Mako (Kōno Makoto), the young lovers who fought Miko's fatal cancer until the last day of her life. A student at the prestigious Doshisha University in Kyoto, Miko died after undergoing very difficult surgery that eliminated one half of her face, including the cheekbone, nose, and the jawbone supporting her mouth.

The year of Ōshima Michiko's death was 1963, one year before the Tokyo Olympic Games. It was also the time when Japan's economy was gradually and steadily gaining confidence after the devastation of WWII followed by the US Occupation. The postwar baby boom had created a surge in the youth population, and urban nuclear families were increasingly being housed in modern, government-subsidized high-rise apartment complexes called *danchi*. Each apartment was equipped with a new space called a "dining kitchen," containing a dining table and chairs, as opposed to the traditional arrangement where the family would sit on the floor around a low table.[2] The dream of owning "my home" had not yet reached the population on a national scale—that was to be a distinctly post-1970s aspiration. To be sure, people worked very long hours, but the concept of exclusive loyalty to the employer had not permeated the salaried class just yet. The family unit was slowly yet inexorably heading toward disintegration, but for the meantime the fiction of the "happy home" remained tenable.

In common with other industrial, non-socialist nations, 1960s Japan presented a mixed picture: these were times marked by fierce clashes between the forces of stability and rebellion. The rising middle-class ideal of the peaceful urban nuclear family life was challenged by student radicalism in the street. Demonstrations against the US-Japan Security Treaty were joined by protestors opposing the treaty normalizing relations between Japan and South Korea in light of Japan's decision to ignore North Korea in its postcolonial settlement negotiations. Anti-Vietnam War protests increasingly came to attract disaffected groups of various persuasions. Street fights and collisions between police and student protestors often resulted in casualties, occasionally even deaths, while Tokyo University and other prestigious college campuses were turned into fortresses of student activism demanding the liberalization of higher education. At the same time, the economic boom following the Korean War (1950–3) was firmly exerting influence on the daily lives of citizens, albeit in ways reflecting the rapidly expanding class divisions. On the political level, the effects of "the 1955 system" were beginning to be felt, the 1955 system being the euphemism for a peaceful, albeit with tension, coexistence of left and right political forces in Japan.

In 1959, four years before the Miko and Mako tragedy, the nation was captivated by the announcement of the engagement of Crown Prince Akihito (the current emperor, the Emperor of Heisei) to Shōda Michiko, a commoner. The media was filled with extensive coverage of their fabulous wedding ceremony. An unprecedented match between the imperial heir and a non-aristocratic woman was represented as a quintessential example of love at first sight, born on the tennis courts of Karuizawa, a popular resort for the upper classes of the time. The Western-style royal parade, with the royal carriage traveling the eight-kilometer distance from the imperial palace to Tōgūgosho, the Crown Prince's residence, was televised. Sales of TV sets soared from 910,000 in 1958 to over two million in April 1959, when the imperial wedding was shown. The 1960s heralded a new era for romance and love (as opposed to arranged) marriage, which was now available to all, even to a prince.[3]

By the time the anti-establishment movements on various fronts had died away, that is, by the end of the 1960s, Japan was clearly joining the ranks of the industrialized nations—once again. Although the majority of the country continued to live humbly, confined in their tiny *danchi* apartments, there was a steady rise in feelings of national pride and middle-class consciousness on a nationwide scale, permeating every household and preparing the nation for the age of affluence, abundance, and waste in the late 1980s on through the 1990s. But, all of this still lay in the future when the story of Miko and Mako unfolded in the early 1960s.

The story of these two young lovers both reflected the romantic ideal of the day—purity—and laid the foundations for many future romances shaped according to this ideal. Their story was televised, made into a movie, published, celebrated, mourned, and remembered. People were mesmerized by it—this was a story of pure love, or so it was understood, and its hopelessly sad ending glorified its purity all the more. The death of a beautiful young woman, who endured dreadful surgery and the subsequent disfigurement, by losing half of her face, and the bereavement of her lover who stayed faithful until her death, became a national love story. The relationship between lovers, Miko and Mako, it was stressed, was pre-sexual or non-sexual in nature. By the 1960s, in other words, premarital sex had become a taboo on Japan's love scene. Or, at least, pre-sexual (read "pure") love became something that the nation looked up to as praiseworthy and ideal. Further, it was supposed that one had to be in love first, prior to having sex; that is to say, virginity became an emblem of purity.

My purpose in this chapter is to identify the effects of the implementation and institutionalization of love as an apparatus by the newly reemerged postwar Japanese state to ensure the wellbeing, productivity, and reproductivity of the population. I shall be referring to the story of Miko and Mako as a national exemplar as I explore this theme, and consider to what extent and in what ways we can understand love as complex social function of the postwar democratic national state. In my view, the US Occupation of Japan from 1945 to 1952 was a significant culprit in changing the nature of romantic relationships in postwar Japan. Reforms that took place in these seven years abolished institutional mechanism that sustained sovereign love. For example, no longer was the emperor able to issue decrees after 1952. Instead, legislative powers were now encapsulated with the sovereign state and judicial authorities in the name of democracy. Considering that state-imposed policies and projects would take some time to organize themselves into the structure of everyday life of the population, any examination of 1960s Japan would have to take into account the reforms and new concepts which the Occupation brought to Japan.

We have already seen at the end of Chapter 2 that, as soon as the war was over, the previously grotesque sex murderer Abe Sada was quickly reconfigured as a modern and model lover of the new era. We noted that Sada made it clear her sex murder had been premised on love, as if sex and love were two clearly separate entities, and more importantly, we further noted the application of the term pure love by leading commentator Sakaguchi Ango. In this chapter, I shall focus on the 1960s, a period marked by a strengthening in the belief that love was to be a prerequisite to sex (and not vice versa). This task will involve a close reading of the letters exchanged by Miko and Mako, which were published under the title *Ai to shi o mitsumete* (Facing Love and Death) in 1963 and became an instantaneous national best-seller. One important shift I consciously attempt at highlighting in this chapter relates to the role of the sovereign state: whereas in the state of exception, the restored imperial sovereign had unlimited power and was omnipresent and ultra-visible, the postwar Japanese state, which withdrew into the background by reverting to its normal (non-war) state, began to make a different kind of intervention—also omnipresent, but not so easily visible.

1

As I have indicated, the reforms instituted during the Occupation—legal, but above all moral and educational—ultimately had the effect of severing sex from love, installing the former in the bodies of prostitutes (whom the GIs bought freely) and the latter in the bodies of unmarried and marriageable women. Nowhere was this concept more strongly manifested than in education. It was under the Occupation that new sex education guidelines were established and manuals produced. By saying this, I do not mean that the US Occupation personnel directly manufactured sex education in Japan; I am suggesting that we need to bear in mind complex workings of the postwar ethos of Japan's social reconstruction, every branch of which interacted closely with and received tutelage from the concerned offices of the Occupation. The keyword for morality in the area of sex education was *junketsukyōiku* or purity education and it was primarily directed at women, that is, the segment of women who were deemed appropriate candidates as good wife/wise mother.

The Ministry of Education was responsible for the formulation, promotion, and enforcement of the concept of purity education, and the object of its enlightenment was the population of female students or *joshigakusei,* a group of young, educated females that should be categorically distinguished from those involved in the sex industry and prostitution. Originally proposed at a conference of deputy ministers in November 1946, the implementation of purity education was further discussed at the national conference of prefectural directors of social and educational departments in December of the same year. From June 1947, under the Ministry of Education, Junketsukyōiku iinkai or the Purity Education Committee began formulating concrete policies. From 1948, high school guidelines for physical education included sex education as part of instruction related to personal hygiene. In 1949, the middle school health instruction curriculum also came to include items related to sex education.[4] However, curiously, the committee decided not to set up a separate sex education curriculum, instead encouraging teachers of moral education, biology, and physical education to be particularly aware of the need to incorporate sex education as an inconspicuous yet natural part of their curricula, as well as reminding teachers, parents, and community leaders of their responsibility to enforce the tenets of purity education.[5]

According to the relevant Ministry of Education manual, *Junketsukyōiku kihonyōkō* or Fundamentals of Purity Education, "feelings towards the other sex should be as natural, innocent, and healthy as those between brothers and sisters," and for that purpose, for example, the manual suggests that boys be encouraged to get out of bed as soon as they wake up in the morning and girls wear loose underwear that does not rub against the genitals.[6] Further, Andō Kakuichi, MD, who headed the above committee, asserted that *junketsu* meant sexual purity involving the attainment of complete unison between the physical aspects of reproduction and moral standards relating to sex.[7] Here, such standards were not to be set randomly by individual men and women, but by the state. As can be seen in the following passage from the above manual, this was also perceived and portrayed as a matter of utmost importance in the context of national health, in particular with respect to maintaining healthy reproductive capacity:

> After defeat in the war, moral corruption in society becomes preva-
> lent. In particular, there is deterioration in morality between the sexes
> and an inevitable increase in youth delinquency and prostitution. Our
> country today cannot avoid this. Furthermore, due to the confusion
> caused by the thorough defeat at war ... moral ignorance and dis-
> trust are intensifying. Such a social environment will poison the next
> generation ... and lead to national disintegration. Today, the need for
> *junketsukyōiku* [purity education] is becoming ever so urgent.[8]

Of course, one needs to remember that the 1940 National Eugenics Law was still alive and well, with its recommendation that those suffering from the terminal illnesses and disabilities on its list be sterilized due to their inferior genes, since their reproduction would lead to the corruption and weakening of national health. Although the 1940 law was overturned in 1948 and revamped as Eugenics Protection Law in 1949, with economic hardship given as a legitimate reason for abortion, the basic premise of the original law was not discarded.[9] The Ministry of Education's Fundamentals of Purity Education manual connects the reproduction of degenerative genes with *rankō* or uncontrolled sexual intercourse with unspecified, multiple partners and emphasizes that: "human reproduction must prioritize genetically pure blood [*kettō no junsui*] and the improvement of physique [*keishitsu no yūryōka*]; such a condition cannot be attained by *rankō* and must depend on [pure or virgin] marriage and marital fidelity."[10]

Following the publication of the Ministry of Education manual, experts competed to publicize their opinions, the majority never failing to mention *junketsukyōiku* for females. For example, Numanoi Haruo, the author of *Seikyōiku no riron to jissai* or Theory and Reality of Sex Education, who was Professor of Liberal Arts at the University of Tokyo and vice president of the Japanese Sexology Society, emphasized the nature of the female and her important duty in nurturing a loving family:

Women differ from men in nature, firstly because they are the most beautiful protectors of love [*ai*] ... Women's love enables men to take on all sorts of challenges in life, replenishes the source of men's energy, and provides men with comfort when they are tired and disappointed. Secondly, women preserve the human species by way of passing on new life to the next generation ... New human lives are born and nurtured inside the female body.[11]

The almost crude and naïve sexism aside, what is interesting here is that the "comfort" the author is referring to is asexual, while sex is for reproduction. While there is a conspicuous absence of mention of the "comfort" men could receive from prostitutes or other sex workers outside wedlock or prior to marriage, the author goes on warning against *fukenzenna kōi* (unhealthy behavior) on the part of women, including masturbation which, according to Numanoi, could turn women into homosexuals and would ruin their marital happiness.[12] Similar warnings against female sexual self-gratification, focusing on clitoral orgasm as a possible cause of mental illness and frigidity (that is, inability to sexually satisfy her husband), abound in purity education and sex education guidebooks.[13] Authors also offer a method of anatomically identifying a virgin by way of examining the woman's vagina and breasts.[14] One can clearly see that *junketsukyōiku* was really about female virginity and not male sexual purity, about controlling female sexuality (by way of educating men as well as disciplining women), and about dividing sex into marital and extra-marital components from the men's point of view. The surprisingly frugal mention of prostitution in the Ministry of Education manual is indicative of this; if total sexual purity of the population was the purpose of *junkestukyōiku,* why would the manual not criticize and denounce prostitution in the first place? In this regard, it is notable that the concerns of educational and medical experts revolved around female students, *jogakusei,* reflecting the reality of postwar *danjokyōgaku* or coeducation and the anticipated increase in the population of female students compared with the prewar period.[15] Here, again, *jogakusei* are posited as the antithesis of sex workers.

Interestingly, though, there was almost no guide available after one ceased to be a *jogakusei.* So, after marriage, a wife's sexuality was not supposed to be discussed openly, as her role was now defined as reproducer and homemaker. Paralleling with a curious "undercover" sex education, embedded in biology and other related subjects, marital sexuality for women and post-reproduction sex life inside the marriage received hardly any attention from the authorities and experts. Thus, by the time *junketsukyōiku* generation became wives and mothers, bewildering lack of knowledge as well as experience awaited the women. One consequence was that the baby boomers of the 1960s came to regard it as silly or embarrassing to be concerned, overtly or covertly, with the sex life of a wife and her husband, once all of the children had been born. Contrary to the oft-believed myth that Western or American influence corrupted the chaste native women, I may say that in the case of Japan, it was the postwar US Occupation that set the tracks for desexualizing married women and made Japanese marriage sexless.

I am, of course, not saying that it was simply the imposition of Western morality that changed and reconfigured love and romance in postwar Japan. A significant change in the romantic life of the Japanese had already begun to take place from the very beginning of the Meiji period (1868–1912). One example, noted in Chapter 1, was the influence of the Bible on the way "love" came to be translated as *ai;* another was the arrival of the *jogakusei* as the new female embodiment of romance, replacing courtesans and prostitutes. Already, as early as the Meiji period, the objects of pure love—*jogakusei*—and of sex—prostitutes—had been separated. But the postwar shift was swift, drastic, and effective, mobilizing the national-scale effort to make Japan acceptable to the world's powerful, notably, the US. This shift took place during a period when certain memories remained fresh: memories of extreme indoctrination related to the notion of love of/for the sovereign, the institutionalization of army comfort stations, the nationwide experience of teetering on the brink of mental collapse during the war, and devastating defeat after enduring the severe state of emergency, with atomic and hydraulic bombs wiping two Japanese cities from the surface of the Earth.

Not totally unlike the efforts of Meiji statesmen to bring the nation up to Western standards in matters of law and social order, the postwar Japanese state was proactive in its dealings with US Occupation, welcoming the occupiers and enthusiastically cooperating with them. Furthermore, there was an important difference between the Meiji and Occupation reforms: in 1945, the population was far better educated, more critical, and widely informed on global, national, and personal issues, as opposed to the Meiji population, which was organized into a modern nation in a somewhat hasty fashion. Most important was the shift in the *topos* of the sovereign: whereas before it had been in the hands of the restored ancient power, in postwar Japan it was said to rest with the people in the name of democracy.

Moreover, unlike the Western powers that Meiji Japan had to deal with, skeptical as they were of Japan's ability to modernize itself, the postwar US Occupation operated on the premise that Japan had fought formidably in its war against the West; that is, it incorporated a recognition of Japan's prowess, despite the fact that the nation had, in the end, been defeated. More importantly, Japan was quickly emerging as an indispensable US ally in the context of the cold war in East Asia. This can be clearly understood if we consider that the Allied forces' postwar reconstruction of Asia prioritized Japan, the aggressor and colonizer, and neglected and marginalized other Asian nations that had been colonized and pillaged by the Japanese.[16]

The Occupation did not subject the Japanese to total humiliation, either. For example, Japanese national sovereignty was respected, even under the Occupation administration. Further, the Emperor, who in the measure of normal assessment should have been held responsible for the war and Japan's crimes against humanity (including the Nanjing massacre), retained his position of privilege as a new, secular figurehead of the nation. There was one significant omission: the wartime experience of sovereign love was erased from official history, and the history of the army comfort stations was consigned to oblivion and treated with silence. Furthermore, a vast body of evidence testifying to Japan's brutality became the subject of systematic whitewashing on a national scale by being excluded from the standard school history textbooks, buried under the euphoria of postwar economic prosperity. This evidence included accounts related to the forced mobilization of labor from the colonies, cannibalism, and other violence among the Japanese soldiers who were left in the tropical jungles of the Philippines and swamps of New Guinea, the atrocities committed during the war in China (including the rape and massacre of Nanjing), the human medical and biological experiments in northeastern China, brutal treatment of Western and Asian POWs (including the Bataan Death March), and many others. What remained after this erasure were the images of starved, exhausted Japanese prisoners returning from Korea and Manchuria, images of the weary eyes of former Japanese POWs being repatriated from Siberia and China, images of the burnt-down and flattened city of Tokyo, images of children and babies crying for their mothers missing after Allied carpet bombings, and images of the unthinkable destruction of Hiroshima and Nagasaki. The US Occupation, which was already caught up in the rapidly emerging structure of cold war confrontation, secured Japan's new rise from the ashes, and for that, the image of Japan as the aggressor was not very useful—rather, for Japan as well as for the US, the image of Japan the victim was a much better point of departure in order to encourage the defeated nation to rise up again.

The International Military Tribunal in the Far East (IMTFE) ignored the issue of "comfort women" and other forms of sexual enslavement of women who had been methodically and systematically exploited by the Japanese military.[17] In other words, the postwar logic of the victors was also the logic of *male* victors. The victorious men entered a pact with the defeated men, by way of silencing and excluding women and the colonized. But this pact meant that now both groups of men, both the victorious and the defeated, shared the burden of secrecy—and this was related to heinous war crimes, the violation of other human beings: torture, biological experiments, killing, mutilation, rape, and desecration. For example, biological weapons experiments by Japan's Unit 731 during the years 1930–45, using Chinese, Russians, and Koreans in Manchuria whom Japanese soldiers had abducted, were kept secret by the US Departments of War and State, which benefited from the records; in exchange, war criminals such as General Ishii who were responsible for human experiments avoided punishment at the IMTFE.[18]

It needs to be emphasized that the "West" the Occupation introduced to Japan was a cultural model that the dominant class in the West deemed as ideal and not the divided, diverse, and stratified reality of the West, where racial segregation and ethnic discrimination, socio-economic class divisions, and gender disparity were the dominant norm, and where only selected segments of the population benefited from the ideal. In Japan, too, the reforms benefited the population only in a selective fashion. The prewar intra-gender division of women into good wife/wise mother and prostitute continued, and in some sense became intensified in postwar Japan, since the form of relationship the "comfort women" had offered Japanese men was consistently preserved, while no historical reflection was made on this subject in Japan's public discourse for at least three decades. This parallels the way in which the US Occupation opposed prostitution on the surface, while, in practice, GIs wholeheartedly contributed to the prosperity of red-light districts in Japan. Interestingly, the act of offering women to GIs was closely connected, in the mindset of Japanese policy makers, with the concern for national security, as I mentioned in Chapter 2 in relation to the RAA or the Recreation and Amusement Association (see p. 56).

However, there was a fundamental difference between postwar prostitution in Japan and men's involvement with "comfort women" during the war. As I emphasized in Chapter 2, to visit a comfort station was part of military duties for the Emperor's soldiers. It was a mission of loyalty to the Emperor, as "comfort women" represented a gift of love from the Emperor to his soldiers. Postwar sex workers in Japan, on the other hand, had nothing to do with such a meaning. Indeed, they had nothing to do with the Emperor at all, nor, at least on the surface, with the Japanese nation. Rather, prostitution in postwar Japan emerged at the margins of the state, staffed with those seen and referred to as the failed and fallen women, whose capacity to join national reconstruction was viewed as seriously compromised due to their own moral degradation and lack of ability to rectify their situation by gaining more honest and "healthy" employment. Indeed, it was women activists who most strenuously insisted on outlawing prostitution, thereby depriving sex workers of the minimal state protection they had possessed. Female members of parliament were more than willing to label prostitutes as immoral, corrupt, and, hence, a threat to the peace and stability of society and the family. According to Fujime Yuki, female political leaders such as Kamichika Ichiko and other members of the Upper and Lower Houses of Representatives at the time completely failed to grasp the reality faced by the prostitutes, most of whom were economic drop-outs from mining and other working class families, war widows, and single mothers, whose economic circumstances had forced them to enter prostitution in order to raise their children and/or to take care of aging parents. The prostitution abolition movement resulted in the Prostitution Prevention Law, inaugurated right after the Occupation in 1956, and put into full practice in 1958. It outlawed prostitution, pushing the women into the mob-controlled back alleys of the sex industry, thereby multiplying the possibility that they would become subjected to exploitation and violence.[19]

Many legal and social reforms were carried out under the Occupation, including the dismantling of the multigenerational, extended, and patriarchal household registry system, and the introduction of female suffrage. In the area of matrimony, Occupation reforms were aimed at recreating the monogamous Japanese family founded upon conjugal love between the parents, which presupposed mutual fidelity as one of the most important preconditions. Considering that in many parts of Japan, customs such as *yobai* still existed and traditional festivals often allowed sexual license, the US-imported emphasis on monogamy created a gap between the actual marriage and sexual reality of men and women in Japan dictated by the residues of tradition, and the ideal of love and marriage now dictated by the law.

An interesting mixture of cultural norms was thus created for the postwar Japanese wife/mother. While her mind and body had previously been immersed in the sense of procreative mission for the Emperor, she was now told not to think about the Emperor as god and instead, to devote her energies to the creation of a home for her husband and children, members of a new democratic state. As a modern and liberated housewife, she would be paying attention to what was happening in politics and society at large and casting her vote in elections. Now, she would also have to be working—most likely part-time or inside the home (*naishoku*) as a seamstress, for example—in order to meet the monthly payments for the "three godly instruments" (*sanshu no jingi*) of refrigerator, washer, and vacuum cleaner, which all good modern households were supposed to own. Her husband would (ideally) be working in a white-collar job, and as years went by, coming home later and later, due to business-related dinners and drinking get-togethers (involving entertainment by hostesses). In the meantime, children of respectable families were raised with *junketsukyōiku* as their sexual moral foundation. But unlike the 1980s wife/mother whose self-destruction and decomposition became all too obvious, the 1960s wife/mother was able to maintain the family romance of loving parents and adorable children. Above all, compared with former decades, the memory of which they still possessed, the 1960s were good times; compared with later decades, the Japanese were still relatively poor and struggling to reach industrialized middle-class living standards and more nationalistically focused on the task of socio-economic reconstruction. And unlike in later decades, Japanese women were getting married and having children. It was the 1960s, the decade during which love marriages, *renaikekkon,* finally outnumbered arranged marriages.[20]

Just as Japan's public discourse never had a genre for "comfort women" until the late 1970s, another form of sex—sex given as a "comfort" by prostitutes—was not openly discussed in Japan. Once the Prostitution Prevention Law was passed in 1956, female leaders were no longer inter-ested in debating prostitution, while feminism identified housewives or *shufu* as its primary target of liberation. In other words, class divisions were rapidly opening up among Japan's women, rendering it taboo to step into another's territory, such as that of prostitution. In this kind of way, the polite, politically correct convention of not patronizing the most oppressed, the lives of whom one could not even begin to understand, was already kicking in and in a gradual and systematical fashion, the working women, blue-collar women, ethnic minority women, women with disabilities, and women in sex industries effectively came to disappear from the surface of Japan's mainstream feminist discourses.[21] The ongoing presence of US military bases offered, in a sense, a convenient cover for the supposition that prostitution existed only for foreigners and only in enclaves around the bases, while Japanese men (married or unmarried) continued to sustain their relationships with "comfort" (read "sex")-giving women. In the meantime, young women educated in the postwar coed system, marrying and having children in the decades to come, were immersed in the values of *junketsukyōiku,* safeguarding their virginity and sexual purity.

In this way, two principal models of romance came to emerge in postwar Japan: relations with the comfort (sex)-giving woman outside matrimony and the relationship with the child-giving woman inside marriage. This division of labor among women was systematically imposed by the nation-state in various guises, such as through the educational apparatus (including purity education), the popular cultural promotion of "happy" homes and families, and via legal institutions such as laws relating to marriage and nationality. At the same time, the *yin* and *yang* of love, the one that was hidden and the other that was upheld as the national ideal, were steadily and successfully internalized and replicated on the daily level by both men and women. In this process, while sex was quietly pushed in the direction of the women who gave "comfort," the women who produced babies, were made "pure" to the extent that marriage became sexless after procreation. Seen from the position of "good girls," there-fore, sex became available only within the cage of marriage and only until all of the babies were born.

I have argued that previously, in ancient Japan, sex and love were one and the same; they were indissolubly connected. Now, sex and love were separated; love was connected to sex only as its prerequisite. In other words, one had to be in love first before having sex, and having sex without love was a despicable act for a "good girl," since that would be a job for a prostitute. Further, this sex should be primarily for producing babies and should not be required when that objective had been met. Causality of a linear kind was now in place, by way of separating what once was one substance into two. The nationally admired exemplary romance of Miko and Mako needs to be read against this context.

2

Miko (Ōshima Michiko) and Mako (Kōno Makoto) met in a hospital in Osaka, while both were receiving treatment as inpatients. Miko was still a high school student and Mako was attending a college preparatory school. Subsequently, they corresponded for about three years until Miko's death. It is at the beginning of their third year of correspondence that their monograph *Ai to shi o mitsumete* (Facing Love and Death) opens. The first letter printed in the book dates from August 15, 1962, precisely seventeen years after Japan's defeat in WWII. The book enjoyed enormous success, selling 1.3 million copies in 1964 alone. The TV station TBS televised the story and a movie was made starring Hamada Mitsuo and Yoshinaga Sayuri, the extremely popular *junai kombi* or "pure love" screen couple of the time. The theme song by Aoyama Kazuko sold phenomenally well and Aoyama won Japan's 1964 Grand Record Prize.[22]

As of 1962, Miko is a student at Doshisha University, a high-ranking private university in Kyoto. In her letter of September 8, Miko tells Mako that after having discussed the matter with her father, she has decided to leave the college altogether, although her father wants her to take a leave of absence for a semester or two.[23] This may already be an indication that she feels premonitions about the limited time remaining to her. Physicians in Japan at that time considered it more humane and ethical not to reveal pessimistic prognoses to dying patients. Miko, therefore, is not aware of the details of her prognosis, plans for her treatment, or the likelihood of her survival (or lack thereof) at this point.

The opening of the book is a little difficult for readers to follow, since it is not until some pages later that the reader learns about the incident on what both Miko and Mako refer to as Mako's "third night" in Osaka. During the August summer vacation, Mako comes to Osaka (from Tokyo where he is attending college) to work part-time as a beer vendor at a railway station. The third night after his arrival in Osaka, he goes to see Miko in hospital. They talk all night. Towards the end of the conversation, Miko tells Mako:

Since there is no hope for us to be happily together, and I think the time will come [soon] for us to be separated [due to my terminal illness], when it becomes difficult for us, let's stop writing to each other.[24]

Many letters at the beginning of the book refer to this incident—Miko trying to explain that her desire for Mako's happiness made her say such a thing, and Mako trying to convey to Miko that he would not leave her no matter what, even in death.

That meeting in August is the first time they have seen each other for two years. In his letter to Miko, Mako recaptures that moment of reunion:

As soon as I arrived at Osaka University Hospital [where Miko was an inpatient], I went up the stairs to the seventh floor of the eastern wing. Room 711. I could find it easily. The name plate, Ōshima Michiko, in brush-paint. I was overwhelmed by nostalgia when I saw it, since it was the same name plate that I was familiar with from two years before. When I looked into the room between the gap in the curtains, I could see Miko sitting by the window, looking outside. As soon as I entered, Miko came toward me. I wanted to hold Miko tight, but buried that desire. Miko and I took a seat beside the window.
   "How long is it that we have not seen each other?" [Mako asked.]
   "Two years."
   "It was when I was in prep school, so this is our third year."
   "How did you know I was here [hospitalized]?"
   "I received your letter letting me know that you were going to be in hospital again. So, I tried the telephone directory [after arriving in Osaka] and found the Osaka University Hospital number. When I called here, I was told there was an inpatient called Ōshima Michiko."
   "I see."
   "Since when have you been here?"
   "Since the tenth [of August]. I came directly from Kyoto [where her college was]."
   "Oh really? I sent my summer greetings [card] to Nishiwaki [i.e. Miko's hometown]."
   "They [Miko's family] will forward it here eventually."
   Then there was a short silence. Miko said, "Don't you think it's amazing that our correspondence has lasted for two years?" ... I was not happy to hear this. Your comment made me feel as if I was taken lightly. But I did not show it ... I'm sorry I've written something unpleasant ...[25]

In reply, Miko writes to Mako, asking him to be patient, full of apologies for being sick, thereby spoiling their fun.[26] Mako writes, responding to this, that he is no longer able to take their relationship lightly, although he candidly expresses the lack of confidence on his part in his ability to make Miko happy.[27] The "third night" in Osaka is to play a pivotal role in the development of their relationship, which started as a pen-pal relationship, as it is the moment of their reunion. On September 30, 1962, Mako writes to Miko:

> This year is the best for both of us. Our relationship, which started in the kitchen of [a hospital] three years ago, seems to be blossoming into a beautiful flower. Let us both try harder to make [our relationship] bear fruit, even if a formidable demon [Miko's illness] is waiting to assault us ... Tonight, I'm going to confess when I first began feeling love [*ai*] toward [you,] Miko. I'm going to write very seriously and sincerely, and so please read this carefully: I don't think it was this year that I began feeling love [*aijō*] toward [you,] Miko. I'm not certain when my friendship first became transformed into love. Naturally and gradually, it became love. At the end of last year, as I continued to write to you, I was already feeling love toward you. I also sensed the same feeling from your letter of January 14 this year. I think [that night, i.e. the third night] you wanted me to say to you that our relationship was not simply about friendship. But because I was silent, you broke into tears and said "Let me know when you decide to stop writing to me." I don't think you meant it at all. I knew all that, and I understand you'd hate me for that. Your tears were beautiful ... it was then that I experienced the bittersweet encounter with a woman's heart. I'll never torment you ever again. You are already suffering so much from your illness and hospitalization. I'll make you feel safe and secure, so you'll be able to focus on recovery. That's my mission. Miko! I love you with all my heart [*aishiteiru*]. So please try harder to recover as soon as possible.[28]

In October, as the date of Miko's surgery draws closer, the lovers' letters become profoundly emotional—at times painful to read. Both develop a strong fear of death and agonize over the meaning of life, death, and love. Miko, facing difficult surgery, writes in her diary: "Will there be any meaning in life left for me after the surgery, surgery that will destroy half of my face? Would that still be a life?"[29] On October 9, Mako writes the following in reply to Miko, whose wording in letters is becoming evasive, alluding to her fear and despondence:

> I'm rereading the letter from Miko, which I received today, and I find it inconsistent and hard to understand. Let me copy the part that I find strange: "Shall I tell you what it was that pleased me most in your letter yesterday? The part where you wrote about *Acacia Rain*

[a popular song about a sorrowful woman hoping to die under an acacia tree] ... In general, I don't like people who are easily disappointed at their own errors and who cry over them. I think one has to get over them and start over again. So, I was moved by [your, i.e. Mako's] determination and strong will to live. I was convinced that [you,] Mako would be able to overcome [your] difficulties." I was surprised and shocked by the fact that Miko was making herself into the heroine of *Acacia Rain*. What are you thinking about, Miko? I'm going to yell at you, if you're thinking thoughts of futility. I can see through everything, even if [you] try to camouflage the meaning. [Mako understood that Miko was telling him to be strong and go on living after her death.] ... tomorrow, I'm going to take up a part-time job in the evenings. [By earning extra money that way] I'll be able to go to Osaka sooner ... I'll live. I'll live to see the twenty-first century ... But I need a companion and ... that would be nobody else but Miko. Please remember that. Miko, be strong. Try harder and harder. Medicine is progressing day by day ... The day you can cut off all your connections with the hospital [and illness] will come. I'm saying this because I believe it. I'm crying tonight ... I cannot write any more.[30]

On the day Miko receives this letter, she writes in her diary: "Mako says I'm inconsistent. He's very perceptive. He might come to Osaka [soon]. Must write before that and tell him to leave me. Will write tomorrow."[31] Following this entry, Miko writes the following letter:

The fall sky is clear and beautiful, but today, to me, it appears cloudy because I have to write this very sad letter to you. I have been wondering whether I should ask Mr Takezawa [Mako's best friend], my brother, or my cousin to talk to you on my behalf, but yesterday's express mail [from you, Mako] was enough to show that you have perceived something, and I decided not to postpone this letter any more ... Things that I'm going to write below I'll write very honestly, and with no exaggeration as if I were some kind of tragic heroine. If you love me truly, please accept what I'm going to tell you. And please, live your own life anew.

Since learning about my illness four years ago, I have not been able to enjoy youthful health, but everyone's been so kind and loving toward me, and I've lived in a [kind of] happy oasis despite my illness. I met you two years ago. With your constant, warm encouragement, I finished high school and successfully passed the entrance examination for the university of my first choice. Since then, I've been oblivious to my disease and [I have been] very happy ... When this fourth hospitalization was decided, I felt overwhelmed, but did not suspect any worries when my doctor told me: "Let's make sure this will be the last time [to stay in hospital]." I was even happy to know that I did not have to make [further] cumbersome trips to the Outpatients Department.

Then you came to Osaka. Those twenty days went by in a flash ... I was so very happy to receive your letters even after you left [for Tokyo]. Every day was so great. I told my brother and cousin [about our relationship]. Hiroko [Miko's younger sister who met Mako at the hospital] must have sensed what was going on between us. I'm certain my parents are aware about us and are understanding. I felt so happy about this very open and healthy relationship with you and wished it would last forever.

But that dream has been completely shattered. From around the *obon* festival [mid-August], I realized that the behavior of my doctor and my family had become different ... A little later, my doctor told me that there was no prospect of recovery for my condition using today's medicine; there was no data and no prognosis for how many years I'd live—it could be one year or twenty years. I listened to him very calmly. Strange—perhaps I had accepted my fate a long time ago.

I told my doctor: "I'm very happy now. I would regret nothing if I were to die now. If [the surgery] were to prolong my life by only two or three years, I'd rather not have anything done to me now." I longed for death then. Death seemed beautiful. But this fantasy was soon erased. I was told [by the doctor] that I should not be selfish, that I must think about the people around me, particularly my parents, and that rather than imagining that my life would end soon, I should think seriously about how to live in case I were to live for a long time, longer than expected. My doctor told me he'd help me in any way and would do his best [in treating me] and asked me not to hastily conclude that it was all over. He told me that I could work for a social welfare [i.e. disability support] organization during my post-surgery rehabilitation ... Other specialists, such as an ear nose and throat doctor, an ophthalmologist, and a radiologist all came to see me and encouraged me [to risk surgery]. Bewildered and confused, I spent all day thinking about nothing.

... I felt awful about not being able to tell you the truth [about the uncertain prognosis] ... I've known all along that it would be unfair to keep you to myself any longer, since my existence is preventing you from meeting other women. But I did not have the courage to say so and wrote the goodbye letter only in my heart.

I'd said to myself: "Because I'll stay in the hospital until the New Year, I'll continue writing [to Mako]. But, when I start [post-op] re-habilitation, I'll tell him everything and leave him ..." But no, my face is swollen and my temperature remains high [suggesting that the surgery should take place earlier than she had hoped] . . .

Please, please forget about me . . . You taught me how to love another person seriously and with all my heart. I learned from you how important it is to love someone. I'll take this experience with me when I start my life as a social welfare volunteer . . . Although I'll be living in an unknown corner of society, my mind will remain beautiful. I'd like to be born again when I leave this hospital . . .

Mako, the "me" that you have known is already dead. Please remember me as I am now, as I have been for the last two years. Please understand my feelings . . . Thank you, Mako, for bringing a beautiful blossom into my twenty-year life. Please live a happy life. Be happy—twice or three times happier than you are now. Good bye, good bye.[32]

Upon receiving this letter, Mako feels that it is up to him whether Miko is to live or die and he packs for Osaka, writing two short, consecutive, and disjointed letters, emphasizing he is already married to her in his heart.[33]

When Mako arrives at Miko's hospital in Osaka on the evening of October 16, she cannot even be bothered to get out of bed to greet him. She is angry at him, asking him why he has come all this way. When they begin talking a little, Miko suggests that if he loved her so much, they should die together, offering 100 sleeping pills. Mako criticizes her: "If you want to die, do it all by yourself. I did not realize you were such a coward." The following day, Miko's father visits the hospital. The three of them talk it out. Miko is persuaded to have surgery. Miko and Mako go to Osaka railway station to see Miko's father off. On the way back to the hospital, Miko is very happy and almost delirious. Mako wonders if it is truly the case that unless she has surgery she will die very soon, since she looks so full of life. During the few days of Mako's stay in Osaka, Miko cooks for him in the hospital kitchenette and tries to make the most of their time together. They eat together, laugh together, sing songs together, and then, there is the first kiss. Mako goes back to Tokyo, filled with hope and in a triumphant mood.[34]

The November letters open on the topic of the surgery Miko is to undergo. Then, the day arrives. It is a major operation that removes half of her face, including her left eye and the bones surrounding her eye, jaw, and nose. The doctors cut along the left side of her nose and down to her lips, leaving the area from her left jaw up to her left eye hollow. At the time, Miko's disease—cancer of the facial bones—is still very rarely known in Japan, and it is the first time that this surgery has been performed at Osaka University Hospital. After the surgery, Miko undergoes a tracheotomy and is placed on a ventilator, taking fluids through a naso-gastral tube. For forty days, she is unable to open her mouth properly and cannot speak. She coughs endlessly every day due to the phlegm that has accumulated in her throat, and is in severe pain. Cotton balls are used in order to stop the bleeding as well as to support the musculature under the hollow face. It takes one hour to exchange the cotton balls under the skin on her face, causing significant pain. Yet it has to happen frequently and regularly, in order to prevent infection.

When finally Miko begins to feel like living again, she writes to Mako, describing the surgery. Miko is scared and is skeptical of her own survival. She tells him that when she is scared, she tries to imagine their future together and creates an imaginary picture in which the two are healthy and forever young. As if to encourage herself to live on, Miko expresses her eagerness to participate in social welfare activities or disability advocacy as part of the rehabilitation program, which has been initiated by a certain Dr Oka, whose work concerns the improvement of living conditions for persons with disabilities and terminal illnesses. It would be useful to remember that in those days in Japan people with disabilities were often institutionalized in seclusion, hidden from the rest of the society. Miko is expressing the wish to participate in helping others in those settings. Referring to her left eye, which doctors have removed, she writes: "I gave my left retina to someone who needed it. I hope that person can make good use of it."[35]

Anyone who has learned about her life cannot help but be most deeply moved by the way Miko tries to regain her will to live after this tough and challenging surgery. A prominent Japanese novelist Inoue Hisashi eloquently describes this:

> What we see is courage, true courage, with which she continues to live, fighting against the terror of her own death . . . She even helps taking care of other patients, with laundry, boiling water for their hot water bottles, making tea for them, cooking noodles for them, changing their diapers. In her, we recognize a genuinely virtuous humanity.[36]

The New Year passes and on February 3, 1963, Miko celebrates her twenty-first birthday in her hospital room. Mako writes to her, emphatically declaring she would never die because he is with her. Mako writes of the eternal nature of love and promises he will protect her against all enemies.[37] Mako also calls her on her birthday, and then writes to her the next day. The phone call is the first time they have spoken over the phone after Miko's surgery in November the year before, and in his letter he asks whether Miko was crying. His letter is wrought with fear. Now—unlike in the previous letter—he finds death "beautiful." He talks about dying—dying *first*, that is, before Miko dies, revealing his fear of losing Miko and his desire to swap the roles of being lost and losing.[38]

In her reply, Miko writes:

> Let me assure you once again. Death has moved away from us. I thought you never liked the word "death." Don't think that death is beautiful . . . But if you are going to die now, I'll follow you immediately. If you were to say "Let's die together," I'd die with you gladly and with no regrets.[39]

Soon after Miko's birthday, her condition worsens. The doctors discover that the surgery, despite the severe burden of unbearable pain and the disfigurement Miko has suffered, has not removed all of the cancerous cells. Miko's father writes to Mako, telling him that although the prognosis is uncertain, the doctors want to perform one more operation, and adds that he himself is feeling despondent.[40] Amidst the hesitation and doubt felt by all involved, it is decided to undertake the second operation. With surgery again imminent, Miko writes to Mako, asking what he is to her, telling him that she cannot simply call him a lover (*koibito*)[41] and that he could be her god (*kamisama*).[42]

From around this time, Mako's resignation becomes evident in his letters. He starts using the past tense when referring to their relationship and, at times, writes as if Miko is already dead. His letters are becoming more and more self-absorbed, for example, where he states that he would return all her letters to her father and would request the return of all his letters, as if she were already dead, even writing that going to heaven would be better than living blind, with reference to Miko's loss of an eye.[43]

One sees that their perception of life and death oscillates wildly. Early in the book, Miko is the one who fantasizes about death and its beauty and Mako criticizes it. Their positions are later transposed, as the prognosis becomes more and more pessimistic. Also, their approaches to living with the consequences of Miko's blindness change: Mako earlier assures Miko that his feelings would remain unchanged even if she were to lose her eyesight, yet later, as has been noted, he changes his mind, saying it would not be worthwhile to have a relationship if she were not able to read and write letters. In one of his "past tense letters," Mako reminisces that he had known for the past three years that Miko would be destroyed by the disease.[44] In return, Miko writes painfully about love, declaring she does not understand what love is, but only knows that she loves him— "That's enough for me," she emphasizes.[45]

There is a curious (and sad) discrepancy between their letters. Fearful of Miko's departure, Mako is trying to rehearse for the future without her, by using her as an interlocutor. Miko, on the contrary, is trying to figure out how to cope with the strong feelings she continues to have toward him, and tries to do her best to make her remaining time in this world meaningful.

Amidst this mutually illusory exchange, Mako asks Miko to prove to her parents that she has had no sexual relations with him, that their relationship has been one of *junketsu* (purity). Miko does not agree with the request, however, suggesting that it is nobody else's business what kind of relationship they have. It is interesting to see that, for Mako, Miko's *junketsu* needs to be declared because, perhaps after Miko's death, he wants to make sure that others understand that they (and more importantly, he, the survivor) remained pure and he is worried that unless Miko declares it *before* her death, it will not look persuasive if Mako is to do it himself alone afterwards. We can see that the value of *junketsu*, the efficaciousness of this concept brought in by the Ministry of Education in the late 1940s, is alive and well in 1963. We can also see that the concept of *junketsu* as internalized by Japan's 1960s lovers continues to focus on the female body as the main site of purity and that the burden of proof of virginity continues to rest with women. But, for Miko, these matters no longer have so much relevance:

> Mako, what do you mean by *junketsu* [purity]? Some people may be pure physically, but mentally impure. I wonder. I personally do not think it would be impure to permit everything in the case of someone I love most, before I marry him, although I know morally that would be wrong . . . I'm sure most people would assume that we have a so-called "deep" relationship. If they want to imagine so, let them do so. We were strongly united spiritually, but never physically [note the past tense]. If I had known I was going to become like this, I would have liked to give you everything (although you never asked for it), but at the same time I think our *junketsu* is what makes our relationship beautiful.
>
> I think our love can simply stay within just the two of us . . . But, I also wonder if [our love] can give strength to those people who were disappointed in love because of their illnesses and disabilities. But above all, I'd love to let the whole world know that there exists a man like Mako who possesses such wonderful love [*aijō*] . . .[46]

A bit later on, Mako tells Miko the reason he wanted her to tell her parents about their purity was because he wanted her father not to misunderstand their relationship. Here again, the burden of proof is borne by Miko, the daughter, while the agreement is supposed to take place between the father and the daughter's lover. Also, whereas for Mako, the concern for *junketsu* is physio-anatomical, i.e. the fact that there has been no penetration of Miko's body on his part, therefore preserving her hymen, for

Miko, although she does not state so clearly, purity is a matter more of the mind or spirituality, while one can see that the weight of moral discourse then in dominance in Japan is closing in on her. Most importantly, whereas for Mako, it is Miko's father who needs to know that there has been no physical contact between Miko and Mako, thereby preparing for Mako's own future, Miko's concern is how to be helpful to people with disabilities and terminal illnesses, those who, according to social norms of the day influenced (of course) by eugenicist values, are assumed not to be entitled to have romantic involvements of any sort. One can see from Miko's stance that to challenge *junketsu* values is also to challenge eugenicist values, because both are primarily concerned with the female body, the former with virginity and the latter with fertility.

Seen more broadly, the question "How should one live?" is taken by Miko and Mako in different ways: whereas Miko is examining and contemplating her own inner worth, will power, and integrity, Mako is concerned with external recognition of his good character. Mako's good character, in this picture, needs to be acknowledged by Miko's father and, by the same token, by the fathers of his future lovers. Miko, on the other hand, facing her imminent death, is able to look both at and beyond her life and her desire to be in touch with the external world, and is only concerned with declaring her happiness and the beauty of their love. Love for her and love for him, thus, are different. For her, to love is to live, precisely because her death is near: Miko gains *bios* by loving, through love, since loving makes her life socially meaningful. This is not to say that her sociality is limited to her relationship to Mako, but that her love goes beyond herself and Mako, reaching out, at least spiritually, to people with disabilities and illnesses. Her comments also suggest that, politically, she views herself as a practitioner of anti-eugenicist, non-reproductive love, and that, philosophically, she sees herself as undertaking the task of going beyond oneself, trying to touch part of the heart of the humanity at large. (But her conviction is fragile—see p. 85.)

For Mako, on the other hand, it is more complicated, since he faces the possibility of a double loss: first, losing control of himself by being in love and then, losing his lover through an event or conditions that are beyond his control. In order not to lose himself in this maelstrom of turmoil and pain, Mako is looking for a "square one" from which to start his life over; hence his need to establish his (or more precisely, Miko's) *junketsu* by way of using her words as proof. The irony is: because she knows she will die shortly, she knows how to live a socially meaningful life; because he does not know when she will actually die, he does not know how to live, what the meaning of life with or without her is, and how to make his own life socially meaningful.

By this point, Mako and Miko are living in different time/spaces: Mako preparing for a future when Miko is gone, and Miko being left alone in timeless space contemplating death. Death for Miko is not perceived as the end of physicality, despite her disfigurement, pain, and illness. Rather, she appears to perceive it as something like a cosmological closure. Hence, she faces it calmly with inner strength and is not afraid. Death for Mako, by way of contrast, is terribly fearful and something that befalls the body. Thus, when Miko loses half of her face, including her left eye, Mako feels death is close, and his fear is augmented. Immediately afterwards, therefore, Mako gets drunk and tries to commit suicide by overdosing on the sleeping pills that he himself had taken away from Miko during the previous summer.[47]

From the next few letters, one learns that the two have talked on the phone about the possibility of separation—yet again—but from mutually different perspectives. While Mako apologizes for not being able to have fulfilled his lover's due and thanks Miko for having showered him with such deep love, Miko is incredulous, as she "thought Mako was joking."[48] She writes, apologetically stating that she never really thought they should be separated, although she may have said things that alluded to separation and the ending of their relationship. She confesses that she is torn, not knowing how she could go on living if she were to lose him now; but at the same time, she is aware she cannot bind him to her, because her health is failing, as if to suggest that a sick person does not deserve love, revising her earlier position.[49] Recognized is an interesting association between love and health, or more precisely, the reproductive health of the female—as long as this point is concerned, the lovers are in agreement. For them, love is available only between a reproductively healthy woman and a man whose health is, curiously, not questioned. For, at this point, Miko is hopeful that she might live, might happen to live longer than anyone expects, including Mako. Then, what should she do with her life and love? Should not she give it up because she is unable to give birth to their children? For Mako, the question is already answered: since Miko is disfigured and unable to live a "normal," healthy life, she is not eligible for love, regardless of how much longer she might have to live, yet he loves her and so, should not he kill himself now? Thus, despite their different takes on each other's love, their basic principle converges: one senses here the socio-historically imposed norm of who can love and live and who cannot, i.e. the healthy versus the unhealthy and their uneven participation in love. This is not a perspective that has developed "naturally": as we have seen, it has been historically formulated through the effects of state-imposed *junketsukyōiku* and eugenics.

At the end of March, Mako visits Miko in hospital spending three happy days close together with his beloved. Afterwards, Mako writes to Miko from Tokyo, letting her know of his arrival back home and telling her that he was happy to see her doing better than he had expected. He continues, however, by noting that he was worried how swollen her face had become. He reminisces about the previous year when Miko was bothered by tears from the eye that doctors had operated on, but he now saw this time that eye was gone forever after the surgery that had been performed in November of the previous year. He tells her how unhappy he was to see tears in her one remaining eye, and desperately and somewhat aloofly states that he is no longer able to believe that Miko will be alive two or three more years from now.[50]

In response, in what is a continuing discrepancy in the perception of their relationship, Miko writes to Mako, stating she is hopeful she will be able to go home before the end of that year. She continues to express her interest in, and hope to work for, the social welfare program, helping peoples with disabilities, deformities, and illnesses. Innocently, Miko asks Mako for advice.[51]

Mako responds to her, almost insensitively in the eyes of the reader, distinguishing himself from Miko's "segregated world" of disability and focusing on his own future career, stating that he has never thought he should bury his life in a segregated corner of the society, since it would render his qualifications and college degree meaningless.[52] In this same letter, Mako also writes of the possibility of meeting other women after Miko's death and states that if a new woman who looked like Miko were to appear in front of him, he would give this woman a very gentle kiss of the kind which he could not give Miko and would treasure and love her more than he had loved Miko.[53] In reply, Miko writes, almost cheerfully, at least on the surface, jokingly starting her letter with the claim that she would be envious of his future lover, whom he said he would love more than he had loved her, adding that "I cannot imagine how you can possibly love her more than you love me now."[54]

At around this time, Mako, who has seen Miko's face following the operation, starts insisting on Miko having plastic surgery. Miko, on the other hand, begins to realize the discrepancy between their perspectives: "I felt strange because you used the past tense in your letters. I wondered if our relationship has become a thing of the past for you, wondered if you knew me only as an already dead woman. And if so, I should let you go, set you free."[55] Both of them, it appears, believe that plastic surgery to reconstruct Miko's face would help her get out of the hospital. But it is becoming increasingly clear to physicians that Miko's cancer is spreading beyond their control, and that there is not much point in reconstructing her face at this time. Miko's physicians, nevertheless, do not tell her that—as stated on p. 75, it was common practice in Japan in those days for doctors to protect patients from negative prognoses—as such, they maintain the line that plastic surgery is imminent. One day in the clinic, Miko overhears the doctors' conversation, referring to the rapid spread of her tumor. She realizes that she will not live long. In any case, in June 1963, Miko again undergoes surgery. Mako writes to her, expressing his suspicion of the tumor's recurrence, stating: "I'll endure anything, because I want you to live longer, even just by one day."[56] Regrettably, one cannot help registering that Mako focuses on his own endurance, rather than hers.

By the end of June, Miko's parents ask the doctors not to operate on her any more, as the repeated surgery will simply increase her pain. Mako writes to Miko:

> I want to go live on an island where nobody is around. I've been feeling pity for you ever since you told me that you'd like to go home before the end of the year. No one told you the truth, did they? But I'm sure you've known it all along. My intuition was not wrong— I've always known that this summer you'd face a major crisis.

In this letter he reveals that he has been addicted to sleeping pills due to insomnia and is trying very hard not to go back to the lifestyle of November/December of the previous year, when he was unable to get up all day and would be often up all night.[57] It is not difficult to infer that he is suffering from severe depression, mood swings, lethargy, and exhaustion due to the imminent death of his beloved.

A little later in July, they talk on the phone. Miko tells him that she is no longer able to bear the pain and cannot have any more surgery. Miko is having difficulty walking. Mako senses that the end is very near. He hurries to Osaka. Their last meeting is full of emotion, but the two try hard to leave warm memories of each other. Miko can only nibble at the canned tangerine oranges, and Mako puts segments into her mouth one by one. Miko tells him: "I wish I could live until your birthday, August 8. I'd like to get you some nice gift. But, I'm not sure if I can."[58]

On August 7, 1963, with her mother present, Ōshima Michiko's twenty-one-year life came to an end.[59]

3

One year after Miko's death, Tokyo was the venue for the Olympic Games, symbolizing Japan's readiness to rejoin the ranks of the world's leading nations. While Japan's domestic living standards remained low, the nation was catching up to Western nations at a remarkable speed. During the 1960s, Japan's average annual economic growth rate was 10.39 percent, more than twice as much as those of Western nations.[60] While Mako, as a poor college student, had to take slow night trains between Tokyo and Osaka, as the Olympic Games commenced, the bullet train started its first trips connecting Tokyo and Osaka in a few hours.

In the 1960s, Japan's economy made a decisive shift from labor-intensive to capital-intensive. There was a drastic decline in the percentage of the population engaging in agriculture, and government subsidies to the agricultural sector increased. Coal mining and textile-related businesses increasingly ceased operations. On the other hand, there was an exponential increase in the number of employees working for large companies. This increase in the white-collar sector changed the structure and ethos of the labor movement and trade unionism. Meanwhile, more women found employment (part-time or full-time) in the service sector. In 1950, the population of female salaried employees totaled 3.63 million, amounting to one quarter of the total number of working women; in 1967, it exceeded ten million, amounting to half the total number of working women.[61]

Japan also experienced strong population growth in the 1960s. From 1960 to 1971, the rate of population increase (per 1,000 people) grew steadily from 8.4 to 14.1. The exception was 1966, the year of the fire horse, a very bad combination in the Chinese zodiacs falling every sixty years and considered an inauspicious time to have children.[62] We have already seen that by 1967 Japan had achieved the prewar population goal of 100 million. In other words, the 1960s was a decade of procreation and the blossoming of the baby boomers. (The demographic balance was to shift again in the early 1970s.)[63]

It was during this decade that the oft-witnessed image of Japanese business men in ties and dark suits getting drunk, throwing up in public, and flirting with hostesses in bars, began to appear. Likewise, the image of the absentee father married to his job, turning Japanese families into virtual single-mother households, is also a post-1960s fixture. In other words, the transition to a capital-intensive economy did not mean shorter working hours. On the contrary, due to the white-collar nature of work, labor hours increased in a more insidious way, especially if we add up after-hours obligatory drinking and weekend commitments to spend "leisure" time together with colleagues and bosses at golf clubs, for example. The need for blue-collar workers was met by seasonal migrant male workers from rural areas, referred to as *dekasegi* or "leave (home) and earn," leaving agriculture in the hands of elderly parents and wives. This pattern often resulted in the estrangement of the father and disintegration of the family. Thus, by the beginning of the 1980s, Japanese families were predominantly urban, affluent, and dysfunctional.

In the picture of 1960s' "pure love," what needs to be recognized is that the prolonged working hours for husbands and the burden of child-rearing placed on wives, coupled with the ethos of *junketsukyōiku,* began rendering marriages in Japan asexual. The sexuality and sexual desires of wives were suppressed or displaced by watching soap operas in the living room, while those of husbands were redirected outside the home, as in the cases of flirting with bar hostesses or buying prostitutes.[64] From the late-1960s on, overseas sex tours to South Korea, Thailand, or the Philippines became popular among Japanese men. These tours, especially those to Korea, were euphemistically referred to as *kisenkankō* or *kisaeng* tourism, *kisaeng* being a Korean word for the traditional courtesan/ high-class prostitute.[65]

If, in the West, the 1960s sexual revolution brought about by the introduction of oral contraceptives freed sex from marriage, in Japan the 1960s freed marriage from sex, meaning that after the intercourse that was necessary for reproduction, sex was no longer required.[66] Of course, this process happened gradually and it had to wait until the turn of the century for the media to discuss *sekkusuress fūfu* (sexless married couples).[67] It also partly accounted for the increasing gap between urban and rural living standards. As the nation as a whole underwent rapid urbanization, the young rural labor force lost inheritable family occupations such as farming and fishing and rapidly began filling the lower ranks of the workforce in the cities, with female attrition flying into the sex industry. At the same time, women from other parts of Asia began arriving en masse to work as waitresses, dancers, and sex workers.

Placed against this background, who was Miko? What kind of lover was she? What can she tell us about love in Japan? In Miko and Mako's letters, the term *koi* hardly appears. Instead, it is *ai* that denotes love. Although there is a term reserved for romantic love, *renai,* which combines the characters used for *ai* and *koi,* routinely and as a matter of convention "I love you" is translated as *aishiteimasu* and not *koishiteimasu.* Furthermore, whereas *ai* is combined with *jun* (pure) in the term *junai* discussed above, *koi* does not form any conceivable combination with the concept of purity: whereas *junai* is part of public discourse in Japan, *junren* (*ren* being the reading of the character for *koi* used in composite words) is not a possible character combination in the accepted lexicon of the Japanese language.[68] By the 1960s, in other words, *ai* definitively became "superior" to *koi,* since it denoted long-lasting, permanent, unchanging, steady, and pure love, rather than the flame-like, whimsical passion and painful infatuation of *koi,* a state of not being able to control oneself.

The figure of Miko as a female college student played an important role in defining *junai.* From 1969, the percentage of women entering senior high school began to surpass that of men, while the female college attendance rate remained low: in 1955, only 2.4 percent of all female senior high school graduates continued to a four-year university course (the rate for males was 13.1 percent).[69] This suggests that, in fact, Miko was a pioneering figure among Japanese women, receiving a higher education and able to write romantically. We can see, as opposed to the type of language used by Abe Sada, for example, the language of love in the 1960s had been gentrified: *ai* as written by Miko here is premarital and asexual, with the promise of marriage and sexual union, that is, pure love. I may call it "the sanitization of love" in postwar Japan. For, *ai* here is love that implies no longer that ambivalent, double-faced or multifaceted and, above all, confusing term *koi* as it appears in *Manyō* poems. This new love is unambiguous, love that is beautiful precisely because of its *junketsu* (purity)—as Miko wrote. Conversely, love that involves (premarital) sexual relations is impure. But the paradox was that sex *had to* happen once married, in order to produce the offspring, while non-reproductive sex, even inside marriage, was neither noble nor important. Needless to say, this formula did not abolish sex or the sex industry nor, by implication, did it end the continued consignment of socially and economically disadvantaged women to the sex-selling trades. While the wartime sovereign love in the state of exception had intensified it through dividing women into national reproducers and national sex slaves, postwar reforms and intervention by the state in the name of *junketsukyōiku* on one hand and by way of outlawing prostitution on the other reorganized the division in a new environment.

A significant side effect of this division related to the requirement that a marriageable woman be unconditionally healthy, and regimentation was applied to the bodies of young, unmarried women from multiple directions. Mandatory annual school physical examinations, *shintaikensa,* which combined chest X-rays, eyesight tests, TB checks and vaccinations, and biometric measurement of height, weight, and chest and torso size, for example, played a part in enhancing this ethos. Doctors would rank each child's body, its shape, musculature, and nutrition.[70] Side by side with this regime, however, under the Ministry of Education guidelines, no adequate education on sexual health was given at school during the 1960s and 1970s (and even today; see Chapter 4), and young women gathered basic knowledge from older female kin, peers, and comic books. This resulted in a state of affairs marked by confusion regarding sexual intercourse, an imprecise understanding of menstruation, and virtually no preparedness with respect to contraceptives on the part of young women, largely leaving abortion as the most common way to terminate unwanted pregnancy.[71] At the same time, the mysterious inaccessibility of sex-related knowledge, augmented by a prohibition on premarital sex, worked to reinforce the value of virginity, and young girls were groundlessly made to worry, for example, about the possibility of inadvertently breaking open the hymen through excessive physical activities such as competitive sports. The gaze of the state, implemented through institutions such as *shintaikensa,* the school health examination, effectively worked to achieve the self-policing of the (developing) female body, yet this policing, as it were, was based on a low level of scientific informedness.

Childbearing, of course, was a duty of daughter-in-laws from olden times. It has often been documented that until the bride became pregnant, she remained outside the household registry of her in-laws' family. Nevertheless, with the much watered-down intervention of the Confucian code (as compared with neighboring cultures such as Korea), reproductive capacity was not, unanimously and in totality, an imperative attribute for a Japanese wife. Childless marriage was routinely resolved by adopting an heir either from among extended relatives or non-relatives. Given that existing demographic research strongly suggests that Japanese households typically took the form of small (three to four people), two-generational (as opposed to multigenerational in the case of Eastern European farming communities, for example), and basically nuclear composition,[72] it would at least be safe to say that procreative sex did not play a central role in the sexual lives of men and women in Japan consistently in history. We can also see this by considering the existence of customary sexual institutions such as *yobai* and noting that sexual pleasure independent of marital and procreative concerns constituted an important play activity for ordinary Japanese. As I have argued in Chapter 1, for much of history until relatively recent times, genitorship of a child was not necessarily an important aspect of identity and, similarly, virginity of the young female population was not considered an important factor when entering a romantic relationship or marriage. However, as can be seen, by the 1960s, consanguinity or more precisely, childbirth (i.e. giving birth to one's own blood) and virginity became important criteria when judging health with respect to kinship and marriage in Japan.

With the intervention of the nation-state in rearranging local sexual customs as part of what would be called modernization from the late nineteenth century, the intensification of eugenicist and pronatalist reproductive control under the wartime military regime, and the postwar imposition of the value of virgin marriage, marital fidelity, and conjugal love, Japanese (good) romantic relations from the 1960s (at least for a short period of two decades or so) came to be characterized by the following type of scenario: an asexual, premarital romance leading to marriage and procreative sex, creating a "happy" nuclear family that operated according to the mechanism of a non-sexual relationship between parents. In reality, this often created excessively codependent mother-child relations on one hand and an increasingly invisible absentee father on the other.

Importantly, love that led to marriage in this way came to be reserved for the healthy female population, while the "other love" that did not lead to marriage (i.e. sex for "comfort") came to be consigned to women of poor health and by implication, lower morals. The agony of Miko, who loved Mako to her maximum capacity, revolved precisely around this point: the lack of possibility for her to give him children rendered marriage with him impossible, and this, perhaps even more than her death itself, was a serious factor in making her hesitate to love Mako more deeply and expect the same in return. However, as far as we can tell from the text, Miko's concern over the lack of possibility of giving birth did not derive directly from the problem of her reproductive organs or capacity. It was the fact that, as a result of major surgery on her facial bones, Miko was disfigured and had come to be labeled as disabled and incapable of marriage (and reproduction) in the eyes of both Miko and Mako.

Further, both seem to have resigned to the scenario in which Miko would live in seclusion—if she were to live—helping other people with disabilities that were likewise condemned and banished from the mainstream society. We must remember that deformity was one of the conditions that the state eugenics policy deemed as an appropriate basis for sterilization. Her disfigured body, with its faceless face, it is not hard to assume, was perceived as not entitled to be classed as reproduction-worthy. One can see how narrowly the frame of "healthy women fit to marry and reproduce" was circumscribed in Japan at that time. Miko's agony and sorrow were the effects of eugenics-inspired *junketsukyōiku,* in that it ranked the national population according to health status and placed boundaries by exiling the unhealthy, the disabled, and the disfigured to institutions and seclusion.

At the same time, it is interesting to note that Mako's reproductive health was never questioned. He smoked heavily, got drunk routinely despite his history of stomach ulcers, and was addicted to sleeping pills. However, these were never factors pushing Miko to reconsider the relationship or the possibility of eventual marriage. On the contrary, his unhealthy lifestyle served to boost Miko's womanly concern over his well-being. In other words, maintaining a healthy body for reproduction was solely a woman's responsibility.

Governmental intervention on the basis of eugenics has a long history in Japan. It was more fiercely emphasized as the nation entered the period of imperialist competition, with the Japanese bearing the burden of "leading race" in Asia. The National Eugenics Law of 1940 was a good example. However, importantly, the 1960s baby boomers were different: intrusive state control and heavy-handed indoctrination were no longer necessary, because individuals—men and women, but more specifically women—disciplined themselves in such a way as to care for their reproductive health. We see here the artful fruit of what Foucault terms governmentality: by this stage, demographic policy has penetrated to the level of the individual through state-implemented politico-cultural-educational apparatuses, such as school physical examinations, purity education, biology curricula, and educational films showing, for example, patients with syphilis. Here, individuals have internalized the effects of state political technology and are self-motivated to attain the disciplinary standard of aspiring to be candidates for healthy reproductive marriage, which they have been made to equate with love, *ai.* Furthermore, we need to recognize that it took some time for this governmentality to emerge as a body of concerted efforts and effects, participated in equally by the state and the population. We can see this clearly in the fact that tenets of the 1940 National Eugenics Law continued to be adhered to after the war by those men and women born from around the time of the rape of Nanjing through to WWII, while their fathers were visiting comfort stations. In this sense, the 1940 law and *junketsukyōiku* form part of a genealogical continuum.

Junketsukyōiku, I must also emphasize, was established on an important historical omission or, let us say, erasure. The Ministry of Education manual and other guidebooks locate *haisen* or Japan's defeat in the war as the primary cause of the eruption of tremendous irregularity in sexual conduct, corruption of sexual morals, sexually violent crimes, and sexual perversion.[73] This cannot be true. Think about the rape of Nanjing and the sexual violence imposed on "comfort women." Think about how Japanese soldiers ravaged little girls and old women in the city of Nanjing. Think about that recollection of a Korean "comfort woman," who had to eat rice balls and urinate while lying under three hundred men, each one of whom ejaculated into her vagina one after another, and another, and another (see Chapter 2). We are, in other words, witnessing national amnesia in the way *junketsukyōiku* was set up. (This was to be a curse in the love life of Japanese men and women in later decades, as we will see in Chapter 4.)

With the inauguration of *junketsukyōiku* during the US Occupation, and its implementation throughout the 1950s and 1960s, a national economy of love emerged and was normalized, with women taught and disciplined first to become good guardians of their own virginity, second to become healthy wives that would reproduce multiple children, and finally to become loving mothers to them. The role of men here is minimal. Surprisingly little was said about visiting prostitutes in *junketsukyōiku* books and pamphlets, as I have stated earlier. In postwar Japan, the intra-gender division of labor was firmly established between healthy and morally superior reproductive (child-giving) women and unhealthy, morally corrupt, unreproductive (sex-giving) women. By the 1960s, confounding these two, therefore, looked unnatural.

Seen from a slightly longer historical perspective, we may summarize as follows. After the Empire collapsed and the man-god Emperor became a mere mortal, love between the sovereign and subjects also collapsed. The Occupation reforms were aimed at modernizing and democratizing Japan by severing the link between sovereign and subjects and instead, at connecting subjects themselves to each other as equal, freedom-enjoying, modern citizens. Love between citizens—this was upheld as the moral-material foundation of society, in that "right" love was assumed to lead to "right" marriage, "right" sex, and "right" family. No longer did the Emperor, the ancient imperial sovereign, play any role here. Instead, love could be found in the modern cultural and material ideal of the small, urban, property-owning, automobile-driving, education-conscious, and vacation-loving family, with the bread-winning husband and stay-at-home wife and their own children. Even the heir to the now secular imperial throne married for love on the basis of his own romantic choice—or so it was said. Nevertheless, what happened in reality in the name of love was more concrete, narrowly focused on female virginity and fertility. In other words, it was not the purity of love itself, but that of the hymen that was at stake. As such, *junketsukyōiku* was an effective apparatus of the Japanese state as biopower, working directly on the body of the population. Furthermore, with more women receiving higher education, population control became more cost-effective. In the meantime, behind the obsession with sexual purity, love, as it were, was left unattended to and gradually forgotten.

Miko and Mako's love marked a turning point in the trajectory of twentieth-century love and romance in Japan: it marked a culmination in the process whereby love of/for the sovereign had shifted to love between citizens and as such, it represented part of the fruit of Japan's postwar sociocultural renewal under the auspices of the US Occupation. This love moved the physically interactive component altogether away from the romance of mainstream popular imagination and concealed the way in which the (not insignificant) role of bodily contact played in the nation's traditional romances. After the 1960s, *junketsukyōiku* or purity education no longer wielded real power. Moreover, sex education itself quietly disappeared from the school curriculum altogether, or was maintained at a minimal level. Love in this way was sanitized, away from fleshly contact and the flow of bodily fluids. An excessive emphasis on the body's purity was paralleled with a virtually complete absence of knowledge about actual sexual practices. In other words, paradoxically, the purity of the body was so abstract (with the exception of information related to the anatomy of the hymen) that it erased and hid the body, limiting self-understanding by the young female population.

Ironically, this erasure of the body was to bring about the reification of one's own body by young female students in the 1990s, for whom the body was so far removed from the self that they could place it on the market to be exchanged in order to satisfy their passionate love for European couture house products such as those by Louis Vuitton. Their material desire can only be understood in terms of fetishism and this occult-like effect of the capitalist market begins to resemble the *Manyō* lovers' *tamagoi* magic in that these young girls are desperately trying to cling on to their souls, souls that are otherwise all too ready to leave their bodies, leaving the selves lost and empty. In Chapter 4, I shall turn to this and other practices of love in Japan in more recent times, practices that mark another radical departure, yet make us wonder about tradition, culture, and the other fundamentals of life and death.

4   Body and soul

I've experienced [diverse forms of sex], but I'm convinced my decision [to enter prostitution] was right. Although I started it because I
was so hurt [by unconsummated love], I was able to meet many
different men and see the real world, a world that was different from
the ideal story I had been made to believe . . . Psychiatry was bad for
my soul, but prostitution was good for me. Those people who tell you
that you'll regret it one day don't really know it, they don't know
anything—I will never regret having done this. I'm not selling my
dignity and I'm not humiliating myself. I've regained my pride
[through prostitution] and sometimes, I feel superior [to these men
who pay me for sex].

A Tokyo University junior[1]

Ever since the Meiji period, female students have provoked debate,
inflamed desire, made heads turn, and produced scandal through their
looks, the uniforms they have worn, hairstyles they have adopted, and
even the bicycles they have ridden; in sum, through the variety of fashion
paraphernalia they have created and adopted, and indeed, through their
very existence they have become carriers of love. Their bodies have become
the objects of myth and romance, for, behind their uniforms, they have
come to represent the not-yet-ripe fruits of womanhood or, more concretely,
the unbroken hymen.

Such an image of purity is, however, a relatively recent creation. When
jogakkō or women's prep schools were first established in Meiji Japan
in the late nineteenth century, the public was disturbed by the appearance
of a new kind of girl—what was a strange embodiment or mimicking of
male ambition of academic accomplishment by females. Their broad
shoulders draped in adapted male attire of *hakama,* the signal the Meiji
jogakusei or female students initially sent out to society in the late nineteenth century was that of an untamable shrew. However, by the early
decades of the twentieth century, *jogakusei* had become the frail objects
of sexual desire. Even their preferred mode of transportation, the bicycle,

had become romanticized, along with the way their loose hair would blow in the breeze and their skirts curled up as they rode along, allowing glimpses of their kneecaps. In other words, interestingly, a riding device, which otherwise would inspire images of activeness and masculinity, was here made part of femininity.[2]

By the time the Taisho era (1912–26) had come and gone, *jogakusei* had definitely come to be seen as cute, adorable, and benign. However, wartime sovereign love, with its agenda promoting a rapid shift from girlhood to motherhood in order to achieve efficient reproduction of a strong Japanese nation, meant that *jogakusei* only fully blossomed as an object of romance in the postwar era. The fact that the postwar national romantic heroine, Miko, was a college student, as we have seen in Chapter 3, was no coincidence.[3] Ever since the *junketsukyōiku* or purity education initiated by the Ministry of Education normatized sexual purity by confounding it with pure love (see Chapter 3), placing a disproportionate emphasis on safeguarding premarital female virginity, female students collectively became an embodiment of purity—to the extent that their vaginal purity became an expensive, highly sought-after, and easily marketable commodity in the logic of Japan's late capitalism.

In this chapter, I shall highlight three key sites—*enjokōsai,* which I translate as "aid-dates," a best-selling novel *Shitsurakuen* (Paradise Lost), and a South Korean soap opera *The Winter Sonata,* or the romance transferred and embodied in its fandom. The first site, *enjokōsai*, is a sexual transaction between female high school (and sometimes middle school) students and middle-aged men. This phenomenon peaked in the early 1990s, delivering the revelation that the age of young women who embodied the sexual desire of men was in fact much younger than that of the college coed or *joshidaisei*. I translate *enjokōsai* as aid-date; the aid here, at least in a narrow sense, denotes the financial "aid" that female students would receive from their middle-aged patrons in exchange for dating, the parameters of which are broadly defined. Although in practice, *enjokōsai* means prostitution, sexual services offered by these pre-college girls in Japan comprise a vast array of marketing strategies and promotional activities including commodification of their used school uniforms, handkerchiefs, socks, school athletic wear, school swimwear, and underwear, and distribution of semi-nude, nude, and sex-scene photographs.

Relayed with this phenomenon, the latter half of the 1990s witnessed the burgeoning desire of married, middle-aged (by the then Japanese standard) men and women to enter into adulterous affairs or *furin* with a mature partner, as the market began actively seeking the possibilities of arranging intimate, extramarital relationships—in reality, in fantasy, or in virtuality. This became known as the *Shitsurakuen genshō* or "Paradise Lost phenomenon," after the best-selling tale of extramarital romance entitled *Shitsurakuen* (Paradise Lost) by Watanabe Junichi. In its wake, the new millennium opened with the mass and public adulation of Bae Yong Joon, a South Korean actor who was the main male protagonist in a South Korean soap opera, *The Winter Sonata*. This series enjoyed tremendous success from its first airing in Japan on the publicly operated NHK network in 2003. *The Winter Sonata,* in its turn, embodies a complex assortment of romantically inspired elements from Japan's past and present, including colonial dreams, wartime sovereign love, and the postwar pure love.

The material upon which I draw in this chapter is, thus, heterogeneous in nature. A cluster of marketing activities performed in the terrain of civil society through the anonymous exchange of selves coexists with other practices operating in virtual reality, ultimately confined to texts and screens and needing some kind of translation into the real sexual world of Japanese men and women. What underpins these phenomena will become obvious—the self that is about to be lost, and the desperate efforts to retain it, either by way of recovering the soul or getting hold of the body. The irony is that now one is connected with the whole world by way of the internet, cell phone, satellite TV, and other communication technologies, one is most unprecedentedly alone. Ontological certainty is sought not in human connections, but in a materially distorted form of fetishism—be it directed towards European designer purses or imaginary adultery or a good-looking Asian actor. Love, again, thus faces a crisis, as its estrangement from self and society intensifies.

When clear economic motivation interferes heavily with the body-selling market, the self begins to exhibit a stretched and artificial split between the mental and the material (carnal), thereby completing the destruction of the sacred elements of sex between strangers that had existed in Japan since ancient times. In this chapter, I hope to demonstrate the extent to which, compared with the case of the *Manyō* lovers, love has become estranged from sex and, by consequence, self in modern Japan. One might ask, when sex is reified and alienated from one's self, can one still love? At the same time, in a highly mediated and layered manner, I also hope to demonstrate the continued influence of state-initiated control through socio-cultural eugenics over the sexuality and love of men and women in contemporary Japan. In this way, I try to capture the almost confusingly complex milieu in which love in Japan claims to exist and to delineate some of the key points that should help us see what is happening. Interestingly, as we shall see, the unresolved past of the nation haunts Japan's love scenes like an apparition.

1

At the busy intersection in the heart of Shibuya, I notice an unusual swarm of girls in school uniform—female students, perhaps from a private girls' high school. The scene strikes me as unique—I had not witnessed such a scene before 1985, the year I left Japan for a graduate school in England. And now, in 1992, street corners and the foyers of department stores are full of young females, in these look-alike school uniforms and uniformly thick cotton bobby socks worn in a deliberate loose and wrinkled state. Not only their socks and uniforms, with skirts uncharacteristically pulled up almost high enough to reveal their underwear, their facial expressions and make-up are also identical. Walking by them, even their vocalization emerges as uniform—that shrieking, yet strangely self-confident tone. Kitten-like voices surround you as you fight your way out through the sea of girls in uniform. Their unanimously long, straight, well-kept, and shining hair and dangerously seductive miniskirts and plump thighs, supported by loose bobby socks—little did I know then that I was looking at an army of self-promoting business girls.

It took me several years to realize that these girls were not simply congregating and hanging around for what we would see as age-appropriate fun—they were "working," displaying themselves and offering sexual services in the market place for young bodies, turning the streets of Tokyo into one big shop window. I hardly knew then about *enjokōsai* or aid-dating; little did I realize what kinds of people, ethos, and transactions I shared my metropolitan space of Tokyo with while conducting doctoral fieldwork there in the years 1992 to 1994.

More than once during that same period, I encountered scenes on Tokyo public transportation in which (presumably) Japanese men of middle-age were harassing a different kind of female high school students—Korean students, whose school uniforms revealed them all too easily as Korean, as they consisted of reformed and (let us say) modernized versions of Korean traditional female clothing. One evening, traveling in a jam-packed commuter subway carriage on the Chiyoda Line, I ended up arguing with a man aged about fifty who had grabbed the arm of a Korean student in front of me, making her scream. I insisted he had used violence intentionally; he insisted he had had to grab her, as the train was so crowded. The way he spoke to me was outright offensive, asking me in a rude mannerism whether I, too, was Korean also—"*nanda, omaemo chōsenjin nandarō?*" I could not go on too much, since the student herself was already very distressed and slipped off the train at the following station. The idea that the student might well have had to get off the train earlier than she had to, forcing her to either take the next train or walk a couple of stations, still bothers me.

Here, too, school uniforms worked as a distinct signifier, but what they signified was notably different from the red-bowed, white-bloused, and mini-skirted uniforms of Japanese (mostly private) female middle and high schools.[4] These Korean girls, unlike their Japanese counterparts, did not offer themselves as sexualized objects for Japanese middle-aged men;

rather, they became a prime target of anti-Korean harassment. The same middle-aged Japanese men would, moreover, be gladly paying Japanese female high school and middle school students in exchange for sexual services. What does this reality tell us? Are these events mutually unrelated? Or are they in any way connected? And where does love come into this picture?

In order to think about these questions, let us first consider the aid-date and the location of love in relation to this phenomenon. Miyadai Shinji, a sociologist with long-term research experience in the area of aid-dating, reported in the early 1990s as follows:

> The time when only the delinquent students were engaged in "impure inter-play with the other sex" [*fujun isei kōyū*] is over. Now we live in a time when [ordinary] students work part-time in *burusera* shops [fetish shops selling used school uniforms and athletic wear such as bloomers] and [are involved in] *terekura* [telephone club] hostessing. Multiple students [in a class], including those ones with outstanding academic performance, date the same teacher for fun [*asobi*], and a student who ranks second among his cohorts participates in gang-rape on campus—these are the times we live in.[5]

Miyadai began his fieldwork among female high school students earning pocket money through aid-dating from around the mid-1980s. Time and again, he emphasizes the difficulty of grasping the quantitative reality of aid-dating, not because the girls themselves are uncooperative or feel guilty about aid-dating and therefore, will not talk about it, but because school authorities and parents are so unwilling to admit that their students and daughters are willing or able to engage in such "disgraceful" acts as prostitution—worse still, uncoerced and voluntarily.[6]

The term aid-dating or *enjokōsai* is an umbrella term, capturing a broad range of activities producing an effect of pseudo-intimacy, starting from sitting side by side with a man for a fee to having sexual intercourse in a so-called love hotel. In between, there is an array of *seifūzoku* or sex industries incorporating a broad range of occupations, including part-time telephone companions entertaining clientele with sexual banter to models posing individually or in groups for male photographers in various costumes, including bloomers, school uniforms, swimwear, and underwear.

The fees for these activities vary: a three-hour group photo session with the models wearing body-conscious, tight-fit clothing would cost between 20,000 yen and 25,000 yen (approximately $177 to $221 according to the 2006 exchange rate). Typically, these girls would first register themselves with a modeling agency, through which photo sessions would then be arranged; if one introduced one's friend to pose for photographers, one would receive half of the friend's earnings as commission; if a particular individual photographer wanted a private session, one would raise the price.[7] Some men pay between 70,000 yen and 300,000 yen per month for expenses related to these types of services, including the rent for a condominium leased especially to use for rendezvous with their steady girl-concubines.[8]

Miyadai is quite clear that it is not always the case that the family backgrounds of these girls are dysfunctional or abusive, or that they have particularly indifferent parents; on the contrary, he claims, these parents are by and large "good" parents, concerned with their children's well-being.[9] Rather, Miyadai asserts, this situation is an outcome of the post-1980 fantasy of the *tomodachikazoku* (friend-like family) the family that is non-hierarchical, egalitarian, and peer-like in the way parents and children are related.[10]

The reality is that there emerged no such a thing as a democratic, egalitarian, friend-like family in postwar Japan—the aspiration towards a democratic, friendly parent–child relationship resulted in reserved, guilt-ridden parents who were unable to intervene meaningfully at any critical moment with regard to moral and behavioral issues concerning their children. In the meantime, children became superficial—adopting what Miyadai calls "role-playing"—in their relation to parents, in particular by playing the role of a "good" child by coming home on time and never missing school, while engaging in aid-dating in their spare time. When asked about their parents, girls would typically respond that they felt sorry (*kawaisō*) for their parents if they came to know about their daughters' involvement in aid-dating. There is a notable distance between their role as "good" children at home and that of business-savvy aid-daters on the street.[11]

By way of contrast, Hayami Yukiko, a journalist who has also been closely following the activities of aid-dating students for some time, highlights the primary role played by fathers in pushing their daughters into aid-dating. Euphemistically and in an uncannily practical manner, girls use the term "papa" to refer to the regular middle-aged patrons who lavish them with posh dinners, three-star hotel rooms, fees for sex, and cash allowances, in addition to clothing and other personal adornments. Hayami is highly critical of the lack of imagination and understanding on the part of fathers, who tend to be pedantic, rank-oriented, and aloof in their relations with their daughters.[12] This is in contrast to the role of mothers, assigned to take care of children at home single-handedly and thus incapacitated in their roles as supervisors and role models for their daughters—here, the mother becomes a domestic worker/companion, a "friend" who accompanies daughters on shopping expeditions to department stores, but with no role as mentor, let alone disciplinarian. The resulting pattern of domestic relations, with authoritarian, over-rigorous father who is out of touch with the reality of his daughter and principle-less mother whose closeness to her daughter comes in exchange with compromised discipline, creates an extreme form of asymmetry where daughters lack a dependable older figure to provide them with a balanced sense of self, coaching them into maturity and womanhood.

Hayami and Miyadai are, however, in agreement that low self-esteem on the part of the girls is the major motivating factor leading them to enter prostitution. Miyadai reports this from his interviews with college students who used to be involved in aid-dating as high school students, others currently engaged in aid-dating and/or prostitution, and one case of a student at Tokyo University, whose comment I quoted on p. 95. His findings recognize the degree of self-doubt experienced by an elite student at the nation's top-ranked institution, with the respondent confessing to him that the (paid and unpaid) sex led to a restoration of her self-esteem and dignity and feelings of superiority in relation to the men she was involved with.[13] Hayami asserts that after the initial wave of aid-dating in the early 1990s, those girls that had entered the profession through peer-pressure were weeded out, and that, by the mid- to late-1990s, it was the ones that were suffering serious domestic problems, such as non-communicative parents or a dominant father, that remained.[14] To summarize: while differing in emphasis, with Miyadai pointing to a lack of communication inside the home and Hayami focusing on the negative role of the dictatorial father, Miyadai and Hayami both trace the arrival of this new "girl culture" or business in Japan to certain aspects of the modern Japanese domestic environment that effectively destroys the self-esteem of the girls. Those that find themselves in non-communicative situations at home get directed into aid-dating, in order to regain their self-worth and fill the void through bodily communication with the "papa."[15]

In connection to the above, Miyadai explores the gradual and steady loss of *seken* (the outside world) as a basis of measuring good and bad, and claims that this structural factor has brought about dysfunctional communication in postwar Japanese society at large.[16] It appears that the views expressed by Miyadai (and, by implication, Hayami) represent a critical revision of the understanding of Japanese society as a harmonious, culturally unique society. As such, their research calls into question images related to two dominant schools of thought adhered to in Western academic writing: one associated with the notion of the *ie* (household) society and the other with an understanding of Japanese social relations as consisting of inter-personal, socially intimate, and interdependent selves.

The first school of thought, represented by Chie Nakane and other scholars commenting on Japan as a household-oriented society, was a product of the highly successful Japanese economy of the 1970s and 1980s. This school of thought or cluster of discourse is usually referred to as *Nihonjinron* (literally, theory of Japanese people) but more comprehensively known as the thesis of Japanese cultural uniqueness. The spokespeople of this school disseminated the idea that Japan's cultural uniqueness was manifested in the reality where Japan remained culturally Japanese despite having achieved Western levels of modernization and industrialization, creating the Japanese management style of big businesses and key industries, according to which employees' families were looked after by paternal and benevolent employers and employees enjoyed lifelong guarantees of employment. In this picture, Japan Inc. looked like a family-like, caring, and nurturing community in which people lived harmoniously.[17]

The second school of thought starts from Takeo Doi's corpus on the Japanese psyche, rekindled by culture-and-personality school anthropologists in the US and in many different incarnations thereafter. According to scholars in this school, the Japanese self is interdependent, socially intimate, and weak in terms of self-determination, as opposed to a Western self that is independent and strong in terms of self-determination. By extension, Japanese society can only be cordial, harmonious, and communicative in nature. Unlike the first trend, which seems to have gone out of fashion, studies of the Japanese self continue to be popular in the Western academe.[18]

Placed against these stereotypical theories of Japanese society and self, the work of researchers such as Miyadai and Hayami has revealed a nation that is strongly oriented around hedonistic consumption and the momentary material gratification of uncontrolled and undisciplined desires in a post-affluence, late-capitalist age. Their work has also suggested that it is young, unmarried women who seem to be blazing the trail as pioneers in this regard.[19] Far from being harmonious and communicative, as we have noted, researchers such as Hayami and Miyadai cite failure of social communication and destruction of the self's interconnectedness as the primary cause of this.

Interestingly—as Miyadai puts it—the emergence of this new species of young girls was accompanied by the process according to which girls perceived themselves to be, collectively, a sexualized brand called *joshikōsei* or female high school students.[20] This can be understood in the way the school uniforms worn by female students were made into pricey commodities during the 1990s by way of selling them in *burusera* shops, for example.[21] If the middle-aged clientele fetishized these girls' school uniforms, then, the girls themselves fetishized European designer brands. These forms of desire were intertwined, as they both related to bodily intimacy with others, while the individuals residing in these bodies themselves were not the genuine objects of desire. If so, what has this got to do with "communication" as asserted by Miyadai and Hayami? For, in my view, the scar of these girls is repaired with material satisfaction as a quick fix. There is, in other words, no communication between the girls and the men—*pace* Miyadai and Hayami, this hardly seems to support the view that aid-dating occurs due to the discommunication or serious lack of communication inside the family, implying that aid-dating is a substitute for humanly communication.

The structural cause of aid-dating is hard to grasp. It could be a combination of capitalist market logic, cultural assumptions, socio-economic fad, peer-pressure, broken families, and the like. But one point I want to emphasize is that the way the girls have come to look at their youthful bodies as an alienable commodity is closely related to the postwar moral education and its culmination in the separation of sex and love, which is in turn closely related to the self's failure to care for its holistic existence, as can be seen in the way body is subjected to alienation from soul.

But there is one more twist. Let us remember that the figure of the *joshikōsei,* the female high school student, as a sexual or sexualized brand name, is primarily visualized through the medium of their school uniforms. Enter the other school uniforms here. As I described earlier, this other visual image, the image of Korean dress modified into girls' school uniforms, is the object not of flirtation and sexualized desire, but of insult, harassment, and violence. Students wearing this uniform attend schools operated by the General Association of Korean Residents in Japan, or Chongryun in its Korean abbreviation. Chongryun was founded in 1955, following the tumultuous decade of transition in Japanese society from the end of the war through the US Occupation and the emergence of the so-called 1955 system, by which the forces on the right and the left in Japan came to a state of peaceful, albeit tense, coexistence. Chongryun associates itself with North Korea.[22]

As a result of colonial policies in general and more concretely, the wartime forced labor mobilization of people from the Korean colony by the Japanese government and military, there were about 2.4 million Koreans in Japan at war's end in August 1945. Most headed home to Korea soon after the war. However, about 600,000 remained in Japan for various reasons. These included those having established livelihoods in Japan and those who found it impractical to relocate their households to a Korea which had been partitioned and placed under foreign occupation.[23] Koreans remaining in Japan were given little civil and residential rights, let alone Japanese citizenship, because the Japanese nationality which they had possessed as a result of colonial policy was unilaterally rescinded in 1952 as part of the terms of the San Francisco Peace Treaty between Japan and the US. Subsequent to the partition of Korea in 1945 into the American-ruled south and the Soviet-occupied north, and the emergence of separate regimes in Korea in 1948, Koreans in Japan failed to gain any national affiliation. This is of no small significance—they became naked human beings in a world in which being national was seen as a precondition for being human.[24] Unlike Europe after the war, Japan did not face a flood of stateless immigrants. Instead, it created stateless people within itself by depriving Koreans (and other former colonial subjects) of Japanese national status. Helped by Japan's strong postwar demographic growth, it was Koreans and other former colonial subjects and the rural poor (and not foreign immigrants) that sustained the supply of lowest-strata labor, with no social security and bare-minimum wages.

From the outset of their postwar expatriate political movement, Koreans in Japan, the predominant majority originating from southern provinces of the peninsula, had been divided into supporters of the northern and the southern regimes respectively. Northern regime supporters outnumbered the other group for several decades after the war. This is because, in their postcolonial nationalistic zeal, Koreans in Japan identified the northern regime as an authentically Korean government, as the northern regime headed by Kim Il Sung and other former anti-Japanese guerrilla fighters appeared to them as a truly national government, as opposed to the southern regime that was headed by Syngman Rhee, a US returnee married to a foreign wife.

The emergence of Chongryun in 1955 was the result of a reorganization of North Korea supporters who had been persecuted severely by US Occupation forces and the Japanese government by the end of the 1940s.[25] Reflecting the mass support it enjoyed, Chongryun successfully built up a school network offering education at all levels, from kindergarten to graduate programs, using North Korea as the source of its pedagogical doctrine and adopting a decisively nationalistic stance. This was reflected from an early phase in the uniforms of the girls at Chongryun schools, which consist of short bodices and long pleated skirts. The two long ties that are placed askance on the bodice are a characteristic of this outfit, which is altogether a modified version of Korean traditional dress. It is unmistakably unique, and all Chongryun female middle and high school students wore identical uniforms throughout Japan until around 2002, when the anti-North Korean hate crimes against Chongryun's female students came to so seriously endanger their safety that Chongryun schools had to renounce the use of traditional school uniforms outside the school premises (see below). (Male students' uniforms have always been in conformity with its Japanese counterparts.) Currently, it is said that a total of 13,000 students attend 130 Chongryun schools nationwide. This figure represents a minority: more Korean students in Japan attend Japanese schools.[26]

Whenever North Korea became the target of international criticism, Korean female students' uniforms were made into soft targets for physical and verbal abuse. For example, in the year 1994—at the peak of general public interest in the aid-dating phenomenon—a total of 154 incidents of abuse towards Korean school students was reported between April and July alone, the majority of the victims being female students whose school uniforms were cut, torn, and soiled.[27] On the other hand, I have yet to come across any reports of Korean female students aid-dating Japanese middle-aged men. Of course, this does not deny such a possibility and, considering that more Korean students attend Japanese schools, it is possible that Korean girls are or have been engaged in aid-dating. My point is, however, that as a signifier, the Korean school uniform does not function to trigger the sexualized desire of aid-dating; it is a signifier that invokes hatred and violence among some Japanese. One group of high school female students is made into the representative of fantasy, dream sex, and pseudo-incestuous father ("papa")-daughter romance; the other group is made into the embodiment of evil and a threat to Japan's national security. What can we see behind the workings of these two different significations produced by one identical item—school uniforms? And what does this say in regard to love, sex, men, women, society, and the nation of Japan?

The contrasting register of Korean and Japanese school uniforms wrapping the youthful bodies of female students, in my view, tells us something about the workings of Japan's state apparatuses. For those Japanese middle-aged men, a Japanese student's body is not simply sexual or sexualized, it is the national-sexual body, as opposed to that of the Korean female student, which is a non- or even anti-national body. I am, of course, not saying that aid-dating is a better form of treatment than violent assault, but I am suggesting that violent contact directed towards young Korean bodies derives from the body's non-Japanese identity. Needless to say, the same middle-aged men may well have sex with non-Japanese prostitutes or sex-workers in Japan, and many of these women may well be underage. My point, however, is this: as long as we use the sexualized brand *joshikōsei* as an index for 1990s sexual culture in Japan, the underlying principle is that these are (and have to be) *Japanese* girls.

This brand—ephemeral, transient, and supple—is time-sensitive and its season is limited, as the girls will soon no longer be *joshikōsei*. This particular brand—unlike hostesses, escorts, barmaids, and prostitutes, with whom the middle-aged men can also have intimate bodily contact—is nationalized, and this is not unrelated to the fact that *joshikōsei* are confined within one of the most pervasive and effective of ideological state apparatuses, that is to say, school education. These young females, whose education is not yet complete, and who are on their way to becoming full members (citizens) of the Japanese state, present themselves as a particular commodity on the national body market, namely, the object of pedagogical discipline. For the older men, therefore, sex with them comes with the additional mission of coaching, teaching, and mentoring them with respect to love, sex, and life, making them into fully participating adult citizens of the Japanese nation. The nationalized sexual bodies of Japanese female students are placed at the opposite end of the spectrum to those of Korean students, a potentially subversive, anti-national, and hence disposable, element within. The way Korean female students' uniforms were cut in the assaults noted above reveals a desire on the part of the perpetrators—a desire to uncover the bodies of the wearers of this foreign, anti-national clothing. Here, the bodies behind are not objects of sexualized fantasy, unlike the case of their Japanese counterparts, but objects that can be (and should be) wounded.

It is no coincidence in my view that aid-dating girls report that many of their clients try to preach to them about careers and life in general, using their own success stories as a model.[28] One does not have to be a psychoanalyst to see the transference of the fatherly love of these men, who are failures in their real families and therefore try to compensate in the fantasy world and sexual family by relying on capitalist market logic. Is this love? If it is, it is closer to the original meaning of *ai,* love, formerly used in the Buddhist lexicon to mean obsession, meaningless desire, clinging, and fetishism. If it is love, for those men, aid-dating creates a pseudo-family romance, an incestuous and intimate space resided in by only two members of the family, "papa" and his favorite girl. The fact that some men obtain a condominium for the purpose of seeing their steady girls might support this. One can see that the economy of love, initially instated through the Ministry of Education's *junketsukyōiku* (purity education), of which perfection we recognized in Miko and Mako's love story, had been eroded from within by changing concepts and practices of love, as embodied by the new generation of female students. For, thanks to *junketsukyōiku,* the new generation of girls was raised by parents, teachers, and a society whose excessive emphasis on the protection of virginity effectively contributed to making them realize not only what a precious and hence, expensive, commodity virginity could be, but also that it was they who owned it. No longer did virginity belong to the gods (as in Babylon or ancient Japan) or to the patriarch (as in Rome or Confucianist Korea); it was now the property of the girls themselves.

Considering that the main clientele of the girls was drawn from the group of men that were born in the late 1950s and early 1960s, when *junketsukyōiku* was exerting a significant influence on social values, we can recognize in the aid-dating that the value of purity continued to produce an intensified focus on the body. Deflowering the *joshikōsei*'s body, feeling her firm and small breast in their hands, stroking the pristine and supple thighs, kissing or ejaculating in a mouth whose lips did not know how to talk back: all became priceless commodities that these men could purchase. Paradoxically, it was the postwar *junketsukyōiku* that pushed men to look for pure bodies again and again.

Then, we may wonder, why not Korean girls? Was it not the case that, in the recruitment of "comfort women," Korean girls were targeted and, in some ways, preferred due to the well-established Confucian tradition of protecting the virginity of unmarried women?[29] Is it simply the case that while colonialism had made the bodies of Korean women into "national property" in the 1940s, Korean women's bodies in the 1990s were non-national, just because Korea was no longer a colony of Japan? In order to see what lies behind this, I would first single out a definitive moment when the Korean body was made "national" (or more precisely, "imperial"): the 1939 household registry reform in the colony. Through this reform, Korea's position as a colony was topologically redefined vis-à-vis the Emperor. Traditionally, Korean clans worshipped their ancestors, not the head of state or the king. Clan borders formed exogamous borders, and any man and woman that both had the same clan origin (embodied in the patrilineal family name, recorded in the family genealogy) were not allowed to marry. This was even the case when these individuals had never met before and had no known familial or kin-like relations, since such a marriage would nevertheless constitute a crime of incest (and therefore polluting and calamity-inviting). In Japan, by contrast, marriage between cousins was not taboo, widows could remarry, daughters could inherit lineage through the adoption of the husband by their parents, and adoption not only of son-in-laws but also of individuals that were kin or non-kin, older or younger than the adopters, was widely practiced. Further, as was seen in Chapter 1, a high degree of sexual license was available for married and unmarried men and women in the community, and the identification of the patriline was often hardly ascribed any meaning. Unlike in Korea where patrilineage was sacred, Japan had no strong tradition of patrilineage, except for the samurai class in the Tokugawa era.[30]

As stated earlier in this book (see Chapter 2), when the Emperor was restored as the head of the nation in 1868, he did not simply become the highest political office holder—he became the living ancestor of all Japanese people, representing the unbroken lineage of the Sun Goddess, virtually rendering them into *tennō no sekishi* (babies of the Emperor). This was reflected and contained in the household registry in Japan, which was reformed under the Meiji government. The registry or *koseki* was supposed to be not simply a bureaucratic tool, but also to be a membership ID system, testifying to the fact that each person belonged to the Emperor's large family. The Meiji *koseki* was multigenerational, incorporating bilateral families as well, and the household head or *koshu* was assigned the moral-ideological duty of ensuring the loyalty of members of his household to the revered Emperor. As such, the *koseki* became a sacred document that connected Japanese families to their Emperor.

Korean household registration could not have been more different from that of the Japanese *koseki*. To begin, Korean households could have more than one family name in one set of the registry: the name of the head of the household, his wife's maiden name (which remained unchanged after marriage) and, if he was the first-born living with his parents, his mother's name. This was because the Korean household registry was a document testifying to the person's loyalty to their ancestors: by not marrying a woman of the same clan (recorded by way of entering their wife's family name into the registry), one paid homage to one's clan. From the Empire's point of view, allowing the Korean household registry to remain as a vehicle for ancestor-worship would be tantamount to be allowing Koreans to have their loyalties diverted away from the imperial sovereign.[31] Thus, under the new system, the Korean household registry came to follow the Japanese style, registering every member of the household under one family name, the name of the head of the household, which was now assigned a worth equivalent to a terminal unit of the large imperial family. It should be remembered that it was only after this reform, that is to say, after Korean kinship relations came to be incorporated into the sovereign order, that Korean men and women became "eligible" to legitimately serve the Emperor's army—men as soldiers and civilian subordinates, women as "comfort women"; although private companies had begun the recruitment of Korean men and women as workers (industrial and sexual) in the late 1930s, it is the household registration reform that eliminated legal hurdles for the government and the military to maximize the mobilization of men and women from the colony to Japan's war effort.

As soon as the war was over, the situation changed fundamentally. Japan was stripped of its former colonies and colonial holdings, including Korea, Taiwan, Sakhalin, and the Pacific islands. With this, the nationality of former colonial subjects who continued to reside in Japan became ambiguous. Ultimately and, as I stated earlier, with the blessing of the US in 1952, simultaneously to the end of the US Occupation, all former colonial subjects (including those who remained in Japan proper) lost their Japanese nationality: the denationalization of Koreans was complete.[32] (It is no coincidence that the last decree of the Emperor of Showa was the 1947 decree to allow the exclusion of Koreans and other former colonial subjects remaining in Japan from Japanese nationhood.) Thus, Koreans in Japan became stateless, since Japan did not recognize South Korea until 1965, and to this day still does not recognize North Korea.[33]

Although postwar democracy granted the Japanese people sovereignty, and despite the Emperor becoming a mere figurehead, a more fundamental principle related to the emergence of Japan as a modern nation, that is, membership of the national community by birth (*jus sanguinis*), was preserved or, more precisely, reinvented in its fullest strength. For, although Japan's empire-building was burdened throughout by tension between the need to expand beyond areas contiguous to Japan's national boundaries and the anxiety of including non-Japanese inside, measures were taken to incorporate peoples who were not Japanese by birth into the Empire, as can be seen in the Korean household registration reform discussed above.[34] With the end of the war and the Empire, these measures were abruptly terminated without any rescue strategy for those who fell in the zone of ambiguity in between the former imperial system and the renewed national state system, as Japan reverted to a nation only of the Japanese. This meant that Koreans in postwar Japan were no longer (even second-class) members of the Japanese nation or indeed any nation in any sense. This zone that they were confined was not only ambiguous but also devoid of law, in the sense that there was no law that granted them any social and civil status—they existed purely as naked humans, no more, no less. With no travel document, no nationality, no citizenship, their life in Japan came to resemble a life in a concentration camp.[35]

The allocation of desire, divided between the national-sexual body of the Japanese *joshikōsei* and the foreign, disposable body of the Korean female student, as opposed to the aggressive use of female bodies from the colonies during the war, needs to be understood in connection to the postwar topological reorientation of Koreans and other non-Japanese in the map of Japanese national membership. As such, it would not be too much to say that *junketsukyōiku* or purity education worked not only to reinforce the idea of the purity of the female body, but also that of the nation. By the same token, we may also say that love in postwar Japan has been systematically nationalized by limiting the object of desire within the boundaries of its nationals (but see section 3).

The observation of female students in the 1990s confirms some interesting aspects of love in modern Japan. Let us remember Origuchi Shinobu and his abstraction of *koi* from the ritual *tamagoi*: during the time of the *Manyō* poems, the bereaved woman performed this magic, longing for the soul (*tama*) of the dead to return to the body from which it had just departed (see pp. 16–17). Here, the separation of body and soul was recognized only in death. The 1990s aid-dating girls, who had mastered the ontological skill of separating themselves from their bodies by distancing themselves from them or using them in the provision of paid sexual services could, in a way, be said to be heading for the territory of the dead: their souls having already departed their bodies. This arid sexuality was not, however, devoid of love. Girls often had a steady boyfriend, with whom they were romantically involved and from whom they kept their aid-dating secret, and they cared about their parents, whom they wanted to protect from being exposed to this knowledge; it was only that love seemed to have become far removed from sex.

After all, what *is* love? I said in the Introduction that I would take love to be a complex social function. As such, it cannot simply be an emotion. I have argued in Chapter 1 that for *Manyō* lovers, sex and love were inseparable. In the sovereign love of the Empire, men and women entered intimate relationships by way of revering the Emperor, that is to say, under His benevolent gaze. In the process of the postwar rebuilding of the Japanese nation, the key principle became guarding the purity of national sexuality, borne primarily by the body of the young female. But the lack of proper historical consciousness and critical reflection, not only in relation to wartime imperial sovereign love as embodied in the rape of Nanjing and the exploitation and abuse of "comfort women," but also with respect to folkloristic heritage (such as *yobai*), combined with the superimposition of Occupation-inspired moral pedagogical values such as *junketsukyōiku* contributed to an artificial separation of body and soul, thereby endangering both of them. Love's social function, one might wonder, may be to retain body and soul in a mutually meaningful state and therefore, when one of them—either body or soul—is alienated from the self, love becomes unable to function.

I also locate the structural cause for love's crisis in a more fundamental, historical, and moral context—the way Japan reidentified itself in the postwar era as a national community by ignoring its own past or, more precisely, certain aspects of its past, such as the "comfort women" and the rape of Nanjing. For, a nation that has violated others' bodies in building its own national body or *kokutai* cannot possibly start again, simply presuming a clean slate and "victim status" on the basis that it was defeated at war, even though it is true that the Japanese endured horrendous suffering as a result of Allied attacks. The nation needed to have thoroughly reflected upon the violence and violation it had committed against other people and before emphasizing the purity of its national sexuality, it needed to have recognized the sexual nature of the past violence that it had committed against others. In this sense, there is a logical connection between the lack of proper sex education and proper history education in Japan's postwar national education system.

It comes, therefore, as no surprise that, in recent years, voices arguing for improved sex education, gender-awareness education, and accurate history education have been ferociously silenced by the state, supported by the rightist forces. For example, in 2002, a booklet entitled *Rabu & bodei bukku* (The Love and Body Book), issued and distributed free of charge by Boshi eisei kenkyūkai (Mother–Child Hygiene Study Group), a satellite organization of the Ministry of Health, Welfare, and Labor, was recalled, resulting in truckloads of the books being burnt. The booklet intended to give middle school students basic knowledge about sex and contraception. Its recall was triggered by a female representative of the Lower House, Yamatani Eriko, who criticized the booklet for promoting the use of contraceptive pills and thereby supposedly encouraging students to have more sex. The media joined in, relying on the emphasis on chastity education under George Bush in the US as a major point of reference. In the same year, the Tokyo Metropolitan Government under Governor Ishihara Shintaro demoted and suspended the principal of a special education school on the basis of the basic sex knowledge taught at the school, in addition to administering pay cuts and strict warnings to a total of 102 teachers, principals, and deputies of twenty-two other schools on the basis of "excessive" sex education, although the so-called sex education in question involved teaching students body parts by singing a song called *Karadauta* (The Body Song).[36]

This same Tokyo Metropolitan Government has adopted for its public schools a new edition of a Japanese history textbook, which met with strong protests in China and South Korea due to its merely passing reference to Japan's military atrocities in Asia and its failure to mention the sexual slavery of the "comfort women." Its education committee has also decided on a policy of punishing teachers when members of their classes fail to stand up in respect to sing *Kimigayo,* Japan's national anthem, a song closely associated with the nation's imperialist past.[37]

It is no coincidence that knowledge on proper sex and that on proper history have to be simultaneously missing from Japan's national school education: these are the sites that necessitate national reflection on imperialist legacy—one on colonial responsibilities of massacres, atrocities, sexual violence, and forced labor mobilizations, and the other on proper settlement of the compensation for former "comfort women," the process by which sexual exploitation of women (both Japanese and non-Japanese), for example, will have to be revealed in full and faced by Japan's younger generations. Indeed, if one looks at the "comfort women" issue, it becomes clear that sexual violation and colonialism heavily overlap. Not only that: implementing proper sex education and history education will reveal an ongoing sexual division of labor among Japanese women, exploitation of foreign sex workers, fundamental gender disparity, and uneven distribution of power, all continuously sustained in society. Again, it is no coincidence that they are missing from the Japanese state's education apparatus.

Overall, adolescent students are left with little concrete knowledge regarding HIV/AIDS, sexually transmitted diseases, and contraceptives, resulting in unfounded stigma and prejudices.[38] In a 2002 poll of high school students, 36.2 percent of female respondents and 31.3 percent of males stated they did not use contraceptives for their first sexual intercourse; as for repeat intercourse, 56.7 percent of female students and 40.4 percent of males answered that their use of contraceptives was inconsistent; 18 percent of females and 14.3 percent of males said they never used them. Meanwhile, the number of induced abortions for females aged between fifteen and nineteen rose from 2.4 per 1,000 in 1965 to 3.1 in 1975, 6.2 in 1995, and 13 in 2000.[39] On the other hand, a recent poll shows that only 13 percent of the population thinks that further apologies to Asian countries with regard to Japan's past colonial atrocities are necessary.[40] The ignorance of sex-related knowledge and that of Japan's history of atrocities go hand in hand through the postwar process of "purification" of the national body and national memory.

2

In the late 1990s, following the aid-dating shock earlier in the decade, a new trend was noted among Japan's mature men and women, becoming known as *Shitsurakuen genshō* or the Paradise Lost phenomenon, after the best-selling novel of the same name by Watanabe Junichi. The story was originally serialized in the national newspaper *Nihon Keizai Shinbun*, subsequently published as a two-volume book in February 1997, made into a movie, and televised as a drama series on the nationwide network running from July to September 1997. The novel sold three million copies in Japan during that year alone. The movie took in just a little shy of $30 million at the box office, and the TV series became one of the top-rated shows of the year. Following the theme of the novel, the term *Shitsurakuen* came to denote extramarital affairs, adultery, and infidelity. There was a dramatic increase in the number of introductions organized by online dating agencies called *deaikei* matching men and women for romance—extramarital or not. On one such site, the home page reads: "*Hitozuma, warikiri, shitsurakuen, soshite furinzuma: furinshite mimasenka? Deaikei shitsurakuen*" or "Married women, decide [to do it], Paradise Lost, and adulterous wife: Would you like to cheat on your spouse? This is the Dating Agency Paradise Lost."[41]

The novel describes an adulterous relationship between Kuki, a fifty-four year-old publishing company editor and Rinko, a thirty-eight year-old calligrapher. They are both already married; Kuki not unhappily on the surface, with a grown-up daughter, and Rinko, very unhappily to a successful medical doctor. Kuki's career has been thwarted: about a year earlier, he was suddenly removed from the position of chief of the Publications Department and demoted to the Research Department. Rinko is a beautiful, well-brought-up upper-class woman who is yet to discover the profundity of her own sexual potential. Through an intimate erotic journey with Kuki, Rinko blossoms fully into a pleasure-loving, explosively sensuous, and ultimately desirable woman.

The story is simple. After many dramatic and incredibly luscious dates at five-star hotels in romantic destinations, countless attendances at exquisite and rarefied artistic performances involving *nō*, *kagura*, and other traditional art forms, gourmet dinners complete with vintage French wines, Kuki and Rinko commit a tragic joint suicide. This they achieve by swallowing poison while their lips and genitals are connected, climaxing in bed in the summer villa that Rinko's deceased father owned in Karuizawa, the resort town where the "pure romance" between the current Japanese Emperor and Empress was reported to have been born—as if to declare the end of such romance and the beginning of the carnal age of adulterous affairs. As it happens, Japanese readers enthusiastically welcomed the novel.

Every date starts with Kuki's sexual opening, always producing a similar response process in Rinko: initial reluctance inexorably leading to carnal inflammation, suggesting that, once aroused, she is completely capable of enjoying sexual pleasure, but somehow unable to know what she knows and wants herself, hence needing Kuki's guidance. Rinko's body is—again, predictably for a novel written by a post-mid-life crisis male writer —anatomically reduced to the metaphor of flower parts—bud, stamen, and petals. Another rather conventional element of the plot is Kuki's procrastination of his divorce, indicating his inability to cut off his wife, as if to suggest that he needs the domestic security while enjoying sex outside the home. Kuki's wife, who appears in the novel most of the time as a faceless, voiceless, and characterless woman and has not had sexual contact with her husband for more than ten years, is yet another typically mundane representation of today's Japanese marriage.

While supposed to be a heterosexual love story, the underlying subtext is a story of male competition to demonstrate superior virility. Kuki is obsessed with outscoring Rinko's husband (whom he never meets). His jealousy and passion become intensely aroused whenever he thinks about this professionally accomplished male that is younger than himself and hence, supposedly more potent sexually. Kuki thus takes great pleasure in the thought of outdoing him. As such, this romance is in fact about two men's tacit competition over one beautiful woman. Can anything be more formulaic than this, one might wonder? Similarly, Kuki's desire flares up when Rinko, upon Kuki's request, sneaks out of her father's funeral, in traditional Japanese mourning attire. Kuki makes love to Rinko wearing kimono, as if to suggest that violating the taboo of defiling a mortuary rite of her father would ensure Rinko's transfer to Kuki from her father.[42]

Throughout the novel, surprisingly little is said about love. Dialogue between Kuki and Rinko is dominated by references to bodily pleasure and is characterized by Kuki's sagacious use of diverse yet high-cultural expressions of maturity on one hand, and Rinko's lack of clarity, choice of childish vocabulary, and routinely incomplete sentences, on the other. Also, the detailed descriptions of nudity, sexual acts, physical reactions, and climaxing, which fill almost each and every episode, are one-sidedly observed from Kuki's male gaze (although the novel does not take the first-person narrative of Kuki's voice). In many sex scenes, Rinko appears as "*onna no karada*" (woman's body), "*nyotai*" (woman's body; classical expression), or simply "*onna*" (woman), as if to suggest that the personhood of Rinko has little meaning and it is her body that matters. In a similar way to *junketsukyōiku,* the anatomy of the breasts and the vagina are accentuated in the text.

Interestingly, the two lovers invoke Abe Sada.[43] Between their sexual fusions, Kuki reads out to Rinko from Sada's interrogation record. Showing

particular interest in the parts where Sada describes in detail how she felt
so close—much closer than before—to the dead body of her lover Ishida,
and where she then, finally decides to cut off his penis and testicles,
Rinko revises her opinion of Sada: "I have completely misunderstood this
woman called Abe Sada. I've always thought of her as a scandalous,
perverted woman, since she cut off a man's [genitals]. But, I was wrong.
She is honest, lovable, and really wonderful."[44] Having studied the case
of Abe Sada, the two look out of the window and appreciate the graceful
soundless fall of cherry blossom petals. It is late at night. In bed, their
conversation returns to Abe Sada. Rinko says, "It was not good, because
she alone lived." Kuki murmurs, "She alone . . .?" Rinko responds, "Yes,
they should have died together. Then they would have been with each
other forever and never lonely."[45] This rendezvous provides them with
decisive momentum towards their eventual joint suicide.

Martha Nussbaum's words might help us here, when she states that
lovers "inflict pain on one another" and they do so because their "condition of neediness is experienced as an open hole, a lack of self-sufficiency,
accompanied by weakness," in the hopes of achieving fusion with "the
object to which they have ascribed such exalted importance."[46] Death by
love (or joint suicide)—is this a "proper" route of following one's passion?
Or is (as in Sada's case) murder by love the "correct" way? How should
one love? Indeed, how should one live and die? Is fusion a necessary
objective of love? Which is more beautiful, killing the other or dying
together? Does love have to hurt, injure, and kill, as opposed to heal,
protect, and nurture? Strangely, we seem to be able to reason why Sada
had to kill Kichi—she was tormented by her love for him, which suffocated her, almost leading her to killing herself. The desire to eliminate
(thereby completely possess and overcome) the object of pain and suffering
in order to achieve control over oneself, or even killing the other in order
to defend and preserve oneself, has been recognized as justifiable and
hence, good, from the Classical Age in the West. We can see this in the
way self-defense is justified in our law. Similarly, crime of passion is
more likely to receive a jury's sympathy, as opposed to premeditated
cold-blooded murder. However, joint suicide by two individuals, neither
of whom owes anything to their parents or spouse, does not make quite
such sense.

Joint suicide, of course, is a recurring theme in the genre of Japanese
love stories ever since medieval times. Nevertheless, a supporting sub-plot
has to be in existence, normally coming in the form of a pre-existing,
insurmountable obstacle for the lovers, such as parental disapproval or
the impossibility of divorce. In the case of Kuki and Rinko, that sub-
plot is missing: Kuki's divorce is slowly, but finally forthcoming, while
Rinko's passive-aggressive husband, despite the repeated harassment he
has inflicted on Kuki, eventually discrediting Kuki professionally, cannot

really do much to stop Rinko. Certainly, Rinko is saddened by her mother's displeasure but, ultimately, she is not financially or psychologically dependent on her. Kuki is portrayed as independently wealthy, regardless of his salary. They are economically capable of making a new home for themselves, while their remaining families are taken care of. They are both well-educated and cultured, able to enjoy a high-class lifestyle complete with exquisite art and taste. Most importantly, neither is bothered in their conscience by the fact that they are in an adulterous relationship. There is no logical necessity for them to cancel out their lives in the manner they did. The rationale is missing. Why didn't they want to live on, loving each other, when that would have been completely possible? The absence of reason, in the case of Kuki and Rinko, renders their affair somewhat unlike love suicide, something of an aesthetic anomaly.

What I see as significant in this novel in trying to understand recent love in Japan is, in fact, not so much the connection between Kuki and Rinko, but Kuki's marriage. His marriage has long ago become sexless. As I have suggested in Chapter 3, after *junketsukyōiku,* sex inside the domestic sphere had become focused on procreation. According to the novel's setting, Kuki is 54 in 1997, his wife, 48, and Rinko, 38; Kuki was born in 1943, amidst the heat of the Pacific War, his wife, in 1949, the year of *junketsukyōiku*'s inauguration, and Rinko, in 1959, the year of the imperial couple's love marriage and at a time when Japan was beginning to feel its first taste of the postwar economic boom. Here, Kuki's wife is the person whose life history coincides with the most intense period of purity education. Kuki, being male, would have experienced it much differently, as I have argued in Chapter 3. His wife, by way of contrast, would have been fully immersed in the values and principles of *junketsukyōiku.*

Kuki's wife is aware that her husband has had many affairs before this one involving Rinko. Until the last moment of their marriage, she is devoted to her husband in the proper sense. For example, she prepares a change of clothing for Kuki, who has begun living with Rinko in a small apartment and has not returned home for a long time. Most importantly, she does not ask questions, the questions that would inevitably raise skepticism regarding the very foundations of their marriage. In the end, it is she who requests a divorce, but it is done in such a way as to almost be doing a favor for Kuki, rather than for herself. She does all of this not because she loves Kuki, but because she wishes to correctly fulfill her positional function as wife.

The novel became popular in Japan not because of the joint suicide, but because of its reference to an adulterous relationship. It inspired a possibility for married men to have extramarital sex not with prostitutes, but with an upper-class, well-educated, and beautiful woman who is younger, but nevertheless mature. Surely, it was the male who settled the bill, but no sex-for-cash transaction was involved. On the other hand, the novel demonstrated that the intra-gender division of labor in Japan is intact: a childless mistress is love's sexualized heroine and a once reproductive (premenopausal?) wife is sexless and proper. In some ways, *Shitsurakuen* symbolized the exhaustion of love's resources in postwar Japan. If, in the early 1990s, young girls demonstrated that the purity of their bodies was a highly marketable commodity, in the late 1990s, mature, married women entertained the possibility of adulterous affairs for the sake of pleasure and adventure, while other mature, married women lost sexuality altogether. It demonstrated that purity education had gone bankrupt. To be sure, the novel showed a form of self-assertion through sexual liaisons, but do we see here that love had gone astray in this process? Where was that *koi* that connected men and women in the most intriguing, yet certain of ways, linking body and soul?

3

Japan's new millennium opened with middle-aged women intensely competing to publicly demonstrate their adoration for a South Korean actor. This actor, Bae Yong Joon, was the male lead in a TV drama called *Fuyu no sonata* (*The Winter Sonata*), televised in Japan repeatedly following its 2003 debut on the public-owned NHK network. The critics agree that his popularity derives from his soft speech and gentle demeanor, in addition to his agreeable looks. Contrasting with machismo and muscle-oriented sex appeal or samurai-like determined and aloof grace, Bae's attraction is *iyashi,* comforting. He has a shy smile like a little boy (although he is in his thirties), and has non-dominant, caring mannerisms, and a warm, yet assuring gaze; his characteristics are therefore, let us say, the antithesis of those of the Olympian male beauty. Nothing about him would remind the viewer of the sexual virility exhibited by Kuki, for example. My purpose in this section is, however, not to find out the secret of his popularity, but to envision how Japan's love, which was nationalized throughout the postwar decades, is now being denationalized, albeit in an uncertain and clandestine fashion, despite the efforts of the government's guard; I see in the story of *The Winter Sonata*'s popularity some indications of how this might be happening.

In November 2004, when Bae briefly visited Japan, about 3,500 fans, mostly women, came rushing into the airport in order to have a glimpse of him. Jostling with each other to get a better look at Bae, some ten women were injured and sent to hospital. News of his visit was first announced via bulletins superimposed on the screen during afternoon variety shows on many TV stations, almost dominating the original content of the programs. The DVD version of *The Winter Sonata* sold 360,000 copies in Japan. According to research by a think tank organization, the economic boost for 2004 generated by the series amounted to a massive 122.5 billion yen in Japan.⁴⁷

According to one source, a total of 2,000 women aged between 30 and 60 spent between 70,000 yen and 120,000 yen during 2004 on pilgrimage tours to South Korea, visiting locations, including houses and buildings, featured in the drama. The same source also mentions the growing number of *Winter Sonata* divorces (*Fuyusona rikon, Fuyusona* being an abbreviation of *Fuyu no sonata* or *The Winter Sonata*) inspired by the loving character of Bae, which contrasted with that of their uncaring husbands. Reportedly, this has sparked off a new international matchmaking service helping Japanese women to find their dream Korean male. Following the tsunami disaster at the end of 2004 in South and Southeast Asia, when Bae Yong Joon made a donation of about 30 million yen to World Vision, a nonprofit Christian relief organization, female fans in Japan followed his example: more than two hundred women, identifying themselves as Bae's fans, donated 5,000 yen to 10,000 yen to World Vision Japan. Its website was "overloaded with fans trying to access the page after Bae's donation was reported."⁴⁸

So, what is this drama about drama? What is *The Winter Sonata* about? It is a story of what we would normally refer to as platonic love between high school sweethearts. Yujin, portrayed by Che Jiu, a beautiful, popular actress, and Jungsang, portrayed by Bae Yong Joon, are high school seniors. They fall in love, and according to the drama's depiction, it is innocent, youthful, non-sexual—what we might call puppy love. Jungsang, a quiet, almost withdrawn transfer student from one of Seoul's most competitive high schools, is a mysterious oddball in this provincial high school class, while Yujin is a lively, extroverted, and very popular girl. Both Yujin and Jungsang have been raised by single mothers; Yujin's father passed away years earlier, while it is not clear at the beginning of the drama what has happened to Jungsang's father. Yujin and Jungsang develop, just as in the *junketsukyōiku* ideal, a sibling-like friendship, which eventually turns into romantic feelings—and there is the first kiss, just like in the case of Miko and Mako.

Suddenly, however, the hands of destiny pull their lives apart. Jungsang gets injured in an accident and loses his memory. The two do not meet for the next ten years, and when they are reunited, Yujin is with Sanghyŏk, her childhood friend who has loved and cared for her ever since they were little. But the reappearance of Jungsang, who now calls himself Minyŏng due to the amnesia, deeply disturbs Sanghyŏk and, of course, Yujin.

It happens that Sanghyŏk's father, Yujin's deceased father, and Jungsang's mother were college friends, always hanging out together. Sanghyŏk begins suspecting that Jungsang's birth father was Yujin's deceased father, due to various coincidences. But this suspicion is violently revised by Sanghyŏk's own father's confession that Jungsang is in fact his own son, that is, Sanghyŏk's half-brother. By then, Jungsang's memory is back and, with it, his love for Yujin is fully revived. Jungsang also learns from Sanghyŏk's father that Jungsang was his son. Sanghyŏk and Jungsang each agonize over their family secret and their love for Yujin.

Yujin, on the other hand, feels deeply for Sanghyŏk and struggles with her love for Jungsang which, she dreads, will deeply hurt Sanghyŏk. Nevertheless, Yujin's love for Jungsang, the story goes, is so pure and strong that even life's whims cannot change it. In the meantime, Jungsang discovers that his health is seriously threatened—his eyes are blurry and he eventually discovers that he is losing his sight due to a brain tumor behind his eye and that he might not live long. In a characteristically rushed final episode, Jungsang and Yujin both head abroad, the former to the US for medical treatment and the latter for France to further her studies and gain qualifications as an interior designer.

At this juncture, Jungsang asks Sanghyŏk to love Yujin forever and make her happy, alluding to the possibility that he won't be around for long. Jungsang also comes to see Yujin and, memorably and movingly, tells her that he wants to remember her beautiful face. Sanghyŏk, having recently discovered that Jungsang is suffering from an incurable disease, decides to give up Yujin for Jungsang's sake. He goes to see Yujin and offers her a ticket to New York to travel with Jungsang on his journey to seek medical treatment. By the time Sanghyŏk and Yujin get to the airport, however, Jungsang's flight for New York has already departed and Yujin and Jungsang are torn apart once more.

Three years pass—all during this same last episode, that is. Yujin is back from France and discovers that Jungsang is in a hospice that looks just like a house that Yujin tried to design in the past. She goes to look for Jungsang, but Jungsang, now blind, has just gone out for a walk with his caregiver. Yujin strolls around. Then, all of a sudden, Jungsang returns to fetch something and senses someone is in the building. "Is that . . . you, Yujin?" Jungsang asks. "Yes, it is I . . ." answers Yujin. The two give each other a long, warm embrace, determined not ever to let the other go.[49]

From August 15, 2004 to May 31, 2005, Kodansha, one of Japan's top popular publishers, took online votes, asking whether *The Winter Sonata* was the "best of dramas, very, very moving" or "not as good as the rumors [would suggest]." Votes were disproportionately divided, with an overwhelming 89 percent (7,407 persons) voting for the first option and 11 percent (881 persons) for the second.[50]

In a drama that invokes notions of purity—sexual purity by all means, but purity of mind as well—what do Japanese women find so attractive? Bae Yong Joon's soft and gentle manner is surely a key factor. But the story itself is also hard to ignore. There is no mention of sex or sexual consummation; there are no lines or scenes even alluding to sex. Further-more, an incurable disease is suffered by one of the lovers. It is unmistakable that this drama revives the "pure love" of Miko and Mako and *junketsukyōiku*.[51]

Under the heading "Japan Gripped by Obsession with Pure Love," Kaori Shoji, writing for *The Japan Times,* declares: "2004 was the year of *jun-ai* (pure love)," and continues:

> Yes, the once-chic *otegaru na kankei* (casual affair) is out . . . Nothing is tackier than having a string of *sefure* (sex friends) but no real *kareshi* (boyfriend) with whom to take walks, dinners and enjoy long, meaningful conversations. The important thing (for women, anyway) is to get into *rabu modo* (love mode) before they throw themselves into a full-fledged relationship, to be ready for romance so that when the *daarin* (darling) does come along, he will spot the signs [of love] immediately. Then they can both launch into that most coveted of states: *uru-uru na ai* (starry-eyed love).[52]

She continues by noting that, according to many *rabu ankēto* (love surveys) in Japan's women's magazines, women long more for intimacy than sex, and wish to be like the heroine in a "pure love" story.

What is particularly interesting in this phenomenon is that the new (or old) type of love, that is, pure love, is now accompanied by the figure of the non-Japanese male. As Shoji goes on to observe:

> What a lot of women say . . . is that the young men of this country are too thick to understand this need for emotional drama. Twenty-nine-year-old Minako says resignedly: "*Kono kuni no otokowa fukami ga nakute nijigenteki sugiru*" (The men in this country have no depth and are too two-dimensional).[53]

The popularity of Bae and Korean TV dramas along with music and other popular cultural products, now forming part of what has come to be known in Korean and Japanese respectively as *hanryu* or *kanryū* (the Korean wave), is related to nostalgia—nostalgia for the 1960s pathos of purity as represented by the romance of Miko and Mako and its tragic yet beautiful end. It is also, if I may assert, related to nostalgia felt by older women for the days of their youth and their early romantic memories. Further, this phenomenon is colored by memories of a less affluent, yet more compact and morally united Japan. Seen in this way, it is highly significant that bearers of values symbolizing a beautiful past have come from across the Japan Strait, and from the peninsula that used to be Japan's possession in the "good old" colonial days, a place that is perceived to be less developed and still catching up with Japan and, therefore, unspoilt.

More curious is the fact that the Korean wave had to arrive in Japan at this moment in history. Koreans, Korean neighborhoods, and Korean culture, albeit in marginalized, fragmented, colonial, diasporic, and Cold War-torn ways, have always existed in Japan throughout the colonial and postcolonial decades. I have already pointed out that, far from being unknown to Japanese society, Korean signifiers such as female students' uniforms are clearly visible. Furthermore, collective, faceless persecution is not the only story that Koreans in Japan can tell. On the personal, individual level, Koreans meet Japanese all the time, as co-workers, friends, lovers, and spouses. The majority of Korean students study at Japanese schools and most Koreans live outside so-called Korean ethnic neighborhoods.

Romance between Korean and Japanese individuals is not at all unusual in Japan. In fact, more Koreans in Japan fall in love with Japanese than with fellow Koreans. This state of affairs has existed ever since the colonial period and continues to this day. Statistically, since the mid-1970s, marriages between Korean and Japanese persons have consistently outnumbered those between Koreans in Japan. The majority of these inter-cultural or inter-ethnic marriages are between Korean females and Japanese males.[54]

In 2002, one year prior to the airing of *The Winter Sonata* in Japan, news broke of past abductions of Japanese citizens by North Korean agents. It was, predictably, received with naked hostility in Japan, and this anger was particularly directed at Korean girls—yet again. Within the span of one year, Korea had become the object of adoration. Of course, reactions to the abductions were directed at North Korea as an evil entity, while the focus of the "Korean wave" fever was South Korea.[55] In between, there was a conspicuous absence of awareness of the fact that North and South Korea were recent creations resulting from the disastrous settlement following the era of Japanese colonization. Similarly missing was recognition of the existence of the Korean diasporic community in Japan, present from the early twentieth century.[56]

To me, an interesting question would be: "why are the inter-ethnic romances of Koreans and Japanese not discussed publicly?" or more precisely, "not discussed as love and romance?" When scholars discuss this issue, it is usually as part of ethnic politics in general and the crisis of Korean identity in Japan in particular.[57] Usually, Korean and Japanese marriages are not arranged, i.e. they are love marriages, and families on both sides would typically oppose them vehemently, rendering stories of parental harassment commonplace. What would be the difference between, on the one hand, the love story in *The Winter Sonata,* in which a young man and woman stay true to their love despite all sorts of obstacles and, on the other hand, love and marriage between Korean and Japanese persons who achieve their goal of being together, despite fierce parental opposition, societal ostracization, and complications in allocating children's nationalities and in other areas related to raising them? Why is it that inter-ethnic romance is largely frowned upon, while the inter-ethnic fandom of Bae Yong Joon dominates society?

One possible reading could be that an ideal foreign male beyond the border is desirable, since he could never be reached in the first place. Romance is, therefore, eternally one-sided and, because it is one-sided, fans can be forever in love with him from a safe distance. This parallels idealization by followers of a charismatic leader.[58] But it also reminds us of the sovereign love of wartime Japan, in that since the gaze of the Emperor was perceived to be everywhere, even though he was nowhere, the subject lived and died for him. Similarly, since the TV character exists nowhere in reality, the idea or image of him can exist everywhere in the lives of the fans.

By way of contrast, the invisible foreign element eroding the national body from within is perceived as a threat to the internal somatic consistency of the nation. Particularly when this element is undetectable, superficially identical with the rest of the nationals, it can be perceived to be deceptive, confusing, and, therefore, more dangerous. Hence, animosity and disapproval of inter-ethnic romances that happen *within* Japan. But, interestingly, once the object of passion comes from across the ocean, not only is it seen as safe, but it also procures value, just like the *marebito* or stranger=deity discussed in Chapter 1. Upon closer examination, however, it can be seen that foreign elements have been selectively put to use by various offices of the government in recent history. For some time, the Japanese government has been importing foreign brides, mostly through services run by local municipalities in depopulated agricultural areas. This measure is entirely focused on marrying Japanese men to foreign women from Asia and Latin America.[59] This itself indicates that Japan's national love scenes are not so nationalized any more.

What is interesting in the case of Bae Yong Joon fever is the gender reversal in terms of Japanese and non-Japanese counterparts. For example, it used to be the Japanese men that went to buy the sexual services of women in Asia, including Korea, Thailand, and the Philippines. In terms of Korean-Japanese marriages in Japan, as mentioned earlier, most coupling is between Japanese males and Korean females. However, now the practitioners of border-crossing are predominantly women, departing for pilgrimage tours to South Korea and the various destinations visited by the star of the above show, spending fortunes on DVDs and DVD players and working hard to learn how to use PCs, scanners, digital cameras, the internet, and other technical gadgets that are required of the efficient fan, even flocking to Korean language and culture classes in the hope of being able to speak the language the star speaks and to appreciate the culture which the star calls his own.[60] Most of the fan base is found among those aged in their 30s and older. However, as I stated earlier, among younger women also, it is no longer fashionable to have "sex friends," and Japanese men receive low scores when it comes to emotion and spirituality: remember the comment quoted earlier: "*Kono kuni no otokowa fukami ga nakute nijigenteki sugiru*" (The men in this country have no depth and are too two-dimensional).

This is an alarming turn of events for the Japanese government that is already suffering severe stress as it faces the prospect of depopulation, aging, and a low birth rate. Unlike those middle-aged and senior fans of Bae Yong Joon, who have, in any case, gotten married and given birth to the nation's children, younger Japanese women today are marrying late or not marrying at all, while within marriages, the birth rate hit a record low of 1.29 or less in 2003 and 2004. The government-run National Institute of Population and Social Security Research predicts that Japan's total population will drop to about 100.6 million in 2050, from 126.93 million in 2000, peaking at 127.48 million in 2004. It also estimates that in 2050, the population aged under fifteen will be 10.8 percent of the total population, the population aged sixty-five or over, 35.7 percent, and the working-age population (fifteen to sixty-four) will be 53.6 percent.[61] Existing marriages are becoming highly unstable: the number of divorces jumped approximately 20 percent between 1990 (157,608) and 1993 (188,297), and a further 48 percent between 1993 and 2003.[62]

The government has long predicted this development and, concerned that the social security system would become seriously undermined in future, has tried to come up with incentives for women to marry and have children. In 1994, the Angel Plan, a basic plan related to future child-rearing support measures, was formulated, and the Five Year Emergency Measures for Childcare Services were launched. In the following year, paternal leave became possible under the Childcare and Family Care Leave Act. In 1999, a new Angel Plan was formulated. Both Angel Plans (1994 and 1999) were aimed at improving the support system for child-rearing, but critics claim that neither has yielded significant results, mainly due to the government's failure to establish viable social support for working women.[63]

Some attribute this to the lifestyle choices on the part of women, but this should be understood in tandem with a realization that gender roles have remained unchanged in Japan.[64] These are characterized by an asymmetrical distribution of household chores between men and women, with the latter basically bearing the double burden of raising children and working for supplementary income, or a triple burden involving the additional care of elderly parents-in-law. This state of affairs structurally discourages women from embarking on married life.[65]

Given the situation that the Japanese government faces, it may not be surprising that various aspects of the lifestyle of the population have become subject to both overt and covert scrutiny of all levels of the national state. And love stands at the forefront of this operation. For example, in June 2005, the Nara prefectural government issued a 128-page book entitled "The World's Happiest Words of Love," consisting of a total of 119 marriage proposal lines. The prefecture's Children and Families Division is hoping that the book will boost the zeal for love marriage.[66] From April 2003, married couples who are undergoing infertility treatment have been entitled to 100,000 yen in government subsidies.[67] Yamatsuri, a small town about 70 miles north of Tokyo, decided to offer 500,000 yen (approximately $4,600) for each newborn, and promised a further $460 a year for ten years as a small incentive in order to retain young, procreative married couples and ease the intensifying depopulation crisis.[68] The anxiety of Japanese politicians and lawmakers can be clearly seen in a statement by former Prime Minister Mori, who commented that it would be wrong for women who did not give birth to expect social security.[69]

It is ironic, then, that a nation that is concerned about its future demography is unable to produce a national romantic idol, and has to rely on a foreign import. But, considering that, not only men but also women can now pass on their Japanese nationality to their children (due to the Japanese nationality law reform in 1985), romances between Japanese women and non-Japanese men have the potential of creating Japanese nationals. It is, therefore, rather astounding that the imagination of the Japanese government (both central and local) is limited to encouraging Japanese women to marry Japanese men or Japanese men to marry foreign women (and live in Japan). In other words, the government consistently prioritizes patrilineal ideology, while it fails to see that Japan's love is already being denationalized.

It needs to be emphasized that cases and materials illustrated in this chapter have shown that governmentality and its effects are produced through a complex entanglement between various components and bodies of state power and the agency of individuals. The intense mutuality of interaction between these is the key to understanding the events this chapter has examined, events that have not always occurred in concerted unison and, indeed, have often mutually contradicted one another. For example, sex education has not been opposed and suppressed in a unified and consistent manner by all branches of the state apparatuses. As has been shown, it was the Ministry of Health, Welfare, and Labor's satellite organization that created and distributed the sex education booklet, which came under ferocious attack from a group led by a female member of parliament and supported by media-engineered sex-education-bashing. There was also the active endorsement by Tokyo Metropolitan Governor Ishihara of severe, public punishment of personnel that were sympathetic to sex education. The popularity of *The Winter Sonata* on the other hand appears to have been a spontaneous oppositional response by older women in Japan to state prioritizing of patrilineal association when determining eligibility for national membership. Upon closer examination, we recognized that it was the opposite: purity education, which was a postwar state project, and the values associated with it have deeply penetrated and shaped the agency of older generations of women, and their nostalgia for pure love reflects this. As such, rather than being a resistant and rebellious passion, the behavior of Bae Yong Joon fans is in sync with the sex education ideals of the post-war Japanese state. Yet, at the same time, the consequence of love's denationalization, along with a low birth rate, emerges as a threat to the state's ideal of national romantic integrity.

We have done an ironic, full circle: the decade that started with the intensification of sex/body commodification, as witnessed in the aid-dating phenomenon, which I characterized as an historical consequence of *junketsukyōiku* or purity education, came to a close with the cravings for comforting love on the part of older women via a commercial fad for adulterous love. In this picture, love's whereabouts is becoming all the more uncertain. For, the conceptual protagonist here appears to be what we in the West would readily call "sexuality." But, what *is* sexuality in the Japanese context, where sex and love existed together, historically speaking, in a relatively uncensored way, relatively freely available to boys and girls, men and women, whether they be married or unmarried (as opposed to the Victorian West, that is)? If aid-dating was the culmin-ation of love culture on the part of middle-aged men, men who were brought up immersed in love's male double standard of combining sex-(read "comfort"-) giving females and child-giving females, Bae Yong Joon fever was the culmination of love culture on the part of middle-aged women, in which they matured craving warmth, adoration, and, above all, sexual purity. In between, young aid-daters demonstrated that as long as the society maintains gender disparity, sexual division of labor among women, and the lack of proper sex and history education, body and soul are eternally alienated and no love is possible, no matter how many European designer goods they were to own.

If we remember the romantic endeavors of the *Manyō* lovers, it would be difficult not to ask: since when did men and women in Japan come to be this far apart and since when did sex and love in Japan become estranged from each other? The historical engineering force here, I assert, is the modern nation-state. In the case of prewar Japan, because of the para-doxically ancient nature of the restored imperial sovereign, total loyalty was required, making the Emperor the object of absolute love for His subjects. Love and devotion for the sovereign were a powerful meta-phorical tool as well as a weapon for the state and the military to invoke when mobilizing the nation on a mass scale in times of war, as can be seen in the cases of Nanjing, the institution of comfort stations, and eugenics law. The postwar redefinition of nationhood, the role of the sovereign and, accordingly, the *bios* of citizens, turned love back to its "normal" state and state intervention became covert, rather than overt. This was manifested in the way the Ministry of Education's purity education was set up, that is, not in a separate framework, but insidiously, behind the façade of the regular curricula. The ethical background to postwar purity education was the false assumption that the defeat at war had corrupted national sex morals and the nation was on the verge of moral decay—as if sexual perversion and corruption had never existed before. The ensuing urgency with which the notion of purity was imposed on women is at least in part responsible for the emergence of sexually self-marketing young females finding a niche satisfying the sexual and pseudo-loving needs of middle-aged men, followed by an avid pursuit of pure love on the part of middle-aged female fans beyond the national border.

In the meantime, as noted above, the government is under serious pressure due to the fast-approaching depopulation and aging crisis, while still not having sufficiently attended to historical debt including contemplation of its own responsibility for men and women in the former colonies. At the same time, it has failed to properly educate its men and women about the past, an example being the way in which "comfort women" issues were accorded thirty years silence and remain unsatisfactorily treated to this day. As such, the question of love is as much a question about self as a question of the nation-state. Reducing it to the personal level or calling it simply "popular culture" would, therefore, fail to touch the depths of its question. Blaming the girls for commodifying their sexuality or calling Japanese middle-aged men and women "strange" would not resolve the matter, either. Only when we try to grasp the role of the state, the ethos created thereby, and the complicity and participation on the part of the population together in a comprehensive way, can we begin to see some answers.

In lieu of conclusion

Although this book has dealt with the case of Japan, it is by no means simply about Japan. For, in today's global modernity, love everywhere is in question and on trial. The question of love raises the question of self. If, as Anthony Giddens and others have asserted, self in modernity is inherently reflexive—capable of critically assessing, observing, and re-evaluating its own environment, conduct, thoughts, and relationships with others—then, it is inevitable that love in modernity becomes immensely complex, uncertain, and insecure.[1]

When love is certain—as in the case of Japan's wartime sovereign love for example, with its focus on the center of the collective whole—it can, however, only be abnormal, grotesque, and perverted. This love, more-over, has a tendency to expand, in a one-sided and even extremely violent fashion, imposing itself on people who refuse or do not understand it— as in 1937 Nanjing. We have seen examples similar or identical to Japan's sovereign love throughout the history of humanity, but particularly during the last century and the early years of this one. Further, these have tended to be marked by greater intensity, and have come in the form of war, terrorism, massacre, and mass rape. Since antiquity, humans have destroyed and exterminated others in the name of love—of God, religion, the nation, justice, and democracy—and this pattern, unfortunately, continues today.

Sovereign love parallels what Isiah Berlin has called the positive notion of freedom in his discussion of two concepts of freedom.[2] It assumes that we as a collective entity attain freedom under a charismatic leader, influential doctrine, and what is deemed as correct guidance. In a similar manner, sovereign love touches everyone under it collectively, and elevates them to a higher level of existence, granting them *bios*; a socially meaningful life, at least in the minds of those who adhere to it.

When one falls out of love with the sovereign, does one move on to claim self-determining, self-controlling, and above all, free love? Berlin's negative notion of freedom might help us think about this question. In this freedom, self is the primary unit to have, defend, and enjoy love. The idea that one needs to be left alone in order fully to enjoy one's right to be oneself is the manifestation of such an idea of freedom.[3] In the negative concept of freedom, self appears to be imminently in charge; in the positive concept, the determination to live and die rests with the head of the state, i.e. the sovereign or other equivalent leaders. For a further explication, I must return to the notion of sovereign.

Using Carl Schmitt's definition of the sovereign as "he who decides on the state of exception," Agamben asserts that such a state entails a return to an original set of conditions where no differentiation exists between juridical, religious, and political powers, and power—absolute power—resting in the hands of the head of the state is "essentially grounded in the emergency linked to a state of war."[4] It is more than suggestive that the emergence of Japan as a modern state came about involving the restoration of and return to power of the original, ancient sovereign, the Emperor.

The state of exception is, according to Zygmunt Bauman, "not the chaos that preceded order but rather the situation that results from its suspension."[5] As I stated in the Introduction, just as Japan at war was going through precisely this kind of extended suspension of order—"comfort women" and Nanjing need to be located within this suspension—postwar *junketsukyōiku* in some ways represented the restoration of order in the name of democracy, in the name of equality of citizens before the law. Thus, it can be said that the state of exception was abolished and everyone was now invited to participate in their own love. The state receded into the background of ordinary lives, ensuring, however, the sustained reproduction of governmentality by publicly educating, economically planning, and clinically managing a population that was now supposedly enjoying sovereignty through democratic representation.

Such is modernity, according to Giddens, where individuals' sovereign rights as citizens enable them to experiment and be active in love. Writing about modern love, which he names "confluent love," Giddens suggests that love and lust are indissolubly connected in confluent love, and he views this love as fundamentally different from premodern romance, where they did not coincide. For Giddens, furthermore, love is now being superseded by sexual plasticity, which would become a more dominant form of interpersonal relations. In this way, we may say, Giddens finds in sex a rational checkpoint against which selves can confirm their identities.[6]

As has been demonstrated in this book, I differ from Giddens in that I do not think it is possible to connect the rapprochement of love and lust with modernity at large. In the case of Japan, it is the ancients that took love to be a holistic endeavor combining sexual union and the exchange of souls, while Japanese moderns have a severed reality of mind and body with heightened reification of self suffocated by capitalist market logic. In the case of the *Manyō* lovers, love holistically incorporated physical consummation. We have seen that the aim of *junketsukyōiku* or purity education, launched by the Ministry of Education in the late 1940s, was to emphasize love's purity, but we have also seen that its primary consequence was to preemptively prioritize sexual purity, thereby throwing love out with the bath water. More importantly, once love was estranged from self and sex in socially available public discourse, love itself became something else. I am not saying that the Japanese had true love when they had an institution such as *yobai* and that they lost it when they began confining men and women in monogamous marriages. I am, however, saying that the process of estrangement of love from sex coincides with the rise of modern national state and intensification of capitalism in Japan, which was not accompanied by the equality between the sexes and equality among women. I am further saying that under these conditions, where certain women continue to be subjected to sexual exploitation, violence, and the body's commodification, love is endangered.

In this sense, sex and love are indeed separated, but note that it is a different state of separation from the one that Giddens envisions: whereas Giddens portrays modern sexual plasticity as a historical outcome of love's freedom in modernity, I am suggesting that, in the case of Japan at least, the intervention of the state to control love (love's "unfreedom") resulted in love's estrangement from sex. As such, this estrangement, I suggest, appears not as a pre-distributed conceptual ingredient to compartmentalize classes, cultures, and civilizations, but as an end-product of a historically specific intervention by the nation-state. It is in education apparatuses such as the purity education curriculum, institutions such as the comfort stations, laws such as the eugenics law and, above all, through the state of exception in times of war that love's estrangement from self, sex, and society is bred and implemented as a means of controlling the population.

Now, we must consider the role of the state in this connection. As I stated in the Introduction, I have deliberately avoided the question: "What is love?" Instead, I have suggested that we may find a better starting point for thinking about love by looking at it as a complex social function and as a political technology of the state. In modernity, the nation-state needs to control the population, intrusively concerning itself with sperm count and the quality of eggs. As the nation-state's sophistication as a biopower intensifies, human marriages become yet more important as primary sites through which to control, discipline, and reproduce men and women. However, not just any men and women—for these are nationals. In this process, love becomes a key institution, both discursively and culturally, making men and women voluntarily subject themselves to state apparatuses, thereby making them into model "national lovers." And this is closely related to the notion of the national sovereignty in modernity: if human rights in the post-WWII world—as Arendt has noted—were attained only by being a national, and not by being a naked human being, love (the right to legitimately love and be loved) is available only within the boundaries of the nation-state.[7] Unlike what is popularly believed, love knows national borders very well.

Seen in this way, thinking about love is to think also about life, death, and the nation-state. Indeed, many forms of love are related to life and death—we have seen that Japanese men and women tried to gain *bios* or socially and politically meaningful lives by way of loving the Emperor during WWII. Such lives would not be achieved purely by adhering to and defending personal freedom, Berlin's negative freedom; it necessarily requires the notion of collectivity and the social realm, approximating love to the positive concept of freedom; that is, collective liberation from unfreedom. Inherently, then, socially meaningful love has the potential to assume the form of what I have called sovereign love in this study, swayed by a charismatic leader or the direct and organized intervention of the nation-state. To varying degrees, elements of sovereign love exist in other kinds of love, be it the worship of a movie star, the fetishization of sex, virginity, or French designer goods, or the valuing of purity. Through this notion of freedom of love the state as biopower gets hold of the *bios* of men and women.

As long as the global modernity presupposes the world's nation-state system, loving remains an act that necessarily brings modern individuals into the realm of nation-state control through interventions in the areas of education, reproduction, discipline, lifestyle, and so on. Men and women still have to enter this realm in order not to remain at the level of *zoē*, mere, basic life. Here lies the conundrum of modernity: in order to gain a socially meaningful life (and death), one has to renounce one's most individualistic freedom: the freedom to be self-sufficient and left alone. And it is for this reason that I believe it is not possible to discuss love as if it is a purely personal endeavor or emotion, removed from the history of the society in question, which in modernity almost always takes a national and nationalized form. To reinstate my argument: when we think about love in modernity, we need to be aware that this will necessarily entail thinking about life and death, which, in turn, will inevitably require acknowledging the existence of a nation-state that makes individuals into loving beings with meaningful lives and deaths, that is, acknowledging the nation-state as biopower.

At this juncture in modernity, state intervention comes in various forms: through public discourse, legal measures, health checks, and educational policies, in some cases emphasizing crises related to depopulation and social security, the lack of prospect for viable care for the aged, and the need for moral guidance of the young, and in some other cases emphasizing crises of overpopulation, environmental peril, scarcity of natural resources, and political instability. Needless to say, as we have seen, state intervention in postwar Japan has taken much more subtle and supposedly innocuous forms in line with the mechanisms of the capitalist market. These do not always work hand in hand and at times appear mutually contradictory.

In the case of Japan, it is gravely concerning to witness today the nation hastily veering toward the right, trying to amend or reform Article 9 of the postwar Constitution—that which renounces war—turning itself into a nation that is able to start and join a war. If, as Agamben emphasizes, it is in times of war that the sovereign can most effectively exercise the state of exception[8]—martial law—it is not surprising that Japan's current Prime Minister Junichiro Koizumi, a conspicuous practitioner of paying homage at the Yasukuni shrine, sanctimoniously commemorating Japan's dead soldiers in WWII, is determined that the above article be amended. Let us remember: in times of war the sovereign demands unlimited executive power and total loyalty and devotion from the national citizenry or subjects, as we have seen in the case of what I termed sovereign love.

This is not to suggest that the state conspires to make individuals into passive dupes, to say that no matter what individuals do, they are to profit and serve the state—this is only one half of the picture. For, the relationship between the individual and the nation-state involves a process of mutual interaction and reinforcement, penetration and intercourse, producing closely intertwined forms of collaboration, codependence, and, shall we say, a love–hate relationship—what Foucault called governmentality. To look at love in close connection with governmentality, as I hope to have done in this study, enables us to incorporate in our examination of love the workings of institutions that are seemingly indifferent to personal relations such as nationalism or sovereignty. As such, thinking about love is an organic part of modern life or *bios*. The question I asked on the first page of this book, how should one write about love, thus comes back to us in altered form, how should one love, which is the question that also leads to another, how should one live—and die.

Notes

Introduction

1 Quoted in Soble (1989: 58) and see Lewis (1960). Weil also classifies friendship in its true sense as the most noble and sacred form of love (1951). See Nussbaum (1994) for an inspiring study of *philia* or friendship. In theology, there is another distinction between agape and eros. For a most classical study, see Nygren (1953).

2 For care of the self among the Greeks, see Foucault (1988).

3 Western conventional wisdom has it that in premodern societies such as, for example, "peasant society" (e.g. Chayanov 1966 and Shanin 1990), men and women simply copulated; they only had lust, one of the seven sins. Love, it was maintained, belonged to the educated and refined classes (e.g. Stone 1988). Goody (1998) brings in another distinction, that between literate (Eurasian) and non-literate (African) societies: in Goody's view, only in writing can love be borne permanently; only in writing may it be fully expressed and grow rich. And, of course, see Malinowski (1926). There has been a growing body of literature in this area in recent years, especially in anthropology, including Constable (2003), Yan (2003), Ahearn (2001), Rebhun (1999), Illouz (1997), Jankowiak (1995), and Abu-Lughod (1986), to cite only a few.

4 See Foucault (1977).

5 See Nicholi (2002: Ch. 7) for Freud on love.

6 The fact that Takamure's scholarship has been greatly understudied is, needless to say, related to the male-centered practices of Japanese academic and literary circles. Having said that, Origuchi is much underestimated as well, due to the glory monopolized by the more orthodox former bureaucrat Yanagita Kunio. This may be related to the fact that Origuchi was homosexual, although others argue that Origuchi is unduly worshipped despite imperialistic undercurrents in his thought, an issue needing to be critically addressed. See Murai (1992) on Yanagita and Murai (2004) on Origuchi.

7 Arendt (1958: 52).

8 The reader must have realized by now that the approach which I have taken above not only relies on Foucault's notion of governmentality, but also on aspects of the work of Althusser. Needless to say, whereas Althusser focused on the workings of state apparatuses and came up with a rather narrow analysis in his exploration of the subject, invoking a ritual-like response reaction that he called interpellation, Foucault's gaze upon the workings of the subject is microcosmological. But Foucault, too, necessitates expansive interpretation on

the part of the reader, especially in relation to so-called non-Western societies and cultures. See Althusser (1984) and Foucault (1979).
9 Agamben (1995) and also Arendt (2000).

1 Sacred sex

1 Origuchi (1966 vol. 10: 357). Tosa and Awa are located on the modern-day Japanese island of Shikoku.
2 Herodotus (1954: 87–8). I need not remind the reader of the rich documentation found in *The Golden Bough,* with its reference to "ruder races in other parts of the world," communicating with vegetation deities through rituals involving sexual intercourse in order to invite a good harvest (Frazer 1922: 156–9, 166, for example).
3 All quotes from Caillois (1959: 119, 118).
4 Qualls-Corbett (1988) calls these ancient customs of sexual encounters between strangers inside the temple and other sacred premises "sacred prostitution." The temple priestess appears in one of the oldest human narratives, *Gilgamesh* (Gardner and Maier 1985). It should be emphasized here that my reference to ancient sexual love has nothing to do with sociobiological concerns arguing for laws related to species preservation and human procreation in the name of love. A good example of sociobiological discussion is Fisher (1992).
5 There are many other similar examples that parallel these. See Ōwa (1993: Ch. 1). Perhaps another custom that anthropologists are familiar with would be the Trobriand *Bukumatula,* as depicted by Malinowski. But, it seems that the *Bukumatula,* in the words of Malinowski, lacks a distinctly religious underpinning (Malinowski 1926: 59–64).
6 Ōwa (1993: 15). See also Saeki (1987: Ch. 1).
7 Huizinga (1950: Ch. 1).
8 Caillois (1959: 152–62) and (1961: Ch. 1). To me, the divide between Caillois and Huizinga seems relatively minor, rather than fundamental. See note 45 on p. 135.
9 Itō (1996: 95). *Ai* was also used in other senses. See p. 33 in the text. I do not agree with the anachronistically nation-centered approach of Itō, given that at the time of *Manyōshū,* the borders between the Korean peninsula and the small and large islands that make up today's Japan were blurred; as such, many poets who contributed to the collection traveled between the peninsula and archipelago.
10 In the early Japanese feminism, *renai* meant a resistance to *kekkon* or marriage. *Renai* in that historical context immediately implied a free love, rather than simply love itself. Love based on free choice was not available for all and sundry, and especially not for women, and theorists such as Takamure insisted on love's radical freedom (Takamure 1967 [1926]). Feminists' use of the term *renai* in this sense was consciously political, although it came with its own weaknesses, such as blindness or indifference to Japan's colonial expansion. I have discussed elsewhere Takamure's view of *renai* (Ryang 1998).
11 Itō (1996: 105–10).
12 Itō (1996: 111–16).
13 Song No. 20, *Manyōshū* Book 1, by Nukatano ōkimi (Satake, Yamada, Kudō, Ōtani, and Yamazaki 1999: 28).
14 Lee (1989: 79–81).

15 See Yasumoto (1990: 39). I'm indebted to Dr Jan Bardsley of the University of North Carolina, Chapel Hill, for this source, as well as the Lee Young Hee book.
16 Origuchi (1966 vol. 9: 41–2).
17 Song No. 86, *Manyōshū* Book 2, by Ihahime kōgō (Satake, Yamada, Kudō, Ōtani, and Yamazaki 1999: 86).
18 Origuchi (1966 vol. 9: 41–2).
19 Origuchi (1966 vol. 9: 55). Not only territories of love and death lay in dangerously close proximity to one another, but also love in the *Manyō* ethos covered a wide range of human connections. No notable distinction existed between strong connections between, say, brother and sister or parent and child, as opposed to those between the lovers (Sekiguchi 1993, for example).
20 Origuchi (1966 vol. 9: 42).
21 Lee (1989: 79).
22 Takamure (1953: 255–6).
23 Takamure (1953: 1204–5).
24 See Malinowski (1926). We have earlier noted that Trobrianders have the institution of the *Bukumatula,* a bachelor house, in which young men and women, without getting married, court each other (see note 5 on p. 132). However, in the case of the *Bukumatula,* it is the women who visit the men. The Japan case, on the other hand, seems to be much closer to Nayar matrilineal marriage (Gough 1959). According to *Kojiki* (AD 712) and other recorded myths of Japan, Japan's ancient rulers were brother and sister, paired as *hiko* and *hime*; the same pattern recurs in other myths, as in the pairs Izanami and Izanaki, Ameno Uzume and Sarutahiko, and Amaterasu and Susanoo. Himiko, the ancient priestess, according to the old Chinese document, was not married and ruled the country with the help of her brother (Saigō 1967: 38–9). Interestingly, as seen from a matrilineal angle, the office of the ancient priestess was handed down to her niece (Saigō 1967: 147–8). In this case, from the succeeding priestess's point of view, it was between her and her father's sister (not between the mother's brother, or avunculate uncle, and son as among Trobrianders) that the matrilineal unit was formed.
25 *Marebito* is discussed in a number of volumes in Origuchi's (1965–6) collection. The parts that I have relied on in the text come from vol. 1 (p. 5) and vol. 2 (pp. 33–4). It is important here, as will be argued in the text below, that the notion of *marebito* was a dual one: both sacred and cursed. Some *marebito* were deities, while others were monsters or traveling beggars that carried curses. See note 47 on p. 135.
26 Kawazoe (2002: 17–18) paraphrasing Fujii (2000). The reinterpretation of *The Tale of Genji* and other works by medieval female writers is actively carried out in the context of today's feminist scholarship in Japan. The difference between Imai (1990) and Fujii (2000) offers an interesting example. Whereas Imai suggests that *Genji* is a story of multiple rape, Fujii veers toward an interpretation of sexual liaisons as depicted in the tale as sacred marriage. See also Noguchi (1985) and Akiyama (1987), and Seidensticker (1978) for the English translation.
27 Song No. 3101, *Manyōshū* Book 12, *Mondōka* (Satake, Yamaka, Kudō, Ōtani, and Yamazaki 2002: 188).
28 Takamure (1953: 57–8).

29 See Morgan (1871) and Engels (1941). It is not clear whether *kagai* was based on the idea of *punaluan* kinship or more like the idea of moiety (See Lévi-Strauss 1949).

30 See Takamure (1953: 205–6) on the dual registration of the Nara period household registry. It seems, however, erroneous to group *tsumadoi* and *mukotori* under the term *shōseikon* or inviting-the groom marriage, as does Takamure, considering that in today's Japanese, the character *sei* has the meaning of *muko*, most commonly understood as son-in-law, rather than "husband"; *tsumadoi* did not offer the possibility for a man to be a son-in-law of the family, as it was a form of courtship and liaison largely based on individual choice, albeit with asymmetry between the gender.

31 Origuchi (1966, vol. 9: 53–4). According to Takamure, however, even in the case of *tsumadoi*, if the visitor (*marebito*) was of prominent origin, his visit was declared (in contrast to the usually clandestine manner of visits) by the announcement, "*Uruwashiki kami kitari*" (Here cometh the beautiful god), and women of the hosting clan gathered around the visitor's bedside, obviously hoping to beget his child. In this picture, one cannot distinguish *kagai* from *tsumadoi*, simply on the basis of randomness/openness and selectivity/secrecy (Takamure 1953: 177).

32 Song No. 3102, *Manyōshū* Book 12, *Mondōka* (Satake, Yamada, Kudō, Ōtani, and Yamazaki 2002: 188). *Tarachine* consists of the characters used for the verb *tareru* (to hang down), and those for *chichi* (breast) and *ne* (roots). Until the time of the *Manyō*, reflecting the matrilocal residence of children, *tarachine* referred exclusively to the mother, and only after the eighth century, gradually coming to mean parents. See Takamure (1953: 224–5).

33 Origuchi (1966, vol. 9: 54–5).

34 Teruoka (1989: 22). The eleventh/twelfth centuries constitute the end-period of the practice of *tsumadoi*. Subsequently, the Confucian ideology of a woman marrying into her husband's family became predominant, reflecting the stability of the samurai rule and of patrilineage, although lower class practices deviated considerably from this principle, and local diversity persisted. Indeed, variations of uxorilocal, matrilocal, and matrilineal marriage even existed until the twentieth century. For example, in the Shirakawa district of the Gifu prefecture, except for firstborn sons, all younger sons had "commuting" marriage through *yobai* or nightcrawling. Children born as a result of commuting marriages were raised by the mother's household, and the husband and wife never lived together. For this and other such marriages, see Ryang (2004a: Ch. 4).

35 Quoted in Ōwa (1993: 91–2).

36 This custom persisted for a long time. In the late nineteenth century, foreign travelers in Japan also recorded that the open practice of what to them was prostitution in Japan was astonishingly prevalent. See more on this, Macfarlane (1997: Ch. 17).

37 Saeki (1987: Ch. 1).

38 Yanagita (1962). Pace Ōwa, I do not think Yanagita's view was as clear as is depicted; his view toward *miko* was more complex and ambiguous. Tatsukawa Seijirō, an acclaimed scholar of Japanese literature and doctor of law, on the other hand, clearly insisted that *yūjo* had its origins in Korea, where, according to him, customs were corrupted; as such, in his view it was foreign to traditional Japan, where higher morality dominated (1965: 66).

39 Fukutō (1990), quoted in Ōwa (1993: 172–3).

40 Saeki (1987: 90–2). Perhaps not surprisingly, Saeki's views have received a somewhat hostile reaction. From a feminist point of view, the way *yūjo* figures in Saeki's theory is upsetting, since it risks depicting prostitution as something mystical, romantic, and sacred, while from an empiricist stance, the anchoring of her interpretation in intratextual data is weak and unfounded. However, obviously her work remains influential. See Fukutō (2002) and Koyano (1999a and 1999b). Saeki's two representative books are: Saeki (1987) and (1998).

41 Ōwa (1993: 169).

42 See Ōwa (1993: Ch. 8). For more on Goshirakawa, see Yasuda (1986) and for a recent study in English, see Kawashima (2001).

43 Morris (1964: 43).

44 Agamben (1995: 79).

45 Caillois (1959: 35). Taking the ambivalence of the sacred into consideration, Huizinga's near-equation of play and the sacred, perhaps, is a misstep. However, as can be seen in the text, in the ancient and medieval Japanese context, *asobi* (play) is an important concept in understanding the sacred.

46 It is worth noting that in so-called primitive societies, according to Frazer, the blood of the sovereign is seen as both sacred and cursed and hence, upon his execution, utmost caution was taken not to spill his blood on the ground (Frazer 1922: 265–8).

47 Aside from *marebito*, *ijin* (stranger, outsider) is also used among folklorists. Many villages in Japan have legends of villagers' murdering and robbing wandering blind beggars or poor traveling monks, who happened to pass the village. These are examples of *marebito/ijin* persecution. See Komatsu (1985). Amino Yoshihiko, a revisionist Japanese historian, casts light on *hinin* (lit. nonhuman) and *yūjo* in medieval Japan, as a social group that existed outside ordinary social norms. In his study of people below the ordinary social order, he emphasizes that *hinin*, largely seen as the ancestors of today's *burakumin* outcastes, served the imperial family, originally holding important ritual positions pertaining to mortuary rites, among others. See Amino (1994), for example.

48 See Takamure (1953: 47–8), Amino (e.g. 1978, 1994), and Fukutō (e.g. 1995, 1996).

49 Wakita (1985: 145–7).

50 I should like to emphasize that the secularization of the market as witnessed in modernity is only relative. Values, discourses, and practices that reflect some belief in the supernatural are still found in market transactions in Japan and elsewhere, including in the industrialized nations. For example, many Japanese firms have company shrines on their premises.

51 Akamatsu (1995: 76–7).

52 Whereas in the northeast, the hierarchical kin organization called *dōzoku* dominated, in the southwest, a relatively egalitarian non-kin cooperative organization called *kōkumi* dominated the village. Such a division, however, is heuristic; between the archetypes, a wide range of diverse practices existed. See Ryang (2004a: Ch. 4).

53 Akamatsu (1994b: 51–3).

54 Mori (1949 [1909]: 21–2). Mori's novel was originally published in 1909 in a literary journal entitled *Subaru*. After the publication of Mori's novel, *Subaru*'s publication was suspended because the authorities deemed it pornographic.

55 Akamatsu (1995: 152–3). See also Akamatsu (1994a) and Akamatsu (1994b). An interesting yet provocative exchange on the subject of sexual culture between

Akamatsu and feminist scholar Ueno Chizuko can be found in Akamatsu and Ueno (1995).
56 See Ryang (2004a: Ch. 3). Akamatsu stresses that the existing ethnological enterprise, created by Yanagita Kunio and followed by his loyal disciples, effectively corroborated with the state-intervened cultural cover-up of what could be seen by Westerners as immoral (Akamatsu 1994b: 110–16). Interestingly, Ivy notes that the Japan National Tourist Organization to this day "hesitates to distribute information about Japan's phallic festivals to foreign tourists" (Ivy 1995: 33).
57 Johnston, referring to the decrease in the practice of *yobai* in modern Japan, claims that this came about as a result of its attribution to the spread of sexually transmitted diseases, the installation of streetlights which revealed the identity of visitors, and police restrictions (Johnston 2005: 33–5). I would identify a more fundamental set of reasons, such as the disenchantment with sexual love in the rapidly strengthening capitalist economy on one hand, and state intervention to control the population in parallel with Japan's emergence as a biopower on the other.
58 It is interesting to register that even today we see that shrines and temples on one hand and markets and fairs on the other are located adjacent to red-light districts. Asakusa in Tokyo is a good example (see Nakayama 1974 [1929], for example). For a detailed ethnographic account of frequenting the red-light districts in early modern Japan (with participant observation), see Murashima (2004).
59 Saeki (1998: 15ff.). Saeki also cautiously adds that there was initial confusion—indeed, love was often translated as *iro* during the early Meiji period (1998: 10–11). See also Honda (1990: 153ff.). Initially, translating God's love as *ai* was met with resistance, due to its negative associations with notions of greed and possession (Honda 1990: 155).

2 Sovereign and love

1 Abe (1997: 73). All quotations from Abe Sada's interrogatory record are my own translations.
2 For a recent study of this incident, see Suzaki (2003).
3 Abe (1997: 74–5).
4 Abe (1997: 75–6). Kichi was part of Ishida's first name, Kichizō.
5 Abe (1997: 20).
6 These women were referred to as *karayukisan* or "girls headed for Kara, i.e. China" (Morisaki 1986).
7 Horinouchi (1998: 57).
8 Abe (1997: 42–3).
9 Abe (1997: 63). I think that the fact that Sada and Kichi met in a restaurant was not coincidental with respect to their sexual involvement. Traditionally speaking, eateries such as noodle houses in Japan offered either sexual services by the women who worked there or facilities where men and women could have sex. Even until recent times in the twentieth century, *sobaya no nikai* or the upstairs floor of a noodle house, euphemistically and practically, meant a place to have sex. See Inoue (1999) on the changing relations between space and love in Japan.
10 Abe (1997: 64–7).
11 Abe (1997: 68).

12 Abe (1997: 72).
13 Wakaume (1987: 155–6). See also Marran (2000) for the media representation and public reception of the Sada incident.
14 Ricoeur (1970: 199). See also Freud (1950).
15 She is on record saying that she enjoyed oral sex and could always tell if her partner had experienced it or not as soon as he licked her genitals. See Matsumura and Takahashi (1973: 51). The term "anthropophagic" was used by Lévi-Strauss and was discussed, rather provocatively, by Bauman (1992: 131, 155). Incidentally, having sex with a menstruating woman was an ancient taboo in Japan, as stated in Chapter 1 p. 23.
16 Mutilating Ishida's penis and carrying it in the chest fold of a kimono, as was done by Sada, was a transgression of a taboo in one other sense—that related to castration. Sada's act vividly replayed the primordial fear of male children, as studied by Freud. Freud also connects the femininity of hysteria with the female phobia related to the loss of the object of love, although I do not think Sada's case was hysterical or that it involved castration phobia. For a feminist reading of Freud's notion of castration, see Mitchell (1974: 74–91). The term "hysteria" was widely used by then in Japan in order to denote sexually charged psychological disorders in women, even in farming communities (Embree 1939). Concerns over hysteria are widely registered in *minouesōdan* or life consultations, first appearing in the newspaper *Yomiuri Shinbun* during the 1920s. An interesting selection of these can be found in Kataroguhausu (1995).
17 Freud (1963: 19).
18 Mercuse (1966) and Freud's own essay " 'Civilized' Sexual Morality and Modern Nervousness" in Freud (1963). It is not deniable, however, that Freud's use of ethnography was naïve and perhaps unjustified. See Ricoeur (1970: 191ff.) for a critique. Also, recent psychoanalysts have pointed out that Freud's *Totem and Taboo* (1950) is based on a misconstrued notion of group gene inheritance. Gaylin, nevertheless, suggests that if we strip *Totem and Taboo* of its faulty genetics and biology, its significance becomes obvious in the sense that it tells us of the human capacity to control impulses related to the selfish pursuit of the sexual instinct (Gaylin 1988).
19 Caillois (1959: 117–19).
20 One must not forget the effect of the nationally standardized school education and writing system, which for many people came as almost a foreign version of the Japanese language, forcing them to adopt a more formal form for writing, while maintaining the use of the vernacular and local dialects for speech. For an English study of the language policies of the early modern Japanese state, see Twine (1991).
21 Takamure (1941, 1943, and 1944). While Takamure's complexity is not to be underestimated, it was undeniable that she acted as an outspoken voice for imperial Japan. See Ryang (1998), Oguma (1995), Nishikawa (1982), and Kanō (1979) for a critique.
22 Abe (1997: 76–7).
23 Suzuki (1993: 46–7). Ironically, this goal was to be achieved only in the 1960s. See Chapter 3.
24 Frühstück (2003: Ch. 1).
25 Marshall (1995).
26 Agamben (1995: 1).
27 See Foucault (1979: 135–6).

28 Monbushō or the Ministry of Education published the canonical publication on *kokutai* during the war (Monbushō 1944; see also Monbushō 1949 for a postwar English translation). For Meiji Japan's indoctrination, see Gluck (1985), for example.
29 For the Anglo-Japanese alliances, see Nish (1966 and 1972).
30 On the Shanghai incident of 1932, see Usui (1974: 159–72), for example.
31 Kurahashi (1994: 13–17).
32 According to Chang (1998: 100–1), the International Military Tribunal of the Far East estimated that over 260,000 noncombatants died at the hands of the Japanese. A Chinese researcher also came up with a total figure of over 227,400.
33 Honda (1981: 236–7, 263–4). See also Hata (1986) for a detailed historical study.
34 Chang (1998: 94–6).
35 Schmitt (1922: 5). In not so different a fashion, on March 2, 2006 the US Senate voted for the renewal of the USA Patriot Act, thereby making most of its provisions permanent. This decision was made following unsettling revelations that President Bush had used his executive power to investigate (spy on) US citizens and residents, bypassing minimal required procedures for authorization. He authorized this in the name of the presidency, i.e. supreme executive power, which had been expanded, this expansion having been justified in the name of the "war against terror," which had become virtually limitless. It is no coincidence that he has referred to himself as the "war president." The state of exception constituted by this "war against terror" has given him unlimited power and, unlike President Clinton, whose affair with a White House intern led to impeachment according to the nation's (ordinary) laws, no one is seriously entertaining the possibility of impeaching Bush, precisely because the "war against terror" is thought to be a time of national emergency. See Agamben (2005: 2, 3–4, 21–2). Much of Agamben's thoughts are inspired by Schmitt's work.
36 Senda (1978: 154). It is well-known that most Japanese soldiers during WWII were not aware of the Geneva Convention, and took it as an honor and duty to terminate their own lives once captured by the enemy; likewise they treated Western POWs extremely brutally.
37 Senda (1978: 121), Yoshimi (2000: 68).
38 Yamada (1991: 48–51). Tanaka (2002: 28–9) states that inside the Japanese military, rape was rarely punished, although it was against army criminal law.
39 Senda (1973) and see Kurahashi (1994: Ch. 2).
40 Fujime (1997a) and, for a more extensive example of research in Japanese, see Fujime (1997b) and Fujino (2001).
41 Senda (1978: 7–8), Tanaka (2002: 31).
42 When Japanese local governments abolished the red-light districts in Japan proper due to the tensions related to the war effort, Japanese prostitutes traveled by boat to the Pacific and Southeast Asia. Of course, how much of this action was "voluntary" is controversial. Excellent reportages have been produced, including Yamada (1991) and Nishino (1992). Testimonials of former Korean "comfort women" have become available during the last decade. There is a wealth of recovered documentation, interviews, recollections, art productions, and political activism on this issue. See, for example, Choi (1997), Yang (1997), Chung (1997), Tanaka (1997, 2002), Soh (2000, 2004), and Yoshimi (2000) to cite only a few. The first confessional books on "comfort women" appeared only in the late 1970s. See Senda (1978) and Kim (1976).

While I am aware that Radhika Coomaraswamy, the UN Special Rapporteur on Violence Against Women, adopted the term "sexual slavery" in her 1996 report, I elect to use "comfort women" in quotation marks for this study. This does not mean that I do not think that the setting-up of comfort stations and forcing women to work there was not a form of slavery. The estimated number of "comfort women" ranges from 50,000 to 200,000, depending on the method of calculation and who is calculating.

43 See Tanaka (1997, 2002) for the IMTFE. Crimes of rape and violation of Asian women were less likely to be regarded as war crimes by the IMTFE (Gardam 1998, for example). To this day, not a single Japanese woman has identified herself as a former "comfort woman." As for Korean women, who formed the majority of these sex slaves, for a long time after the war's end through to the 1980s, this issue was completely ignored by the governments of North Korea, South Korea, and Japan. The situation changed when the issue of compensation was raised during state-level discussions involving Japan and the two Koreas in the 1980s. Until then, Korean former "comfort women" were not only forced to be silent about their past, receiving no protection or compensation from any of the governments, but also made to feel ashamed, dehumanized, and desecrated due to their past sexual involvement with the Koreans' archenemy, the Japanese. This post-traumatic secondary oppression was not just the work of Korean men—Korean society as a whole, involving both men and women, at least for some time since the end of the war strongly subscribed to notions of male dominance and patrilineage, combined with a postcolonial repulsion for things Japanese and an over-zealous hunt for "national traitors" and "pro-Japanese elements" in order to eliminate colonial influences, condemning these women to the eternal darkness of a "living death." Even today, after the emancipation of some of these women in both North Korea and South Korea, the controversy over who to receive compensation from (the Japanese government, the Korean government, or Japan's non-governmental fund) and, more acutely, who should be held responsible, seems to know no end. In 1995, the Japanese government set up an Asian Women's Fund, as a result of which a total of 364 former "comfort women" in Taiwan, the Philippines, and South Korea each received $30,000 in "attonement money." However, it was met with strong reactions and political division between activists over the legitimacy of this money, especially in South Korea. In Japan itself, also, opinions were divided about the efficacy and legitimacy of this measure. It was decided that the fund would be shut down by 2007 (Horsley 2005). In December 2000, the Women's International War Crimes Tribunal was held in Tokyo, aimed at reopening the unresolved question of responsibility for the suffering of the "comfort women." See Kim (2001).

44 It was SCAP (Supreme Commander for Allied Powers), the US Occupation authorities, and the US government who ultimately decided on this exemption.

45 The absence of accurate teaching in formal Japanese school curricula regarding what Japan did to its Asian neighbors before and during the war has not only created mass amnesia but also strong resistance toward accepting the nation's past. If one clicks on Amazon.com and searches for Yoshimi's seminal book, *Comfort Women* (Yoshimi 2000), one will find a host of reviews by individuals that can be easily presumed as Japanese because of their names and locations. One person declares everything in the book to be a lie, while the other accuses Yoshimi of being a liar and a communist—obviously, being a communist is a

crime in this reviewer's mind. The third person denies Yoshimi's scholarly credentials and calls his book anti-Japanese propaganda.

46 Senda (1978: 127–8).
47 Nishino (1992: 42, 48, 52–3).
48 Suzuki (1993: 87–90) and Ishikawa (2001: 212–14). As for sexual violence committed by the Allied forces in Japan, see Tanaka (2002: Ch. 6).
49 Suzuki (1993: 81–5). See also Soh (2004).
50 See Norgren (2001: 27–8). For the National Eugenics Law, see Suzuki (1993: 46–7). The Japanese state was engaged in the promotion of eugenicist marriage from early on, and the debate over eugenics continued for decades, involving feminists and anti-feminists alike. See, for example, Otsubo (2005), Ishizaki (1998), and Robertson (2001, 2002, and, to some extent, 2005) among many others. According to this law, doctors were no longer allowed to perform abortions unless the patient could produce evidence of their "inferior" genetic makeup. A total of more than fifty-five diseases were listed as appropriate criteria for sterilization, including not only an array of serious, hereditary illnesses but also some minor illnesses as well.
51 Arendt (1958: 52).
52 This is not to psychoanalyze Japan as a nation. However, it is worth remembering that the national character studies during WWII labeled Japanese culture as "adolescent," with the Japanese referred to as compulsive and their wartime aggression explained in psychological terms. For example, La Barre lists the traits of the compulsive Japanese personality, including sadomasochistic behavior and a love of scatological obscenity and anal sexuality (La Barre 1942; see also Gorer 1943, Minear 1980, and Ryang 2004a: Ch. 1). My purpose here is not to trace the cause of the rape of Nanjing to some abnormal element of the Japanese psyche, but to draw hints from psychoanalysis and draw a parallel between the ontogeny and phylogeny of the taboo and its transgression.
53 I am, of course, referring to *Nineteen Eighty-Four* by Orwell (1949).
54 See Ryang (2000, 2002) for the formation of the self in North Korea.
55 In a somewhat archaic description, this state would have been called "indoctrination," but in today's post-Foucault social scientific language, closely associating this state of seizure-like self-oblivion with the effects of biopower would be more appropriate. For, using the term indoctrination would have the effect of unduly highlighting the cerebral, cognitive aspect of human life, while using a more corporeal and embodied metaphor (such as seizure—see Chapter 1) would have the effect of holistically capturing the ontological state of the human as a living being. I find Lindholm's close connection between charisma and romantic love most useful in this consideration. Lindholm's ideas about idealization and its relation to the concept of authenticity are entirely original and highly sophisticated. See Lindholm (1990, 1998a, 1998b).
56 According to myth, the first Emperor's reign is supposed to have started in AD 660 on the occasion of the Taika reform (see Chapter 1).
57 Abe (1948). One of Sada's biographers of the day, Fuyuki Ken, endorsed Sada's life as most human-like (Fuyuki 1947: 241). Regardless of their motivations, however, Sada's (unauthorized) biographies fell into the category of the semi-pornographic genre then called *kasutori* or bottom-feeder pulp. For an overview of postwar *kasutori* and mass culture, see Yamaoka (1973). A glimpse of postwar sex culture can be found in Dower (1999: Ch. 4).
58 Quoted in Horinouchi (1998: 283).

59 His essay collection *Darakuron* (On Decadence) and his novel *Hakuchi* (Idiot), published in 1946 and 1947 respectively, turned Sakaguchi into an acclaimed writer and commentator of the day (Sakaguchi 1990 [1946] and 1947).
60 Quoted in Horinouchi (1998: 299–308; abridged and emphasis added).
61 Sakaguchi (1991: 241, 243).
62 I am not saying here that there was an internally unified concept of *ryōsaikenbo* during the prewar and wartime period, or that it was unanimously accepted by Japanese women of the day. For more on *ryōsaikenbo* in the years immediately after the war, see Garon (1997).
63 Wittig (1981).
64 Seen from this angle, Sada seriously disrupts the patriarchal sovereign order *from the outside,* in the sense intended by Irigaray, if only temporarily (Irigaray 1985). In this sense, Sada did not even possess the performativity of female sexual identity (Butler 1999 [1990]).
65 Arendt (1958: 50).
66 The appropriation of Sada's feminine agency is an ongoing issue in today's Japan, seen in movies, biographies, and academic writing; and in the West, for that matter, as well. For example, Nagisa Oshima's feature film *L'Empire des sens* (Oshima 1976) and Shimizu (1998: 72). For a short, yet comprehensive recent study of Abe Sada, see Marran (2005).

3 Pure love

1 Ōshima and Kōno (1963: 187). All quotations from Ōshima and Kōno (1963) in the text are my own translations.
2 In 1951, the University of Tokyo's Yoshitake Group publicized a standard floor plan for public apartment complexes, which included the dining kitchen. Public reaction was mixed. Some complained about the Western-style use of chairs, while others worried that the new design presupposed that it would be occupied by a two-generational nuclear family with the aging parents pushed outside the family. Women, understandably, generally welcomed the new living arrangements. See Inoue (1995a: 122–4).
3 Princess Michiko came from one of the wealthiest commoner families in Japan of the day, Nisshin, a flour manufacturing family that had accumulated its wealth through Japan's invasion of China. The Crown Prince's declaration of free love came as a surprise to members of parliament and provoked increased discord among former aristocrats, who had lost their titles under the US Occupation (Watanabe 1991). Numerous books were published and continue to be published about this former commoner-turned-Crown Princess and later, Empress, due in part to the continuing harassment that she is allegedly receiving from the former aristocratic in-laws. The way she raised little Prince Naruhito (Japan's current Crown Prince) was hyped up as a model of good motherhood. See Satō (1962) and Kawahara (1987, 1990). On the postwar abolition of aristocratic titles, see Hirota (1995).
4 Nagasato (1949: 36).
5 See Monbushō junketsukyōiku iinkai (1949).
6 Monbushō junketsukyōiku iinkai (1949: 38–9).
7 Andō (1948: 22). This author and the other advocates of *junketsukyōiku* insisted that reproductive sex had to be based on love, without carefully considering what love was (see, for example, Sadakata, Tanimura, and Ōhira 1949). Amidst

the *junketsukyōiku* zeal, Takamure Itsue declared the death of purity by challenging the Ministry of Education's stance, insisting that love and reproduction did not have to coincide. She forewarned those women who had been made to subscribe to the ideal of viewing "healthy" and "desirable" males as objects of love—regardless of whether the women were virgins or not—that they no longer had purity (Takamure 1967 [1948]). The bulk of her ideas, however, were contained in her earlier work (1967 [1926]). Another noteworthy commentator would be Itō Sei, a prominent thinker and writer of the day, whose translation of D.H. Lawrence's works involved him in a lawsuit due to its sexually explicit nature. Writing monthly essays for *Fujinkōron,* Women's Public Debate, during the year 1953, he advocated the straightforward expression of emotions at home and caricatured those emphasizing the moral and ethical dimensions of love, as represented by *junketsukyōiku.* Itō prioritized sex as the basis for *renai,* romantic love, but clearly distinguished sex from marriage or marital life. See Itō (1960).

8 Monbushō junketsukyōiku iinkai (1949: 3).
9 See Norgren (2001). Norgren's Appendix has the English text of the 1940, 1948, and 1996 laws. I thank Professor Marlene Mayo of the University of Maryland for drawing my attention to Norgren's important study.
10 Monbushō junketsukyōiku iinkai (1949: 42–3).
11 Numanoi (1949: 126).
12 Numanoi (1949: 129–30).
13 Kimura (1947: 101ff.), for example.
14 Kimura (1947: 15–20) and Kusato (1948), for example.
15 Nishimura and Shikiba (1949), for example. All public elementary and middle schools became coeducational and adopted the 6–3–3–4 system (denoting six years of elementary school, three years' middle school, three years' high school, and four years' university) in 1947, following the US model. However, the decision on whether high schools would become coeducational was left to the prefectural governments. As of 1949, 54.6 percent of public high schools were coed, increasing to 63.9 percent in 1954. See Murakami (1974) and Yamazumi and Horio (1976). It was only after the war that the nation's top public institutions of higher education, such as the University of Tokyo, became open to female students.

    example, whereas Korea, Japan's former colony, was partitioned into two, offered such a fate (except in the case of the thirty-year occupa- Cumings (1981). Considering that in Europe, only German, partitions, including those of was a colonizer of other nations. From another angle, in the area of understanding, as can be seen in Benedict's now classic *Chrysanthemum and the Sword* (1946), a charitable reading of Japan's cultural uniqueness became the dominant trend, and postwar US understanding of Japan bore a blindfold ignoring Japan's colonial past. I have argued this elsewhere. See Ryang (2004a: Ch. 2).
17 See note 43 on p. 139.
18 See Gomer, Powell, and Roling (1981).
19 An excellent study on this theme, and its close relationship to the historical context of the labor movement and trade unionism can be found in Fujime (1998).
20 Fukutō (2002: 207).

21 A helpful guide for understanding the shifting feminist momentum of the late 1960s/early 1970s can be found in Mackie (2003).
22 Inoue (1995b: 33).
23 Ōshima and Kōno (1963: 25). I use the ethnographic present when paraphrasing Miko and Mako's story.
24 Ōshima and Kōno (1963: 18).
25 Ōshima and Kōno (1963: 27).
26 Ōshima and Kōno (1963: 28).
27 Ōshima and Kōno (1963: 28–9).
28 Ōshima and Kōno (1963: 40–2). As the reader can see, the letters use the addressee and his/her name (Miko or Mako) interchangeably.
29 Ōshima and Kōno (1963: 45).
30 Ōshima and Kōno (1963: 46–7).
31 Ōshima and Kōno (1963: 47).
32 Ōshima and Kōno (1963: 47–51).
33 Ōshima and Kōno (1963: 52).
34 Ōshima and Kōno (1963: 52–3).
35 Ōshima and Kōno (1963: 88).
36 Inoue (1995b: 40).
37 Ōshima and Kōno (1963: 149).
38 Ōshima and Kōno (1963: 152–3).
39 Ōshima and Kōno (1963: 157).
40 Ōshima and Kōno (1963: 164).
41 When referring to a lover in a respectful, morally decent way, the Japanese translation uses *koibito,* a term consisting of the two characters *koi* (love) and *hito* (person), instead of *aijin,* which consists of the two characters *ai* (love) and *jin/hito* (person). Despite the fact that in all other instances *ai* is used to imply moral love, *aijin* normally implies illicitness and immorality.
42 Ōshima and Kōno (1963: 173–4).
43 Ōshima and Kōno (1963: 176–7).
44 Ōshima and Kōno (1963: 183).
45 Ōshima and Kōno (1963: 185).
46 Ōshima and Kōno (1963: 186–7).
47 Ōshima and Kōno (1963: 190–1).
48 Ōshima and Kōno (1963: 192).
49 Ōshima and Kōno (1963: 192).
50 Ōshima and Kōno (1963: 206).
51 Ōshima and Kōno (1963: 220–1).
52 Ōshima and Kōno (1963: 223).
53 Ōshima and Kōno (1963: 222).
54 Ōshima and Kōno (1963: 226).
55 Ōshima and Kōno (1963: 231).
56 Ōshima and Kōno (1963: 262).
57 Ōshima and Kōno (1963: 267).
58 Ōshima and Kōno (1963: 269).
59 Ōshima and Kōno (1963: 272–3).
60 Embassy of Japan, Washington, DC (2003).
61 Japan Institute of Worker's Evolution (2004).
62 Calculated from Statistics Bureau, Japan (1996–2000).

63 After peaking at 1.27 percent in 1974, Japan's annual population growth rate steadily declined to 0.2 percent in 1995. Life expectancy at birth continued to grow from 74.20 in 1983 to 78.32 in 2002 for men and from 79.78 to 85.23 for women (National Institute of Population and Social Security Research 2005).

64 Writing about a period a little later, Allison (1994) describes how the routine of frequenting hostess clubs is in fact a work duty; a show of loyalty and a form of male bonding. Wives at home are fully aware of this, yet keep their mouths shut. But, of course, things were altogether different for working class, blue-collar families.

65 Matsui (1995). On Asian women heading for Japan's sex industries, called *Japayukisan* (women going to Japan), see Usuki (1992) among many others.

66 After thirty-five years' debate, in December 1999, Japan finally introduced oral contraceptives.

67 Macfarlane notes that there was a long tradition of sexual abstinence within marriage in premodern Japan, keeping Japan safely away from the Malthusian trap by maintaining a low fertility rate (Macfarlane 1997: Ch. 17). My point here is that when conjugal love emerged in postwar Japan, conjugal sex (after reproduction) did not accompany it.

68 Japanese characters have more than one reading; there are "sound readings" (*onyomi*) based on the original Chinese pronunciation of the character and "meaning readings" (*kunyomi*), which use vernacular terms with related meanings. *Ren* and *koi* are, respectively, the *onyomi* and *kunyomi* of a particular Chinese character meaning "love."

69 Office of Gender Equality, Prime Minister's Office, Japan (1996).

70 The Japanese school physical examination was implemented in 1900 and underwent its fifth national reform in 1949 (Makiyama 1949).

71 Hardacre (1997) shows an interesting take on abortion from a religious studies' angle, combined with admonitions routinely given in relation to women's magazines in the form of the curse story of an aborted fetus.

72 Hanley and Yamamura (1977), for example.

73 Monbushō junketsukyōiku iinkai (1949: 3), Numanoi (1949: 25ff.), and Hyogoken kyōiku iinkai (1948a and 1948b).

4 Body and soul

1 Quoted in Miyadai (1998: 279).

990: *passim*). When the New Woman emerged in late Meiji Japan, as Hiratsuka Raichō and the others who founded the Seitōsha or Blue Sto... ...se women were unspeakably ugly. In relation to ... ...4), for example.

3 Many researchers studying Japan have poin... ...*shōjo*(girl)-orientation in recent Japanese culture. In a similar vein, recen... ubiquitous assignment of the attribute of "cuteness" to girls in Japanese p... discourse (see, for example, Treat 1996). The role played by *manga* or comic books in promoting the cute or *kawaii* is undeniable (see Napier 2001, Kinsella 2000, and Allison 1996, for example). I use the term "girls" throughout this chapter and wherever necessary and appropriate in the rest of the book to denote young women and female adolescents. Some readers may find this term politically incorrect. However, in my view, there is no better term to denote adolescent women in the situations that I depict in this chapter.

4 Girls' high school uniforms in Japan used to predominantly consist of a sailor-collared top with pleated skirt in navy blue with burgundy tape trimming. From around the middle of the 1980s, public schools began abolishing the uniforms, allowing students to wear clothing of their own choice, though within the limits of school stipulations. Meanwhile, private schools entered the race to attract applicants (in light of Japan's shrinking birth rate) by offering more attractive, designer-created school uniforms. Some have a variety of color coordination widely seen in the American or European prep-school look, complete with tartan check miniskirt and blazer with Ivy-league look-alike emblems. Skirt lengths began to shrink around this time also, while, as observed in the text, students began making a statement by pulling up their skirts even higher and loosening the bobby socks.

   Although today, *burusera* shops (shops selling bloomers and sailor-collared uniforms traded in by female students) have disappeared from public view, female school uniforms remain the subject of intense attention. *Zukan* (picture encyclopedias), which classify and detail school uniforms according to region (such as Tokyo Metropolitan or Aichi Prefecture, for example) continue to be published and sold. On Amazon Japan, I found twenty-one entries as of July 2005, with prices ranging from around 2,000 yen to 5,000 yen for related books and DVDs.

5 Miyadai (1994: 4).

6 Miyadai (1994: 3–4).

7 Miyadai (1994: 31–3).

8 Hayami (1998a: 92, 203).

9 Miyadai (1994: 9–10).

10 This very much echoes the postwar ideal of the egalitarian, peer-like, and mutually-loving democratic family in Japan as opposed to the prewar hierarchical, seniority-based, patriarchal family. See Kawashima (1950) and my critique of it (Ryang 2004a: Ch.3).

11 Miyadai (1994: 9–10).

12 Hayami (1998a: 89–102).

13 Miyadai (1998: 272–83).

14 Hayami (1998b: 17).

15 It is ironic to think that now that Japan has attained the most advanced level of communicative technology in the world (with pagers, cell phones, and the internet), communication at home with the closest kin is failing. Furthermore, it is these advancements in communication technology that have enabled young girls to gather the information necessary to enter aid-dating. For a recent study of Japanese communicative technology and its related culture, see Gottlieb and McLelland (2003), and more specifically on cell phones, Ito, Okabe, and Matsuda (2005). Tomita (2005) provides a very useful guide for understanding the mechanism of "Q2," "message dial," and "*terekura*" (telephone club), the services which, along with pagers, were actively used by aid-dating girls to arrange their rendezvous in the 1990s. The phone companies have now withdrawn these services.

16 Miyadai (1994: 47). This view is echoed in many different areas of social analysis in relation to Japanese society. Most scholars rely on Benedict's *Chrysanthemum and the Sword*, in which Japanese culture is named a "shame culture," *haji no bunka*, and contrasted with "guilt culture," *tsumi no bunka*. See Benedict (1946 and 1948).

I should add that Miyadai's keyword *seiteki jikoketteiken* (the right to sexual self-determination) has been subjected to criticism, as it obviously comes with an implication of approving prostitution. While the society maintains gender disparity, the concept such as self-determination (especially applied to the more vulnerable group of people such as minors) can be erroneous and misplaced. See Tsunoda (2004) for such a position.

17 See Nakane (1967 and 1970), and also Vogel (1979). I have elsewhere critiqued *Nihonjinron*-related literature from an anthropological perspective (Ryang 2004a: Ch. 5). For a critique of *Nihonjinron* per se, see Dale (1986). In Japanese, Aoki's synthesis is useful (Aoki 1990).

18 See Doi (1971, 1973, and 1988), Caudill (1962, 1973, and 1976) and Caudill and Doi (1963). In this psychologically and psychiatrically charged direction of research, the psychiatric ward has been taken as synonymous with Japanese society. More recently, scholars such as Rosenberger (1989 and 1992), Bachnik (1992), and Bachnik and Quinn, Jr (1994) have maintained that the Japanese self is fundamentally different from the Western self. Also notable here is Ohnuki-Tierney's exposition of the primordial Japanese national self (Ohnuki-Tierney 1993). Recently, social psychologists have assumed a role in building up this theory. See Markus and Kitayama (1994), Kitayama, Markus, and Lieberman (1995), Kitayama, Markus, Matsumoto, and Morasakkunkit (1997), and Kitayama, Markus, and Kurokawa (2000). For critiques of these, see Lindholm (1997) and Ryang (2004a: Ch. 6).

19 Skov and Moeran (1995), for example. Hayami's interviewees emphasize that they would normally carry a lot of cash, in addition to adorning themselves with designer brand goods (Hayami 1998a: 120–2). For a more recent commentary, see Bardsley and Hirakawa (2005).

20 Miyadai (1994: 117–40). Miya (1998) points out the fact that the shelf life of this brand is short—in a few years, girls will cease to be *joshikōsei* (female high school students).

21 See note 4 on p. 145.

22 For a comprehensive study of Chongryun, see Ryang (1997).

23 Wagner (1951: 95). For Korea's partition and the subsequent emergence of the separate regimes, see Cumings (1981).

24 Arendt (2000).

25 Chongryun inherited its infrastructure as well as its ideology from the first postwar leftist Korean expatriate organization, the League of Koreans, which emerged in October 1945 with the purposes of successfully repatriating all Koreans from Japan to Korea and, in the meantime, providing instruction in Korean language and culture to Korean children in Japan. In 1949, following the violent closure under the martial law of Korean schools that it operated, the authorities suppressed the League (see Koshiro 1999, Inokuchi 2000).

26 Statistics from Epstein (2005). As of the late 1980s, a total of about 20,000 out of 150,000 Korean students in Japan attended the 150 Chongryun schools, with the rest going to Japanese schools (Fukuoka 1993: 55). According to Han Tonghyun, a Korean researcher in Japan, the modified Korean uniforms were not one sidedly imposed on the girls, but were worn spontaneously by female students wanting to differentiate themselves from Japanese girls (Han 2004, 2006). I thank Han Tonghyun for imparting her thoughts in a phone conversation and Youngmi Lim for drawing my attention to Han's research.

27 Han (2004: 118). For more recent years, see Johnston (2002) and McNeill (2005) who reports that a Korean female student was spat at.

28 Girls are not interested in learning from their clients. Many express boredom and disgust at these men telling them about which "good" school they went to, what a "great" career they have, etc. (Miyadai 1998: 278).

29 Kim (1976: Ch. 1).

30 I have argued this elsewhere. See Ryang (2004b).

31 There was a heated debate when introducing this legislation to the colony, as some lawmakers thought it would result in Korean blood being mixed into the Japanese national body, eventually corrupting the makeup of the Japanese, while others thought it would be giving Koreans too many privileges, which they did not deserve. See Miyata, Kim, and Yang (1992).

32 Japan's one-sided revocation of its nationality from former colonial subjects remaining on its soil was an exceptional measure when seen from an international perspective. Whereas post-1960s measures with respect to former European colonies in Africa, for example, were carried out in such a way so as not to produce stateless peoples, the 1952 withdrawal of Japanese nationality from former colonial subjects residing in Japan produced a massive number of stateless peoples. See Ōnuma (1979a, 1979b, 1979c, 1980a, 1980b, and 1980c).

33 At the same time, household registry systems in the Korean peninsula, now divided in two, underwent changes: South Korea restored clan-based registration with the incest taboo reinforced in all sorts of ways, for example, by not allowing children born to a same-clan marriage to receive a public education (a measure which has recently been revised), while North Korea completely abolished any record of clan genealogies and reorganized its kinship in a somewhat similar manner to that of the prewar Japanese sovereign state, designating Kim Il Sung as Father of the nation.

34 Also, by the 1925 universal male suffrage, all males from the colonies that resided in Japan proper with official residential registration became eligible to vote and be voted for. (The household registry for those men remained in the colony, while residential registration was made in the local municipalities in Japan.) This was also abolished after the WWII. See Matsuda (1995) for details.

35 Since the 1965 ROK-Japan diplomatic normalization, some measures were taken to stabilize the legal status of Koreans in Japan, including the issuance of permanent residence. Nevertheless, no legal measures revising the 1952 one-sided withdrawal of Japanese nationality has been addressed. Most Koreans in Japan today have South Korean nationality, but their ambiguous belonging (to South Korea) is still present (Ryang 2006).

36 This and other updates are concisely explained in Asai, Kitamura, Hashimoto, and Murase (2003). See also Nohara (2004).

37 "Tokyo Adopts Contested Textbook," *BBC News* July 28, 2005. See also Hogg (2005) and Suzuki (2004: 71).

38 The general public does not have an accurate understanding of how AIDS is transmitted and how to prevent it, for example. As a result, Japan's AIDS/HIV rate is rising rapidly. Some 300 new AIDS cases and 530 new HIV infections were reported in 1999; in 2004, this had risen to a record 1,165 cases of AIDS/HIV infection. See "Japan AIDS/HIV Rate Skyrockets with 80% Condom Use," *LifeSiteNews.com* June 6, 2005, "Japan AIDS Cases Increase by Record 300 Last Year," *Shanghai Star* July 4, 2000, Lies (2005), and Head (2004).

39 Nihon fujin dantai rengōkai (2004: 135).

40 Horsley (2005).
41 Japanese Drama Database (1993–2003), "The Husband Instruction Manual,"
    China Daily News July 19, 2005, and Herskovitz (1997). Watanabe's Japanese
    original (1997a and 1997b) was translated into numerous languages including
    English (Carpenter 2000). For *deaikei,* see Media shisutemu (n.d.) and for a
    study of *deaikei* in English, Holden and Tsuruki (2003). Habuchi (2005) and
    Tomita (2005) give close attention to criminality potentially caused by *deaikei.*
42 Watanabe (1997a: 179–88), Watanabe (1997b: 74–5).
43 Watanabe (1997b: 153–7). For Abe Sada, see Chapter 2.
44 Watanabe (1997b: 100; my translation).
45 Watanabe (1997b: 105; my translation).
46 Nussbaum (1994: 259–60).
47 "Japanese Marriages Falling Victim to 'Yongfluenza'," *Crisscross News Japan*
    July 17, 2004, "Women Swarm Narita for Arrival of 'Yon-sama'," *Japan Times*
    November 26, 2004, "10 Women Hurt While Jostling for Glimpse of 'Yon-
    sama'," *Japan Times* November 27, 2004, and Kaku (2005a). South Korean
    TV dramas, including *The Winter Sonata,* enjoy very strong popularity in Asia.
    According to the Korean Ministry of Culture and Tourism, Korean TV program
    exports recorded their highest level in history in 2004, totaling $71.46 million.
    During that year, Japan took 57.4 percent of Korea's TV program exports,
    Taiwan 15.37 percent, China 10.8 percent, and Hong Kong 2.4 percent (Kaku
    2005b).
48 "Japanese Marriages Falling Victim to 'Yongfluenza'," *Crisscross News Japan*
    June 17, 2004 and "Fans Follow Suit After 'Yon-sama' Tsunami Donation,"
    Japan Times January 7, 2005.
49 Paraphrased from Kodansha Moura (2006a).
50 Kodansha Moura (2006b).
51 It is no coincidence that in 2004 *Ai to shi o mitsumete* (Facing Love and Death)
    by Miko and Mako was revived and reissued in Japan (Ōshima and Kōno 2004).
    The TV drama re-make will be aired on NHK in 2006. I owe this information
    to Ms Yada Shōko, the executive editor-in-chief of Daiwashobō.
        It was around this time that we began hearing more about sexless marriages
    and sexless lovers in Japan. See Wiseman (2004) and Joyce (2005) for a brief
    account. See also West (2005: 145) for a globally infrequent coupling number
    for the Japanese. Kawana (1995) discusses impotence, refusal, and other marital
    sexual problems. However, whereas in the US, for instance, sexless marriages
    can be a serious offence in relation to marital contracts, in Japan, a variety of
    reactions can be found. In the US, therapists and counseling services are routinely
    mobilized with the aim of improving (or normalizing) marital sex life. See, for
    example, Gardner Jr (2003) and "Steps for Outsmarting the 'Sexless Marriage',"
    SexSmart.com July 2003. For a recent polemic in this area, see Kipnis (2004).
    In Japan, couples' therapy is not heard of.
52 Shoji (2004).
53 Shoji (2004).
54 See Kim (1996: 179).
55 Kang Sang Jung, a Japan-born Korean professor at the University of Tokyo,
    contrasts Kim Jong Il, the North Korean leader, seen as the devil incarnate in
    Japan, with the popularity of Bae Yong Joon, and reminds the Japanese that it
    was due to the national partition and the cold war that we now have two starkly
    different Koreas (Kang 2005). For reports related to abductions, see International

Crisis Group (2005) and McCormack (2005). As of the beginning of 2006, no notable progress had been achieved with regard to Japan–North Korea relations.

56 It is said that *The Winter Sonata* fever is slowly promoting the inclusion of Korean residents in Japan in media coverage. For example, Fuji TV has aired a drama in which one of the main protagonists was a Korean resident in Japan. Some have claimed this would in the long run ease the discrimination and bias these Koreans face in Japan (Brasor 2004). I remain skeptical. For a sensible account on the Japanese reception of Koreans in Japan, see Nomura (1996).

57 For example, Fukuoka (2000: Part 2) introduces many personal cases pertaining to this effect.

58 See Lindholm (1990), for example.

59 Lugo and Baba (2001), for example. This service was more popular in the mid-1980s/early 1990s, but due to the frequent divorces that have been reported, it has since experienced declining popularity.

60 Kaku (2005a).

61 National Institute of Population and Social Security Research (2005). In 2005 it went further down to 1.25 ("Fertility Rate Plummets to its Lowest Level Yet, 2006). The birth rate of 1.29 is less than half the rate (3.65) in 1950. See Chapple (2004) for more details. The total number of marriages decreased for the third straight year to 720,429 in 2004, which was 19,762 less than in 2003. See "Concern Deepens over Continuing Slide of Birth Rate in Japan, No Stop in Sight," *Japan Brief* June 10, 2005. Of households consisting only of husband and wife, 21.1 percent were couples where both husband and wife were aged 65 or above in 2002; the same statistic was 6.2 percent in 1975 (Nihon fujin dantai rengōkai 2004: 201).

62 Wiseman and Nishiwaki (2005). For a recent study on the topic of divorce in Japan, see Fuess (2004). The number of divorces was 69,410 in 1960 and 95,937 in 1970, steadily increasing to 284,906 in 2003 (Nihon fujin dantai rengōkai 2004: 192).

63 For example, only 4 percent of the social welfare budget goes to child-related services, while 70 percent goes to programs for the elderly. See "Concern Deepens over Continuing Slide of Birth Rate in Japan, No Stop in Sight," *Japan Brief* June 10, 2005. According to other sources, the government spends about $4.1 billion a year on government-provided child support, or about one third of the amount that it spent to build a little-used bridge in Tokyo Bay. See Wiseman and Nishiwaki (2005).

64 See Jolivet (1997). The young women (and men) who try to stay single and live off their parents are called "parasite singles." For more on this, see Tolbert (2000), Takahashi and Voss (2000), and "'Parasite Singles' Multiply: And Parental 'Hosts' Don't Seem to Mind," *Trends in Japan* May 15, 2000.

65 In a 2000 poll regarding the possibility of men taking childcare leave, approximately 50 percent of women over the age of 45 and 49.5 percent of men of the same age group answered negatively. The response of men aged between 35 and 44 was more or less the same (in the range of 49 to 50 percent), while 33 percent of women of the same age group answered negatively. For this and other related statistics, see Nihon fujin dantai rengōkai (2004). According to a 2003 poll, only 27.9 percent of single women found childrearing to be enjoyable (Chapple 2004).

66 Naraken kodomo kateika (2005).

67 Suzuki (2004: 71), Wijers-Hasegawa (2003), and "Test-tube Babies Pass 100,000 Mark," *Japan Times* January 28, 2005.

68 Wiseman (2005).
69 Quoted in Suzuki (2004: 69).

In lieu of conclusion

1   Giddens (1991).
2   Berlin (1969: 131–4).
3   Berlin (1969: 122–31).
4   Agamben (2005: 6, 21); Schmitt (2005).
5   Bauman (2005: 131).
6   Giddens calls the modern relationship a "pure" relationship, not in the sense that the relationship is pure, i.e. two people exclusively loyal to each other, but in the sense that the relationship exists purely for the sake of relationship and therefore, easily broken at the free will of those involved (1992: 58, 63–4). See the critique on this view in Lindholm (1998a).
7   Arendt (2000).
8   See Agamben (2005: Ch. 1).

References

"10 Women Hurt While Jostling for Glimpse of 'Yon-sama'," *Japan Times* November 27, 2004. Online. Available http://search.japantimes.co.jp/print/news/nn11-2004/nn20041127a7.htm (accessed February 14, 2006).

Abe, S. (1948) *Abe Sada shuki: ai no hansei* [The memoir of Abe Sada: The half life of love], Tokyo: Shinbashishobō.

—— (1997) *Inochi kezuru seiai no onna: Abe Sada "jiken chōsho zenbun"* [The woman who scrapes off her life for love: Abe Sada's interrogatory record], Tokyo: Cosumikku intanashonaru.

Abu-Lughod, L. (1986) *Veiled Sentiments: Honor and Poetry in a Bedouin Society*, Berkeley, CA: University of California Press.

Agamben, G. (1995) *Homo Sacer: Sovereign Power and Bare Life*, Stanford, CA: Stanford University Press.

—— (2005) *State of Exception*, Chicago: University of Chicago Press.

Ahearn, L. (2001) *Invitations to Love: Literacy, Love Letters, and Social Change in Nepal*, Ann Arbor, MI: University of Michigan Press.

Akamatsu, K. (1994a) *Yobai no minzokugaku* [The ethology of nightcrawling], Tokyo: Akashishoten.

—— (1994b) *Yobai no seiairon* [Theory of the love of nightcrawling], Tokyo: Akashishoten.

—— (1995) *Sabetsu no minzokugaku* [The ethnology of discrimination], Tokyo: Akashishoten.

Akamatsu, K. and Ueno, C. (1995) *Waidan: kindainihon no kahanshin* [Sex talk: The lower half of modern Japan], Tokyo: Gendaishokan.

Akiyama, K. (1987) *Genjimonogatari no joseitachi* [Women in *The Tale of Genji*], Tokyo: Shōgakukan.

Allison, A. (1994) *Nightwork: Sexuality, Pleasure, and Corporate Masculinity in a Tokyo Hostess Club*, Chicago: University of Chicago Press.

—— (1996) *Permitted and Prohibited Desires: Mothers, Comics, and Censorship in Japan*, Boulder, CO: Westview Press.

Althusser, L. (1984) "Ideology and Ideological State Apparatuses (Notes Towards an Investigation)," in L. Althusser, *Essays on Ideology*, London: Verso.

Amino, Y. (1978) *Muen, kukai, raku* [Lack of connection, the public sphere, and *raku*], Tokyo: Heibonsha.

—— (1994) *Chūsei no hinin to yūjo* [*Hinin* [non-human] and *yūjo* [prostitutes] in medieval Japan], Tokyo: Akashishoten.

Andō, K. (1948) *Seikyōiku yōkō: shidōsha no tame no* [Sex education manual for mentors], Tokyo: Hakkōkonnichisha.

Aoki, T. (1990) *"Nihonbunkaron" no henyō, sengonihon no bunka to aidentiti* [The transformation of "Japanese cultural studies": Culture and identity in postwar Japan], Tokyo: Chūōkōronsha.

Arendt, H. (1958) *The Human Condition*, Chicago: University of Chicago Press.

—— (2000) "The Perplexities of the Rights of Man," in P. Baehr (ed.) *The Portable Hannah Arendt*, New York: Penguin.

Asai, H., Kitamura, K., Hashimoto, N., and Murase, K. (eds) (2003) *Jendāfurī, seikyōiku basshingu: kokoga shiritai 50 no Q & A* [Gender-free, sex education bashing: Let's learn 50 Q & A], Tokyo: Ōtsukishoten.

Bachnik, J. (1992) "The Two 'Faces' of Self and Society in Japan," *Ethos* 20(1): 3–32.

Bachnik, J. and Quinn Jr, C. (eds) (1994) *Situated Meaning: Inside and Outside in Japanese Self, Society, and Language*, Princeton, NJ: Princeton University Press.

Bardsley, J. and Hirakawa, H. (2005) "Branded: Bad Girls Go Shopping," in L. Miller and J. Bardsley (eds) *Bad Girls of Japan*, New York: Palgrave.

Bauman, Z. (1992) *Mortality, Immortality, and Other Life Strategies*, Stanford, CA: Stanford University Press.

—— (2005) *Liquid Love: On the Frailty of Human Bonds*, Cambridge: Polity.

Benedict, R. (1946) *The Chrysanthemum and the Sword: Patterns of Japanese Culture*, Boston, MA: Houghton Mifflin.

—— (1948) *Kiku to katana* [The chrysanthemum and the sword], Tokyo: Shakaishisō kenkyūkai.

Berlin, I. (1969) *Four Essays on Liberty*, Oxford: Oxford University Press.

Brasor, P. (2004) "Korean Wave May Help Erode Discrimination," *Japan Times* June 27, 2004. Online. Available http://search.japantimes.co.jp/print/features/media2004/fd20040627pb.htm (accessed February 14, 2006).

Butler, J. (1999 [1990]) *Gender Trouble: Feminism and the Subversion of Identity*, New York: Routledge.

Caillois, R. (1959) *Man and the Sacred*, Urbana, IL: University of Illinois Press.

—— (1961) *Man, Play and Games*, Urbana, IL: University of Illinois Press.

Carpenter, J.W. (tr.) (2000) *A Lost Paradise*, New York: Kodansha International.

Caudill, W. (1962) "Patterns of Emotion in Modern Japan," in R. Smith and R. Beardsley (eds) *Japanese Culture: Its Development and Characteristics*, Chicago: Aldine.

—— (1973) "The Influence of Social Structure and Culture on Human Behavior in Modern Japan," *Journal of Nervous and Mental Diseases* 157: 240–58.

—— (1976) "The Cultural and Interpersonal Context of Everyday Health and Illness in Japan and America," in C. Leslie (ed.) *Asian Medical Systems: A Comparative Study*, Berkeley, CA: University of California Press.

Caudill, W. and Doi, T. (1963) "Interrelations of Psychiatry, Culture and Emotion in Japan," in I. Galdston (ed.) *Man's Image in Medicine and Anthropology*, New York: International Universities Press.

Chang, I. (1998) *The Rape of Nanking: The Forgotten Holocaust of World War II*, New York: Penguin.

Chapple, J. (2004) "Dilemma Posed by Japan's Population Decline," *Electronic Journal of Contemporary Japanese Studies*, Discussion Paper No. 5, October 18,

2004. Online. Available www.japanesestudies.org.uk/discussionpapers/Chapple.html (accessed February 14, 2006).

Chayanov, A.V. (1966) *The Theory of Peasant Economy*, Homewood, IL: R.D. Irwin.

Choi, C. (ed.) (1997) *positions: east asia cultures critique, special issue, the comfort women: colonialism, war, and sex* 5(1), Durham: Duke University Press.

Chung, C. (1997) "The Origin and Development of the Military Sexual Slavery Problem in Imperial Japan," *positions: east asia cultures critique* 5(1): 219–54.

"Concern Deepens over Continuing Slide of Birth Rate in Japan, No Stop in Sight," *Japan Brief* June 10, 2005. Online. Available www.fpcj.jp/e/mres/japanbrief/jb_534.html (accessed February 14, 2006).

Constable, N. (2003) *Romance on a Global Stage: Pen Pals, Virtual Ethnography, and "Mail-Order" Marriages*, Berkeley, CA: University of California Press.

Cumings, B. (1981) *The Origins of the Korean War: Liberation and the Emergence of Separate Regimes 1945–1947*, vol. 1, Princeton, NJ: Princeton University Press.

Dale, P. (1986) *The Myth of Japanese Uniqueness*, New York: St Martin's Press.

Doi, T. (1971) *Amae no kōzō* [The structure of amae], Tokyo: Kōbundō.

—— (1973) *The Anatomy of Dependence*, Tokyo: Kodansha International.

—— (1988) *The Anatomy of Self*, Tokyo: Kodansha International.

Dower, J. (1999) *Embracing Defeat: Japan in the Wake of World War II*, New York: Norton.

Embassy of Japan, Washington, DC (2003) *FAQ on Japan, Economy (Business)*. Online. Available www.embjapan.org/english/html/faq/11/economy.htm (accessed March 13, 2006).

Embree, J. (1939) *Suye Mura*, Chicago: University of Chicago Press.

Engels, F. (1941) *The Origin of the Family, Private Property and the State, in the Light of the Researches of Lewis H. Morgan*, London: Lawrence & Wishart.

Esptein, M. (2005) "Diaspora coréenne: Les oublié de Kim Il-sung," *L'Éxpress* July 4, 2005. Online. Available www.lexpress.fr/info/monde/dossier/japon/dossier.asp?ida=433872 (accessed February 14, 2006).

"Fans Follow Suit After 'Yon-sama' Tsunami Donation," *Japan Times* January 7, 2005. Online. Available http://search.japantimes.co.jp/print/news/nn01–2005/nn20050107a8.htm (accessed February 14, 2006).

"Fertility Rate Plummets to its Lowest Level Yet" *Asahi.com* June 2, 2006. Online. Available www.asahi.com/english/Herald-asahi/TKY200606010331.html (accessed August 18, 2006).

Fisher, H. (1992) *Anatomy of Love,* New York: Norton.

Foucault, M. (1977) *History of Sexuality, Volume 1*, Harmondsworth: Penguin.

—— (1979) *Discipline and Punish: The Birth of the Prison*, London: Peregrine.

—— (1988) *History of Sexuality, Volume 3*, Harmondsworth: Penguin.

Frazer, J. (1922) *The Golden Bough,* London: Macmillan.

Freud, S. (1950) *Totem and Taboo*, London: Routledge.

—— (1963) *Sexuality and the Psychology*, New York: Touchstone.

Frühstück, S. (2003) *Colonizing Sex: Sexology and Social Control in Modern Japan*, Berkeley, CA: University of California Press.

Fuess, H. (2004) *Divorce in Japan: Family, Gender, and the State, 1600–2000*, Stanford, CA: Stanford University Press.

Fujii, H. (1999) *Junai no keifu: showa 30 nendai to iu jidai* [A genealogy of pure love: The Showa 30s], in *Ai to kunan* [Love and painful difficulties], Tokyo: Iwanamishoten.

Fujii, S. (2000) *Genjimonogatari ron* [Discussing *The Tale of Genji*], Tokyo: Iwanamishoten.

Fujime, Y. (1997a) "The Licensed Prostitution System and the Prostitution Abolition Movement in Modern Japan," *positions: east asia cultures critique* 5(1): 135–70.

—— (1997b) *Sei no rekishigaku: kōshōseido, dataizai taisei kara baishun bōshihō, yūsei hogohō taisei e* [History of sex: From public prostitution system to prostitution prevention and eugenics system], Tokyo: Fujishuppan.

—— (1998) "Akasen jūgyōin kumiai to baishun bōshihō" [The red-line employees' union and the prostitution prevention law], in S. Ishizaki and Y. Sakurai (eds) *Nihon joseishi ronshū 6: sei to shintai* [Collected essays on the history of Japanese women, vol. 6: Sexuality and body], Tokyo: Yoshikawakōbunkan.

Fujino, Y. (2001) *Sei no kokkakanri* [State control of sex], Tokyo: Fujishuppan.

Fukuoka, Y. (1993) *Zainichi kankoku chōsenjin* [Koreans in Japan]. Tokyo: Chūōkōronsha.

—— (2000) *Lives of Young Koreans in Japan*, Melbourne: Trans Pacific Press.

Fukutō, S. (1990) "Ukareme kara yūjo e" [From *ukareme* to *yūjo*]. In Joseishi sōgō kenkyūkai (eds) *Nihon josei seikatsushi* [History of women's lives in Japan], vol. 1, Tokyo: Tokyodaigaku shuppankai.

—— (1995) *Heianchō no onna to otoko* [Women and men during the Heian period], Tokyo: Chūōkōronsha.

—— (1996) "Seiai no henyō—chūseiseiritsuki o chūshin ni" [Changing love—with the focus on the early medieval period], in N. Kōno and K. Tsurumi (eds) *Onna to otoko no jikū: nihon josei saikō* [Time and space of women and men: Rethinking Japanese women], vol. 2, Tokyo: Fujiwarashoten.

—— (2002) "Renai seiai kenkyū no ima: zenkindai nihonshi kenkyū bunya no seika to kadai o chūshin toshite" [Today's research in love and sexual love: Focusing on studies in premodern Japanese history, their achievements and future issues], in S. Fukutō, M. Yamada, and A. Yoshino (eds) *Renai to seiai* [Love and sexual love], Tokyo: Wasedadaigaku shuppanbu.

Fuyuki, K. (1947) *Aiyoku ni nakinureru onna: Abe Sada no tadotta hansei* [The woman who cries over love and desire: The half life of Abe Sada], Tokyo: Kokusaishobō.

Gardam, J. (1998) "Women, Human Rights and International Humanitarian Law," *International Review of the Red Cross* 324: 421–32.

Gardner, J. and Maier, J. (trans. and eds) (1985) *Gilgamesh*, New York: Vintage.

Gardner Jr, R. (2003) "Generation Sexless: No Sex, Please—We're Married! Between the Kids and the Economy, It's No Surprise That New Yorkers' Libidos Are Shrinking Faster Than Their 401(k)s," *New York Magazine* January 13, 2003. Online. Available www.newyorkmetro.com/nymetro/nightlife/sex/features/n_8228/ (accessed February 14, 2006).

Garon, S. (1997) *Molding Japanese Minds: The State in Everyday Life*, Princeton, NJ: Princeton University Press.

Gaylin, W. (1988) "Love and the Limits of Individualism," in W. Gaylin and E. Person (eds) *Passionate Attachments: Thinking about Love*, New York: Free Press.

Giddens, A. (1991) *Modernity and Self-identity: Self and Society in the Late Modern Age*, Stanford, CA: Stanford University Press.

—— (1992) *The Transformation of Intimacy: Sexuality, Love and Eroticism in Modern Societies*, Cambridge: Polity.

Gluck, C. (1985) *Japan's Modern Myths: Ideology in the Late Meiji Period*, Princeton, NJ: Princeton University Press.

Gomer, R., Powell, J., and Roling, B. (1981) "Japan's Biological Weapons: 1930–1945, A Hidden Chapter in History," *Bulletin of the Atomic Scientists* 37 (October 1981): 43–52.

Goody, J. (1998) "Love, Lust and Literacy," in J. Goody, *Food and Love: A Cultural History of East and West*, London: Verso.

Gorer, G. (1943) "Themes in Japanese Culture," *Transactions of New York Academy of Sciences*, series II, 5: 106–24.

Gottlieb, N. and McLelland, M. (eds) (2003) *Japanese Cybercultures*, New York: Routledge.

Gough, K. (1959) "The Nayars and the Definition of Marriage," *Journal of the Royal Anthropological Institute* 89: 23–34.

Habuchi, I. (2005) "Accelerating Reflexivity," in M. Ito, D. Okabe, and M. Matsuda (eds) *Personal, Portable, Pedestrian: Mobile Phones in Japanese Life*, Cambridge, MA: MIT Press.

Han, T. (2004) "Chakui ni yoru esunikku aidentiti hyōgen to jendā: chima chogori seifuku tanjō o meguru eijenshī to koroniarizumu" [The expression of ethnic identity and gender by way of clothing: Agency and colonialism seen in the birth of Korean traditional school uniforms] in M. Itō (ed.) *Bunka no jissen, bunka no kenkyū* [Cultural practice, cultural studies], Tokyo: Serikashobō.

—— (2006) *Chima chogori seifuku no minzokushi* [The ethnography of Korean school uniforms], Tokyo: Sōfūsha.

Hanley, S. and Yamamura, K. (1977) *Economic and Demographic Change in Pre-Industrial Japan 1600–1868*, Princeton, NJ: Princeton University Press.

Hardacre, H. (1997) *Marketing the Menacing Fetus in Japan*, Berkeley, CA: University of California Press.

Hata, I. (1986) *Nankinjiken—"gyakusatsu" no kōzō* [The Nanjing incident—the structure of "massacre"], Tokyo: Chūōkōronsha.

Hayami, Y. (1998a) *Anatawa mō gensō no onnashika dakenai* [You can only sleep with fantasy women], Tokyo: Chikumashobō.

—— (1998b) "Enjokōsai o sentakusuru shōjotachi" [Girls that opt for aid-dating], in S. Miyadai *et al.*, *"Sei no jikokettei" genron* [A theory of "sexual self-determination"], Tokyo: Kinokuniyashoten.

Head, J. (2004) "Japan's Aids Time Bomb," *BBC News* July 13, 2004. Online. Available http://news.bbc.co.uk/1/hi/world/asia-pacific/3890689.stm (accessed August 11, 2005).

Herodotus (1954) *The Histories*, London: Penguin.

Herskovitz, J. (1997) "Nippon Ad House on a Roll," *Variety.com* December 19, 1997. Online. Available www.variety.com/article/VR111791538?categoryid= 19&cs=1 (accessed July 22, 2006).

Hirota, Y. (1995) "Kyū shisan kaikyū no botsuraku" [The fall of the formerly privileged and wealthy class], in M. Nakamura, A. Amakawa, K. Yun, and T. Igarashi (eds) *Sengo nihon: senryō to sengo kaikaku* [Postwar Japan: Occupation and postwar reform], vol. 2, Tokyo: Iwanamishoten.

Hogg, C. (2005) "Japan Textbook Back in Spotlight," *BBC News* July 13, 2005. Online. Available http://news.bbc.co.uk/2/hi/asia-pacific/4678009.stm (accessed February 14, 2006).

Holden, T.J.M. and Tsuruki, T. (2003) "*Deai-kei*: Japan's New Culture of Encounter," in N. Gottlieb and M. McLelland (eds) *Japanese Cybercultures*, New York: Routledge.

Honda, K. (1981) *Chūgoku no tabi* [A journey to China], Tokyo: Asahishinbunsha.

Honda, M. (1990) *Jogakusei no keifu* [Genealogy of female students], Tokyo: Seitosha.

Horinouchi, M. (1998) *Abe Sada seiden* [A proper biography of Abe Sada], Tokyo: Jōhōsentā.

Horsley, W. (2005) "Korean WWII Sex Slaves Fight On," *BBC News* August 9, 2005. Online. Available http://news.bbc.co.uk/2/hi/asia-pacific/4749467.stm (accessed February 14, 2006).

Huizinga, J. (1950) *Homo Ludens: A Study of the Play Element in Culture*, Boston, MA: Beacon Press.

"The Husband Instruction Manual," *China Daily News* July 19, 2005. Online. Available www.chinadaily.com.cn/english/doc/2004–06/07/content_337178.htm (accessed February 14, 2006).

Hyogoken kyōiku iinkai (1948a) *Seikyōiku shiryō* [Sex education materials], vol. 1, Kobe: Hyogoken kyōiku iinkai.

—— (1948b) *Seikyōiku shiryō* [Sex education materials], vol. 2, Kobe: Hyogoken kyōiku iinkai.

Ihara, S. (1974) *Kōshoku ichidaiotoko* [Grand story of a man who loved color], Tokyo: Meijishoin.

Illouz, E. (1997) *Capitalism and the Romantic Utopia: Love and the Cultural Contradictions of Capitalism*, Berkeley, CA: University of California Press.

Imai, G. (1990) "Onna no kaku monogatari wa reipu kara hajimaru" [Stories written by women start with a rape], in G. Imai, *Ōchō no monogatari to kanshibun* [Royal stories and classical poems], Tokyo: Kasamashoin.

Inokuchi, H. (2000) "Korean Ethnic Schools in Occupied Japan, 1945–52," in S. Ryang (ed.) *Koreans in Japan: Critical Voices from the Margin*, London: Routledge.

Inoue, H. (1995a) *Besutoserā no sengoshi* [Postwar history of the best-sellers], vol. 1, Tokyo: Bungeishunjusha.

—— (1995b) *Besutoserā no sengoshi* [Postwar history of the best-sellers], vol. 2, Tokyo: Bungeishunjusha.

Inoue, S. (1999) *Ai no kūan* [Love's space], Tokyo: Kadokawashoten.

International Crisis Group (2005) "Japan and North Korea: Bones of Contention," *Asia Report* 100, June 27, 2005. Online. Available www.crisisgroup.org/home/index.cfm?l=1&id=3533 (accessed February 14, 2006).

Irigaray, L. (1985) *This Sex Which Is Not One*, Ithaca, NY: Cornell University Press.

Ishikawa, H. (2001) "Sengonihon no sekushuariti no henyō" [Transformation of sexuality in postwar Japan], in S. Yamanaka and H. Ishikawa (eds) *Sengomedia no yomikata* [How to read the postwar media], Tokyo: Keisōshobō.

Ishizaki, S. (1998) "Seishoku no jiyū to sanji chōsetsu undō: Hiratsuka Raichō to Yamamoto Senji" [The freedom of procreation and the birth control movement: Hiratsuka Raichō and Yamamoto Senji], in S. Ishizaki and Y. Sakurai (eds) *Nihon joseishi ronshū 6: sei to shintai* [Collected essays on the history of Japanese women, vol. 6: Sexuality and the body], Tokyo: Yoshikawakōbunkan.

Ito, M., Okabe, D., and Matsuda, M. (eds) (2005) *Personal, Portable, Pedestrian: Mobile Phones in Japanese Life,* Cambridge, MA: MIT Press.

Itō, Sei (1960) *Josei ni kansuru jūnishō* [Twelve chapters on women], Tokyo: Kadokawashoten.

Itō, Susumu (1996) *Nihonjin no ai* [Japanese love], Tokyo: Hokujushuppan.

Ivy, M. (1995) *Discourses of the Vanishing: Modernity, Phantasm, Japan*, Chicago: University of Chicago Press.

Jankowiak, W. (ed.) (1995) *Romantic Passion: A Universal Experience?*, New York: Columbia University Press.

"Japan AIDS Cases Increase by Record 300 Last Year," *Shanghai Star* July 4, 2000. Online. Available www.shanghai-star.com.cn/history/00–07–04/104-aids.html (accessed August 11, 2005).

"Japan AIDS/HIV Rate Skyrockets with 80% Condom Use," *LifeSiteNews.com* June 6, 2005. Online. Available www.lifesite.net/ldn/2005/jun/05060610.html (accessed August 11, 2005).

Japanese Drama Database (1993–2003) "Shitsurakuen," *j!-ent DORAMA database.* Online. Available www.nt2099.com/DORAMA/s_shitsurakuen.html (accessed February 14, 2006).

"Japanese Marriages Falling Victim to 'Yongfluenza'," *Crisscross News Japan* July 17, 2004. Online. Available www.crisscross.com/jp/shukan/234 (accessed February 14, 2006).

Japan Institute of Workers' Evolution (2004) *The Situation of Women in Japan.* Online. Available www.jiwe.or.jp/english/situationworking-html (accessed February 14, 2006).

Johnston, E. (2002) "North Koreans Get Little Sympathy in Japan: Pyongyang's Abductions Spell Fallout for Chongryun," *Japan Times* November 20, 2002. Online. Available http://search.japantimes.co.jp/member/member.html?nn2002 1120c1.htm (accessed February 14, 2006).

Johnston, W. (2005) *Geisha, Harlot, Strangler, Star: A Woman, Sex, and Morality in Modern Japan*, New York: Columbia University Press.

Jolivet, M. (1997) *Japan: The Childless Society? The Crisis of Motherhood*, London: Routledge.

Joyce, C. (2005) "Japan's Sexless Marriages Are Turning It into the Land of Rising Celibacy," *News.Telegraph* (*Weekly Telegraph*) June 3, 2005. Online. Available www.telegraph.co.uk/news/main.jhtml?xml=/news/2005/05/20/wceli20.xml (accessed February 14, 2006).

Kaku, Y. (2005a) "Senior Style: Going DVD for Yon-sama," *Asahi.com* January 15, 2005. Online. Available www.asahi.com/english/lifestyle/TKY200501150159. html (accessed February 14, 2006).

—— (2005b) "Korean Dramas Still the Rage in Japan—But Why?" *Asahi.com* March 19, 2005. Online. Available www.asahi.com/english/Herald-asahi/TKY2005 03190147.html (accessed April 15, 2005).

Kang, S. (2005) "Opinion/Point of View: Yong-sama, Kim Jong Il: 2 Faces of Divided Korea," *Asahi.com* February 24, 2005. Online. Available www.asahi.com/english/opinion/TKY200502240117.html (accessed February 14, 2006).

Kanō, M. (1979) "Takamure Itsue to kōkoku shikan" [Takamure Itsue and the imperialist historical consciousness], in N. Kōno, S. Fujii, S. Terada, M. Sugata, and M. Kanō, *Takamure Itsue ronshū* [On Takamure Itsue], Tokyo: JCA shuppan.

Kataroguhausu (ed.) (1995) *Taisho jidai no minouesōdan* [Life problem consultation during the Taisho period], Tokyo: Kataroguhausu.

Kawahara, T. (1987) *Michikohi* [Princess Michiko], Tokyo: Kōdansha.

—— (1990) *Michikokōgō* [Empress Michiko], Tokyo: Kōdansha.

Kawana, K. (1995) *Jidai wa sekkusuresu* [It's a sexless age], Tokyo: Asahishinbunsha.

Kawashima, Takeyoshi (1950) *Nihonshakai no kazokuteki kōsei* [The familial structure of Japanese society], Tokyo: Nihonhyōronsha.

Kawashima, Terry (2001) *Writing Margins: The Textual Construction of Gender in Heian and Kamakura Japan*, Cambridge, MA: Harvard University Press.

Kawazoe, F. (2002) "'*Genji monogatari*' ni okeru renai seiai" [Love and sexual love seen in *The Tale of Genji*], in S. Fukutō, M. Yamada, and A. Yoshino (eds) *Renai to seiai* [Love and sexual love], Tokyo: Wasedadaigaku shuppanbu.

Kim, I. (1976) *Tennō no guntai to chōsenjin ianfu* [The Emperor's army and Korean comfort women], Tokyo: Sanichishobō.

Kim, P. (2001) "Global Civil Society Remakes History: 'The Women's International War Crimes Tribunal 2000,'" *positions: east asia cultures critique* 9(3): 611–20.

Kim, Y. (1996) "Hoshō: kaisetsu to tōkei no hosoku" [Supplement: Additional explanation and statistics], in Y. Morita, *Sūji ga kataru zainichi kankoku chōsenjin no rekishi* [A history of Koreans in Japan seen from statistics], Tokyo: Akashishoten.

Kimura, F. (1947) *Tadashiku heiina seikyōiku* [Correct and simple sex education], Tokyo: Shikō no nihonsha.

Kinsella, S. (2000) *Adult Manga: Culture and Power in Contemporary Japanese Society*, Honolulu: University of Hawai'i Press.

Kipnis, L. (2004) *Against Love: A Polemic*, New York: Vintage.

Kitayama, S., Markus, H., and Kurokawa, M. (2000) "Culture, Emotion, and Well-Being: Good Feelings in Japan and the United States," *Cognition and Emotion* 14(1): 93–124.

Kitayama, S., Markus, H., and Lieberman, C. (1995) "The Collective Construction of Self Esteem: Implications for Culture, Self, and Emotion," in J.A. Russell, J. Fernàndez-Dols, A.S.R. Manstead, and J.C. Wellenkamp (eds) *Everyday Conceptions of Emotion: An Introduction to the Psychology, Anthropology and Linguistics of Emotion*, Leiden: Brill.

Kitayama, S., Markus, H., Matsumoto, H., and Morasakkunkit, V. (1997) "Individual and Collective Processes in the Construction of the Self: Self-enhancement in the United Sates and Self-Criticism in Japan," *Journal of Personality and Social Psychology* 72(6): 1245–67.

Kodansha Moura (2006a) "Dokoyorimo kuwashii arasuji, saishūwa 'fuyu no owari'" [The most precise story, the final episode "the end of the winter"], *Fuyusona dōri* [Winter sonata street]. Online. Available http://moura.jp/clickjapan/fuyusona/d1/index20.html (accessed March 16, 2006).

—— (2006b) "Anatani totte fuyu no sonatawa . . ." [What is *The Winter Sonata* for you? . . .] *Fuyusona dōri* [Winter sonata street]. Online. Available http://moura.jp/clickjapan/fuyusona/v1/result04.html (accessed February 14, 2006).

Komatsu, K. (1985) *Ijinron: minzoku shakai no shinsei* [On strangers: Re-birth of ethnic society], Tokyo: Seitosha.

Koshiro, Y. (1999) *Trans-Pacific Racisms and the US Occupation of Japan*, New York: Columbia University Press.

Koyano, A. (1999a) *Edogensō hihan* [A critique of the Edo fantasy], Tokyo: Shinyōsha.

—— (1999b) "Romantikku rabu towa nanika" [What is romantic love], in *Ai to kunan* [love and painful difficulties], Tokyo: Iwanamishoten.

Kurahashi, M. (1994) *Jūgun ianfu mondai no rekishiteki kenkyū* [Historical study of comfort women issue], Tokyo: Kyōseishobō.

Kusato, S. (1948) *Seikyōiku kenkyū shiryō* [Sex education research material], Urawa: Hatsunesha seinen kenkyūkai.

La Barre, W. (1942) "Some Observations on Character Structure in the Orient: The Japanese," *Psychiatry* 8: 319–42.

Lee, Y. (1989) *Mō hitotsu no Manyōshū* [The other *Manyōshū*], Tokyo: Bungeishunjusha.

Lévi-Strauss, C. (1949) *Les structure élémentaires de la parenté*, Paris: Presses Universitaires de France.

Lewis, C.S. (1960) *The Four Loves*, New York: Harcourt Brace.

Lies, E. (2005) "Japan's AIDS Stigma Strong, HIV-positive Woman Says," *Reuters AlertNet* July 5, 2005. Online. Available www.alertnet.org/thenews/newsdest/T225807.htm (accessed August 11, 2005).

Lindholm, C. (1990) *Charisma*, Cambridge, MA: Blackwell.

—— (1997) "Does the Sociocentric Self Exist? Reflections on Markus and Kitayama's 'Culture and the Self'," *Journal of Anthropological Research* 53: 405–22.

—— (1998a) "The Future of love," in V.C. De Munck (ed.) *Romantic Love and Sexual Behavior: Perspectives from the Social Sciences*, Westport, CT: Praeger.

—— (1998b) "Love and Structure," *Theory, Culture and Society* 15(3–4): 243–63.

Lugo, L.M. and Baba, Y. (2001) "Foreign Farm Wives See Little of Koizumi Fever," *Asahi.com* July 28, 2001. Online. Available www.asahi.com/english/asianet/kisha/eng_kisha_005.html (accessed February 14, 2006).

Macfarlane, A. (1997) *The Savage Wars of Peace: England, Japan and the Malthusian Trap*, Oxford: Blackwell.

Mackie, V. (2003) *Feminism in Modern Japan: Citizenship, Embodiment, and Sexuality*, Cambridge: Cambridge University Press.

Makiyama, K. (1949) *Shintaikensa to kenkōsokutei* [The physical examination and health measurement], Tokyo: Takudōshobō.

Malinowski, B. (1926) *Sexual Life of the Savages*, Boston, MA: Beacon Press.

Markus, H. and Kitayama, S. (eds) (1994) *Emotion and Culture: Empirical Studies of Mutual Influence*, Washington, DC: American Psychological Association.

Marran, C. (2000) "From Pathography to Pulp: Popular Expressions of Female Deviance, 1930–1950," in D. Slaymaker (ed.) *A Century of Popular Culture in Japan*, Lewiston, NY: Edwin Mellen Press.

—— (2005) "So Bad She's Good: The Masochist's Heroine in Postwar Japan, Abe Sada," in L. Miller and J. Bardsley (eds) *Bad Girls of Japan*, New York: Palgrave.

Marshall, J. (1995) "Foucault and Neo-Liberalism: Biopower and Busno-Power," *Philosophy of Education*. Online. Available www.ed.uiuc.edu/EPS/PESYearbook/95_docs/marshall.html (accessed February 14, 2006).

Matsuda, T. (1995) *Senzenki no zainichi chōsenjin to sanseiken* [Koreans and voting rights in prewar Japan], Tokyo: Akashishoten.

Matsui, Y. (1995) "Ajia no baishunchitai o yuku" [In the red-light districts of Asia], in T. Inoue, C. Ueno, Y. Ehara, and M. Amano (eds) *Nihon no feminizumu* [Feminism in Japan], vol. 6, Tokyo: Iwanamishoten.

Matsumura, T. and Takahashi, K. (1973) "Abe Sada jiken" [The Abe Sada incident], in Y. Uchimura *et al.* (eds) *Nihon no seishin kantei* [Psychological evaluation in Japan], Tokyo: Misuzushobō.

McCormack, G. (2005) Disputed Bones Fracture Japan-North Korea Relations," *OhmyNews* April 20, 2005. Online. Available http://english.ohmynews.com/articleview/article_view.asp?menu=c10400&no=221670&rel_no=1 (accessed February 14, 2006).

McNeill, D. (2005) "Japan's Enemy Within: The Shrinking North Korean Community Feels It Is Under Siege," *Japan Times* January 25, 2005. Online. Available http://search.japantimes.co.jp/print/features/life2005/fl20050123zg.htm (accessed August 10, 2005).

Media shisutemu (n.d.) "Hitozuma, warikiri, shitsurakuen, soshite furinzuma: furin-shite mimasenka? Deaikei shitsurakuen" [Married women, decide [to do it], Paradise Lost, and adulterous wife: Would you like to cheat on your spouse? This is the Dating Agency Paradise Lost]. Online. Available www.shitsurakuen.com/ (accessed February 14, 2006).

Mercuse, H. (1966) *Eros and Civilization*, Boston, MA: Beacon Press.

Minear, R. (1980) "The Wartime Studies of Japanese National Character," *Japan Interpreter* 13(1): 36–59.

Mitchell, J. (1974) *Psychoanalysis and Feminism: Freud, Reich, Laing and Women*, New York: Vantage Books.

Miya, Y. (1998) "Sei no jikokettei to feminizumu no aporia" [Sexual self-determination and feminism's confusion], in S. Miyadai *et al.*, *"Sei no jikokettei" genron* [A theory of "sexual self-determination"], Tokyo: Kinokuniyashoten.

Miyadai, S. (1994) *Seifukushōjotachi no sentaku* [The choices of uniformed girls], Tokyo: Kōdansha.

—— (1998) "Jikokettei genron: jiyū to songen" [A theory of self-determination: Freedom and dignity], in S. Miyadai *et al.*, *"Sei no jikokettei" genron* [A theory of "sexual self-determination"], Tokyo: Kinokuniyashoten.

Miyata, S., Kim, Y., and Yang, T. (1992) *Sōshikaimei* [Creating Japanese-style names and reforming Korean names], Tokyo: Akashishoten.

Monbushō (1944) *Kokutai no hongi kaisetsu sōsho* [Comprehensive handbook of the principles of the national body], Tokyo: Monbushō.

—— (1949) *Kokutai no Hongi: Cardinal Principles of the National Entity of Japan*, (tr.) J.O. Gauntlett, Cambridge, MA: Harvard University Press.

Monbushō junketsukyōiku iinkai (1949) *Junketsukyōiku kihonyōkō* [Fundamentals of purity education], Tokyo: Insatsukyoku.

Morgan, L.H. (1871) "Systems of Consanguinity and Affinity of the Human Family," *Smithsonian Contributions to Knowledge* 17: 1–590.

Mori, Ō. (1949 [1909]) *Uita sekusuarisu* [Vita sexualis], Tokyo: Shinchōsha.

Morisaki, K. (1986) *Karayukisan* ["Karayukisan"], Tokyo: Asahishinbunsha.

Morris, I. (1964) *The World of the Shining Prince: Court Life in Ancient Japan*, New York: Kodansha International.

Murai, O. (1992) *Nantōideorogi no hassei: Yanagita Kunio to shokuminchishugi* [The birth of southern island ideology: Yanagita Kunio and colonialism], Tokyo: Fukutakeshoten.

—— (2004) *Han Origuchi Shinobu ron* [Anti-Origuchi Shinobu theory], Tokyo: Sakuhinsha.

Murakami, N. (1974) *Kindainihon no renaikan* [Perspectives of romantic love in modern Japan], Tokyo: Rironsha.

Murashima, Y. (2004) *Baibaishun to josei* [Prostitution and women], Tokyo: Kashiwashobō.

Nagasato, K. (1949) *Atarashii seikyōiku* [New sex education], Tokyo: Gakuentosho shuppansha.

Nakane, C. (1967) *Tateshakai no ningenkankei: tanitsushakai no riron* [Human relations in a vertical society: A theory of the monoethnic society], Tokyo: Kōdansha.

—— (1970) *Japanese Society,* Berkeley, CA: University of California Press.

Nakayama, T. (1930) *Nihon koninshi* [History of Japanese matrimony], Tokyo: Okayamashoten.

—— (1974 [1929]) *Nihon mikoshi* [History of Japanese shamanesses], Tokyo: Yagishobō.

Napier, S. (2001) *Anime from Akira to Princess Mononoke: Experiencing Contemporary Japanese Animation*, New York: Palgrave.

Naraken kodomo kateika (eds) (2005) *Sekaide ichiban shiawasena ai no kotoba* [The happiest words of love in the world], Tokyo: Zennichishuppan.

National Institute of Population and Social Security Research (2005) *Population Projections for Japan: 2001–2050*. Online. Available www.ipss.go.jp/index-e-html (accessed February 14, 2006).

Nicholi, Jr, A. (2002) *The Question of God: C.S. Lewis and Sigmund Freud Debate God, Love, Sex, and the Meaning of Life*, New York: Free Press.

Nihon fujin dantai rengōkai (ed.) (2004) *Joseihakusho 2004: sekai no nagare to nihon no josei* [White paper on women, 2004: Global trends and women in Japan], Tokyo: Horupushuppan.

Nish, I. (1966) *The Anglo-Japanese Alliance: The Diplomacy of Two Island Empire*, London: Athlone Press.

—— (1972) *Alliance in Decline: A Study in Anglo-Japanese Relations, 1908–23*, London: Athlone Press.

Nishikawa, Y. (1982) *Mori no ie no miko Takamure Itsue* [The shamaness in the forest house—Takamure Itsue], Tokyo: Shinchōsha.

Nishimura, I. and Shikiba, R. (1949) *Gakusei to seikyōiku* [Students and sex education], Tokyo: Kensetsusha.

Nishino, R. (1992) *Jūgun ianfu: moto heishitachi no shōgen* [Comfort women: Testimonials of former soldiers], Tokyo: Akashishoten.

Noguchi, T. (1985) *Genji monogatari o edo kara yomu* [Reading *The Tale of Genji* from the Edo period], Tokyo: Kōdansha.

Nohara, S. (2004) "Seikyōiku basshingu—ima kyōshi toshite omoukoto" [Sex education bashing—what I am thinking now as a teacher], *Sensō to sei* 22: 72–5.

Nomura, S. (1996) *Korian sekai no tabi* [A journey to the Korean world], Tokyo: Kōdansha.

Norgren, T. (2001) *Abortion before Birth Control: The Politics of Reproduction in Postwar Japan*, Princeton, NJ: Princeton University Press.

Numanoi, H. (1949) *Seikyōiku no riron to jissai* [Theory and reality of sex education], Nagoya: Reimeishobō.

Nussbaum, M. (1994) *The Therapy of Desire: Theory and Practice in Hellenistic Ethics*, Princeton, NJ: Princeton University Press.

Nygren, A. (1953) *Agape and Eros*, London: SPCK.

Office of Gender Equality, Prime Minister's Office, Japan (1996) *Advances Made by Japanese Women during the 50 Years since the End of the War, The Present Status of Women and Measures, Fifth Report on the Implementation of the New National Plan of Action toward the Year 2000*. Online. Available www.gender.go.jp/english_contents/e01.html (accessed February 14, 2006).

Oguma, E. (1995) *Tanitsu minzoku shinwa no kigen: "nihonjin" no jigazō no keifu* [The myth of the homogeneous nation: Genealogy of the self-image of the Japanese], Tokyo: Shinyōsha.

Ohnuki-Tierney, E. (1993) *Rice as Self: Japanese Identities through Time*, Princeton, NJ: Princeton University Press.

Ōnuma, Y. (1979a) "Zainichi chōsenjin no hōtekichii ni kansuru ichi kōsatsu" [A study of the legal status of resident Koreans in Japan] 1, *Hōritsujihō* 96(3): 266–315.

—— (1979b) "Zainichi chōsenjin no hōtekichii ni kansuru ichi kōsatsu" [A study of the legal status of resident Koreans in Japan] 2, *Hōritsujihō* 96(5): 529–96.

—— (1979c) "Zainichi chōsenjin no hōtekichii ni kansuru ichi kōsatsu" [A study of the legal status of resident Koreans in Japan] 3, *Hōritsujihō* 96(8): 911–80.

—— (1980a) "Zainichi chōsenjin no hōtekichii ni kansuru ichi kōsatsu" [A study of the legal status of resident Koreans in Japan] 4, *Hōritsujihō* 97(2): 192–269.

—— (1980b) "Zainichi chōsenjin no hōtekichii ni kansuru ichi kōsatsu" [A study of the legal status of resident Koreans in Japan] 5, *Hōritsujihō* 97(3): 279–330.

—— (1980c) "Zainichi chōsenjin no hōtekichii ni kansuru ichi kōsatsu" [A study of the legal status of resident Koreans in Japan] 6, *Hōritsujihō* 97(4): 455–536.

Origuchi, S. (1965–6) *Origuchi Shinobu zenshū* [The Origuchi Shinobu collection], vols. 1–30. Tokyo: Chūōkōronsha.

Orwell, G. (1949) *Nineteen Eighty-Four, A Novel*, New York: Harcourt & Brace.

Oshima, M. and Kōno, M. (1963) *Ai to shi o mitsumete* [Facing love and death], Tokyo: Daiwashobō.

—— (2004) *Ai to shi o mitsumete* [Facing love and death], Tokyo: Daiwashobō.

Ōshima, N. (1976) *L'Empire des sens: ai no korida* [The empire of the senses: Love's bullfight], Tokyo: Sanichishobō.

Otsubo, S. (2005) "Between Two Worlds: Yamanouchi Shigeo and Eugenics in Early Twentieth-Century Japan," *Annals of Science* 62(2): 205–31.

Ōwa, K. (1993) *Yūjo to tennō* [Play women and emperors], Tokyo: Hakusuisha.

"'Parasite Singles' Multiply: And Parental 'Hosts' Don't Seem to Mind," *Trends in Japan* May 15, 2000. Online. Available http://web-japan.org/trends00/honbun/tj000508.html (accessed February 14, 2006).

Qualls-Corbett, N. (1988) *The Sacred Prostitute: Eternal Aspect of the Feminine*, Toronto: Inner City Books.

Rebhun, L. (1999) *The Heart Is Unknown Country: Love in the Changing Economy of Northeast Brazil*, Stanford, CA: Stanford University Press.

Ricoeur, P. (1970) *Freud and Philosophy*, New Haven, CT: Yale University Press.

Robertson, J. (2001) "Japan's First Cyborg? Miss Nippon, Eugenics, and Wartime Technologies of Beauty, Body, and Blood," *Body and Society* 7(1): 1–34.

—— (2002) "Blood Talks: Eugenic Modernity and the Creation of New Japanese," *History and Anthropology* 13(3): 1–26.

—— (2005) "Dehistoricizing History: The Ethical Dilemma of 'East Asian Bio-ethics'," *Critical Asian Studies* 37(2): 233–50.

Rosenberger, N. (1989) "Dialectic Balance in the Polar Model of Self: The Japan Case," *Ethos* 17(1): 88–113.

—— (ed.) (1992) *Japanese Sense of Self*, Cambridge: Cambridge University Press.

Ryang, S. (1997) *North Koreans in Japan: Language, Ideology, and Identity*, Boulder, CO: Westview Press.

—— (1998) "Love and Colonialism in Takamure Itsue's Feminism: A Postcolonial Critique," *Feminist Review* 60: 1–32.

—— (2000) "Gender in Oblivion: Women in the Democratic People's Republic of Korea (North Korea)," *Journal of Asian and African Studies* 35(3): 323–49.

—— (2002) "Technologies of the Self: Reading North Korean Novels from the 1980s," *Acta Koreana* 5(1): 21–32.

—— (2004a) *Japan and National Anthropology: A Critique*, London: Routledge.

—— (2004b) "A Note on Transnational Consanguinity, or, Kinship in the Age of Terrorism," *Anthropological Quarterly* 77(4): 747–70.

—— (2006) "Between Life and Death: Diaspora of Koreans in Japan." A seminar paper presented in Columbia University, March 2006, New York, USA.

Sadakata, K., Tanimura, H., and Ōhira, E. (1949) *Junketsukyōiku* [Purity education], Tokyo: Meijitosho shuppansha.

Saeki, J. (1987) *Yūjo no bunkashi: hare no onna tachi* [A cultural history of *yūjo*: Sacred women], Tokyo: Chūōkōronsha.

—— (1998) *"Iro" to "ai" no hikaku bunkashi* [A comparative history of "color" and "love"], Tokyo: Iwanamishoten.

Saigō, N. (1967) *Kojiki no sekai* [The world of the *Kojiki*], Tokyo: Iwanamishoten.

Sakaguchi, A. (1947) *Hakuchi* [Idiot], Tokyo: Chūōkōronsha.

—— (1990 [1946]) *Darakuron* [On decadence], Tokyo: Toshosentā.

—— (1991) "Abe Sada-san no inshō" [Impressions of Ms Abe Sada] in A. Sakaguchi, *Sakaguchi Ango zenshū* [Collected works of Sakaguchi Ango], vol. 19, Tokyo: Chikumashobō.

Sasaki, H. (1994) *"Atarashii onna no tōrai: Hiratsuka Raichō to Sōseki"* [The arrival of "the New Woman": Hiratsuka Raichō and Sōseki], Nagoya: Nagoyadaigaku shuppankai.

Satake, A., Yamada, H., Kudō, R., Ōtani, M., and Yamazaki, Y. (eds) (1999) *Manyōshū* [Book of ten thousand songs] vol. 1, Tokyo: Iwanamishoten.

—— (2002) *Manyōshū* [Book of ten thousand songs], vol. 3, Tokyo: Iwanamishoten.

Satō, H. (1962) *Hironomiyasama: Michikohidenka no ikuji* [The Crown Prince Hironomiya: Her Majesty Princess Michiko's motherhood], Tokyo: Banchō-shuppan.

Schmitt, C. (2005) *Political Theology: Four Chapters on the Concept of Sovereignty*, Chicago: University of Chicago Press.

Seidensticker, E. (tr.) (1978) *The Tale of Genji*, New York: Knopf.

Sekiguchi, Y. (1993) *Nihon kodai koninshi no kenkyū* [A study of the matrimonial system in ancient Japan], 2 vols, Tokyo: Komashobō.

Senda, K. (1973) *Jūgun ianfu* [Army "comfort women"], Tokyo: Futabasha.

—— (1978) *Jūgun ianfu* [Army "comfort women"] 2, Tokyo: Sanichishobō.

Shanin, T. (1990) *Defining Peasants: Essays Concerning Rural Societies, Expolary Economies, and Learning from them in the Contemporary World*, Oxford: Blackwell.

Shimizu, M. (1998) *Abe Sada o yomu* [Reading Abe Sada], Tokyo: Gendaishokan.

Shoji, K. (2004) "Japan Gripped by Obsession with Pure Love," *Japan Times* December 30, 2004. Online. Available http://search.japantimes.co.jp/print/features/edu2004/ek20041230ks.htm (accessed August 11, 2005).

Skov, L. and Moeran, B. (eds) (1995) *Women, Media, and Consumption in Japan*, Honolulu: University of Hawai'i Press.

Soble, A. (1989) *Eros, Agape, and Philia: Readings in the Philosophy of Love*, St Paul, MN: Paragon.

Soh, C.S. (2000) "From Imperial Gifts to Sex Slaves: Theorizing Symbolic Representations of the 'Comfort Women'," *Social Science Japan Journal* 3(1): 59–76.

—— (2004) "Aspiring to Craft Modern Gendered Selves: 'Comfort Women' and Chŏngsindae in Late Colonial Korea," *Critical Asian Studies* 36(2): 175–98.

Statistics Bureau, Japan (1996–2006) *Population Growth*. Online. Available www.stat.go.jp/english/data/nenkan/zuhyou/y0201b00.xls (accessed February 14, 2006).

"Steps for Outsmarting the 'Sexless Marriage'," *SexSmart.com* July 2003. Online. Available www.sexsmart.com/article_sexlessmarriage.htm (accessed February 14, 2006).

Stone, L. (1988) "Passionate Attachments in the West in Historical Perspective," in W. Gaylin and E. Person (eds) *Passionate Attachments: Thinking about Love*, New York: Free Press.

Suzaki, S. (2003) *2.26 jiken—seinenshōkō no ishiki to shinri* [The February 26 incident: Consciousness and psychology of young officers], Tokyo: Yoshikawa-kōbunkan.

Suzuki, R. (2004) "Ojisantachiga nozomunowa donna onnaka" [What kind of women Japan's middle-aged and senior men want?], *Sensō to sei* 22: 67–71.

Suzuki, Y. (1993) *"Jūgun ianfu" mondai to seibōryoku* [The "comfort women" issue and sexual violence], Tokyo: Miraisha.

Takahashi, H. and Voss, J. (2000) "'Parasite Singles'—A Uniquely Japanese Phenomenon?" *Japan Economic Institute Report* no. 31, August 11, 2000. Online. Available www.jei.org/Archive/JEIR00/0031f.html (accessed August 11, 2005).

Takamure, I. (1941) "Shintō to jiyūrenai" [Shinto and free love], *Fujo Shinbun* December 6, 1941, quoted in N. Kōno, S. Fujii, S. Terada, M. Sugata and M. Kanō (eds) *Takamure Itsue ronshū* [On Takamure Itsue], Tokyo: JCA shuppan.

—— (1943) "Gunji to josei" [Women and the military], *Nihonfujin* November 1943, quoted in N. Kōno, S. Fujii, S. Terada, M. Sugata and M. Kanō (eds) *Takamure Itsue ronshū* [On Takamure Itsue], Tokyo: JCA shuppan.

—— (1944) "Shinkoku goji" [Defending the sacred land], *Nihonfujin* April 1944, quoted in N. Kōno, S. Fujii, S. Terada, M. Sugata and M. Kanō (eds) *Takamure Itsue ronshū* [On Takamure Itsue], Tokyo: JCA shuppan.

—— (1953) *Shōseikon no kenkyū* [A study of inviting-the-groom marriage], Tokyo: Kōdansha.

—— (1967 [1926]) *Renaisōsei* [The genesis of love], in I. Takamure, *Takamure Itsue zenshū* [Collected works of Takamure Itsue], vol. 7, Tokyo: Rironsha.

—— (1967 [1948]) *Renairon* [A theory of love], in I. Takamure, *Takamure Itsue zenshū* [Collected works of Takamure Itsue], vol. 6, Tokyo: Rironsha.

Tanaka, Y. (1997) *Hidden Horrors: Japanese War Crimes in World War II*, Boulder, CO: Westview Press.

—— (1999) "Introduction," in M.R. Hanson, *Comfort Woman: A Filipina's Story of Prostitution and Slavery under the Japanese Military*, Lanham, MD: Rowman & Littlefield.

—— (2002) *Japan's Comfort Women: Sexual Slavery and Prostitution during World War II and the US Occupation*, London: Routledge.

Tatsukawa, S. (1965) *Yūjo no rekishi* [History of the *yūjo*], Tokyo: Shibundō.

Teruoka, Y. (1989) *Nihonjin no ai to sei* [Love and sex of the Japanese], Tokyo: Iwanamishoten.

"Test-tube Babies Pass 100,000 Mark," *Japan Times* January 28, 2005. Online. Available http://search.japantimes.co.jp/print/news/nn01–2005/nn20050128a7. html (accessed February 14, 2006).

"Tokyo Adopts Contested Textbook," *BBC News* July 28, 2005. Online. Available http://news.bbc.co.uk/2/hi/asia-pacific/4724669.stm (accessed February 20, 2006).

Tolbert, K. (2000) "Japan's New Material Girls: 'Parasite Singles' Put Off Marriage for Good Life," *Washington Post* February 10, 2000. Online. Available www. washingtonpost.com/wp-srv/WPcap/2000–02/10/101r-021000-idx.html (accessed February 14, 2006).

Tomita, H. (2005) "*Keitai* and the Intimate Stranger," in M. Ito, D. Okabe, and M. Matsuda (eds) *Personal, Portable, Pedestrian: Mobile Phones in Japanese Life*, Cambridge, MA: MIT Press.

Treat, J.W. (ed.) (1996) *Contemporary Japan and Popular Culture*, Honolulu: University of Hawai'i Press.

Tsunoda, Y. (2004) "'Seiteki jikoketteiken' to baibaishun—baishun yōninron no gimansei o abaku" ["Sexual self-determination right" and prostitution—revealing the deceptive position of tolerating prostitution], *Sensō to sei* 22: 84–97.

Twine, N. (1991) *Language and the Modern State: The Reform of Written Japanese*, London: Routledge.

Usui, K. (1974) *Manshūjihen: sensō to gaikō to* [The Manchurian incident: War and diplomacy], Tokyo: Chūōkōronsha.

Usuki, K. (1992) *Gendai no ianfutachi: guntai ianfu kara japayukisan made* [Modern comfort women: From military comfort women to *Japayukisan*], Tokyo: Tokumashoten.

Vogel, E. (1979) *Japan as Number One: Lessons for America*, Cambridge, MA: Harvard University Press.

Wagner, E. (1951) *The Korean Minority in Japan, 1904–1950*, New York: Institute of Pacific Relations.

Wakaume, S. (1987) "Abe Sada ryōkijiken" [Grotesque murder by Abe Sada], *"Bungeishunju" ni miru shōwashi* [The Showa history seen in *Bungeishunju*], vol. 1, Tokyo: Bungeishunjusha.

Wakita, H. (1985) *Muromachi jidai* [The Muromachi era], Tokyo: Chūōkōronsha.

Watanabe, J. (1997a) *Shitsurakuen* [Paradise lost], vol. 1, Tokyo: Kōdansha.

—— (1997b) *Shitsurakuen* [Paradise lost], vol. 2, Tokyo: Kōdansha.

Watanabe, M. (1991) *Michikokōgō no "inochi no tabi"* [The "life journey" of Empress Michiko], Tokyo: Bungeishunjusha.

Weil, S. (1951) *Waiting for God*, New York: Harper & Row.

West, M. (2005) *Law in Everyday Japan: Sex, Sumo, Suicide, and Statutes*, Chicago: University of Chicago Press.

Wijers-Hasegawa, Y. (2003) "Fertility Experts Urge Health Insurance Help: Japan's Falling Fertility Rate," *Japan Times* October 5, 2003. Online. Available http://search.japantimes.co.jp/cgi-bin/nn20031005b1.htm (accessed February 14, 2006).

Wiseman, P. (2004) "No Sex Please—We're Japanese," *USA Today* June 2, 2004. Online. Available www.usatoday.com/news/world/2004-06-02-japan-women-usat_x.htm (accessed February 14, 2006).

—— (2005) "Towns Hope Cash-for-Babies Incentives Boost Populations," *USA Today* July 28, 2005. Online. Available www.usatoday.com/news/world/2005-07-28-japan-babies_x.htm (accessed February 14, 2006).

Wiseman, P. and Nishiwaki, N. (2005) "Japan Struggles to Cope with Effects of Divorce," *USA Today* July 28, 2005. Online. Available www.usatoday.com/news/world/2005-07-28-japan-divorce_x.htm (accessed February 14, 2006).

Wittig, M. (1981) "One Is Not Born a Woman," *Feminist Issues* 1(2): 47–54.

"Women Swarm Narita for Arrival of 'Yon-sama'," *Japan Times* November 26, 2004. Online. Available http://search.japantimes.co.jp/print/news/nn11-2004/nn20041126a5.htm (accessed February 14, 2006).

Yamada, M. (1991) *Ianfutachi no taiheiyōsensō* [The comfort women's Pacific War], Tokyo: Kōjinsha.

Yamaoka, A. (1973) *Shomin no sengo: fūzokuhen 1945–51 nen sengo taishū zasshi ni miru* [The postwar of the ordinary people: On everyday culture as seen in postwar popular magazines 1945–51], Tokyo: Taiheishuppansha.

Yamazumi, M. and Horio, T. (1976) *Kyōikurinen: sengo nihon no kyōikukaikaku* [Pedagogical concepts: Educational reform in postwar Japan], vol. 2, Tokyo: Tokyodaigaku shuppankai.

Yan, Y. (2003) *Private Life under Socialism: Love, Intimacy, and Family Change in a Chinese Village, 1949–1999*, Berkeley, CA: University of California Press.

Yanagita, K. (1962) "Mikokō" [Thinking about shamanesses], in K. Yanagita, *Teibon Yanagita Kunio shū* [Definitive edition: Collected works of Yanagita Kunio], vol. 9, Tokyo: Chikumashobō.

—— (1963) "Mukoiriko" [Thinking about son-in-law adoptions], in K. Yanagita, *Teibon Yanagita Kunio shū* [Definitive edition: Collected works of Yanagita Kunio], vol. 15, Tokyo: Chikumashobō.

Yang, H. (1997) "Revisiting the Issue of Korean 'Military Comfort Women': The Question of Truth and Positionality," *positions: east asia cultures critique* 5(1): 51–72.

Yasuda, M. (1986) *Goshirakawa jōkō* [Goshirakawa, the abdicated emperor], Tokyo: Yoshikawakōbunkan.

Yasumoto, B. (1990) *Chōsengo de "Manyōshū" wa kaidokudekinai* [You cannot understand *Manyō* poems in Korean], Tokyo: JICC shuppan.

Yoshimi, Y. (2000) *Comfort Women*, New York: Columbia University Press.

Name index

Subject index

Printed in the United States
150069LV00002B/5/P